GUIDE TO

DISTANCE AND ONLINE

LEARNING

PROGRAMS IN THE USA

2001 EDITION

in-depth profiles covering

a complete range of study options

▼

includes undergraduate, graduate

& continuing education programs

▼

feature articles for distance learners

ACADEMIC
THE EI GROUP

:: ACADEMIC

THE EI GROUP

EI Group Ventures Ltd.
205 - 5325 Cordova Bay Road
Victoria, BC V8Y 2L3 Canada
Internet: http://www.TheEIGroup.com
email: service@TheEIGroup.com

National Library of Canada Cataloguing in Publication Data

Main entry under title:

Guide to distance & online learning programs in the USA

Annual.
ISSN 1605-430X

1. Distance education--United States--Directories. I. EI Group.
LC5905.G8   374'.4'02573   C00-900326-6

Printed in Canada by Friesens
Researched in Victoria, Canada by EI Academic

Contents

WHAT. HOW.

Introducing *dramatically* more interactive degree programs.

Sure, you like your laptop, but scrolling through text isn't your idea of learning. You need interaction. That's why **Bellevue University's** innovative **Online Programs** combine the convenience of online access with a dynamic cyber-active® environment. So you can get involved in online discussions and team research, e-mail your professor with your questions and concerns, and meet with students for chat and group study. All this while earning your degree on your own schedule, from anywhere in the world.

Graduate Programs

- Master of Arts in Leadership
- Master of Arts in Management
- Master of Business Administration
- Master of Science in Health Care Administration

Undergraduate Programs

- Business Information Systems
- Criminal Justice Administration
- E-business
- Leadership
- Management
- Management of Human Resources
- Management of Information Systems
- Business Administration of Technical Studies
- Health Care Administration

BELLEVUE UNIVERSITY

www.bellevue.edu

Bellevue University has the distance learning programs you need to go further in your career.
Call us at 402.293.2030, toll free at 800.756.7920 ext. 2030 or email bellevue-u@bellevue.edu

Welcome

We know that choosing the right school is the key to your success. If you want to explore opportunities open to you through distance learning, you cannot do better than EI's *Guide to Distance and Online Learning Programs in the USA – 2001 Edition.*

This guide provides an introduction to distance learning programs available through American universities and colleges. By supplying concise and comparable information about program offerings, this guide provides much of the preliminary information you will need to make an informed decision. In addition, the complete *Fields of Study Index,* a supplemental index of programs and courses by institution, will help you find the schools in this guide that offer majors in your area of interest.

Would you like to know where you can study business administration, electrical engineering or health sciences at a distance? Are you interested in combining your academic studies with full-time employment? Are you eager to discover which universities offer degrees and diplomas through distance education? All of these questions, and many more, are answered in this guide.

The guide is intended to help adult learners, students and educational counselors begin to explore distance learning education in the US. Use the information provided in this guide to compile a short list of potential programs; then seek further information directly from admissions staff or embassy representatives.

All of the schools whose programs appear in EI guides are consulted for up-to-date program information. While we have included noteworthy reputational information, such as awards won, external rankings and prominent alumni, we have imposed no subjective judgments of our own. You are free to assess each school according to the criteria of most importance to you and to rank the schools based on your personal preferences and career goals.

Good luck in your studies!

David Boag
President, The EI Group

CREIGHTON UNIVERSITY

2500 California Plaza
Omaha, Nebraska 68178-0055

SCHOOL OF PHARMACY AND ALLIED HEALTH PROFESSIONS

800-325-2830

402-280-2662

spahp.creighton.edu

anchored in ethics centered on service pledged to excellence

How to Use the Guide

This guide has been set up to help you find the distance learning program that best meets your needs. By following the steps listed below, you will have the tools you need to determine which schools can meet your personal and educational goals.

➤ Review the *How to Read the Profiles* section on page 26 and then read several of the profiles themselves to get acquainted with the format.

➤ Read the article entitled *Successful Distance Learning* and then develop and prioritize a list of criteria that are most important to you. As you do this, consider program details (such as what disciplines are offered, the availability of study at a distance), technology requirements and English language support, if you are a non-native speaker of English. Other items to consider are admission requirements, entry dates and tuition costs.

➤ Read all of the profiles and highlight the programs that strike you as interesting so that you can easily refer back to them. Try to eliminate any program that does not match your search criteria.

➤ Use the *Program Quick Facts* chart on page 20 to quickly compare individual programs based on specific statistics.

➤ Re-read the programs that you highlighted. Based on the criteria you selected earlier, compose and prioritize a list of first choice schools (ones that offer programs that most interest you) and a list of second choice schools (other schools that could meet your needs).

➤ Send in the *Reader Response Cards* (found at the front of this guide) requesting information on all of the schools in your first choice list. It could take anywhere from three to six weeks to receive the information from the schools. You can also contact the schools directly for information.

➤ Once the information arrives from your selected schools, review the calendars and brochures, as well as each school's specific admissions requirements. You may want to consult an academic counselor to ensure that you have the right qualifications. Narrow your choice to a manageable list of schools (approximately three to five) whose admission criteria you meet.

➤ If you have completed any postsecondary education in your home country, find out whether you can obtain advanced standing in some courses. You may be able to save as much as a year of study.

➤ If you are an international student and need to upgrade your English skills, you may want to consider registering for some English language preparation classes and tests. If any of the schools you are applying to have set a minimum English proficiency test score for admission, you should register for the test as early as possible, as you may wish to take it more than once in the hope of increasing your score.

➤ Good luck…you are now ready to complete your applications for admission!

DistanceStudies.com

the website of distance learning programs & courses

DistanceStudies.com is designed exclusively for students who are searching for distance learning degrees, diplomas and short course programs.

Check out the website to

 Search for a wide range of programs, from business and nursing to health, fine arts, teacher education and other academic programs

 Find in-depth information for each program on admission requirements, program options, student services, tuition and more

 Link directly to school websites and other useful websites

 Request application packages online via an automated email system

DistanceStudies.com has the most up-to-date and accurate information available on distance learning programs. All information is verified by the schools.

ACADEMIC
THE EI GROUP

Guiding Students to Success

Successful Distance Learning

There are many reasons to study via distance learning. You may live in a small town, and not have easy access to an academic environment like a college or university. Perhaps you're a busy professional looking to expand your knowledge and possibly obtain a professional designation, a new job or a raise. Or maybe you're interested in a particular subject and would like to take a course for the fun of lifelong learning.

Whatever your reasons, there are many options available to make distance learning an enjoyable and valuable experience. It is up to you to pick the right match.

What is distance learning?

The United States Distance Learning Asssociation defines distance learning as "the acquisition of knowledge and skills through mediated information and instruction, encompassing all technologies and other forms of learning at a distance." Content can be delivered by surface mail, video, interactive or cable TV, satellite broadcast, or various Internet technologies such as message boards, chat rooms and desktop video or computer conferencing.

Many people mistakenly believe that distance learning will offer them an instant or easy education – this is not so. Distance learning is often more adaptable, convenient and flexible than a traditional classroom setting, but that doesn't mean it requires less work. On the contrary, many students report that distance education courses demand more effort, and many institutions state that online and distance courses maintain the same workload and pace as their on-campus counterparts.

If you decide to pursue distance learning, start off with one course rather than a full program of online study, to see if it is right for you. While distance learning is very convenient, it is also a unique study option with some demanding requirements, and some people may find it is not a viable option for them.

What's your learning style?

To be successful in your distance learning program, you must be a self-starter and able to work independently. It is easy to be motivated in a

There are many options available to make distance learning an enjoyable and valuable experience. It is up to you to pick the right match.

classroom setting with an instructor directing your learning; it may seem much harder to be at home by yourself in front of the computer, facing a pile of assignments. Although distance learning allows for scheduled freedom, it also facilitates the temptation to put off your work. Self-discipline is a must. Will you be able to avoid interruptions and distractions and take the time necessary to complete the course?

When choosing a distance learning program, it is important to find one with the right "fit" for you. There are two types of distance studies:

Synchronous classes usually require students to participate in virtual chats or teleconferences, and hand in assignments at specific times

Asynchronous classes let students work at their own pace

While synchronous classes provide some structure, deadlines, and help with motivation, asynchronous classes allow you to work and learn at your own pace, focussing on the skills that are most important to you.

Along with instruction style, it is important to choose the medium that is right for you, since distance learning is available through many technologies. Whether you learn best by listening, reading or viewing, it is critical to find a program that matches

your learning style. If you learn by viewing (through video delivery, for example), a course based solely on reading print material may bore and frustrate you. Instead, try to pick a course with interactive models and graphics that complement your learning style.

The Requirements for Success

Although it may seem like you have to be a whiz with computers to take a distance learning course, that is not the case. Most schools know that the majority of students will not be "techies", or have vast computer experience (although you should have some basic computer skills). However, before you begin any study program, be sure that you have access to all the

ei's guide to distance and online learning programs in the usa - 2001 edition

equipment necessary to complete the course (ie computer, modem, email, etc).

Since nearly all communication for distance learning is written, good writing skills are essential. You must feel comfortable asking questions and expressing yourself in writing. For many, the chance to sharpen their writing skills is just another benefit of distance learning; for some with limited writing abilities, remedial efforts may be required.

Make the Most of It

Because distance learning is mainly self-driven, what you get out of the course depends on what you put into it. Here are some suggestions to make the most out of your distance learning experience:

Participate

When sitting alone at a computer, it is easy for a distance learner to feel isolated. Take advantage of discussion opportunities with your peers such as message boards and any available conferencing times. Many people mistakenly believe that distance learning is impersonal, but taking opportunities to network with your peers can be very fulfilling.

Be Realistic

Online courses require just as much time and effort as traditional courses. Expect to put in four to 15 hours a week, depending on the intensity of the course. Also, try not to get too frustrated over the inevitable technical glitches and problems. Many schools have tech support to help you deal with these issues.

Keep in Touch

Just because you can't physically see your instructor, doesn't mean you can't correspond. Regular contact will allow you to get the extra help you may need, and clear up any questions you may have. If you have problems

with the course, or are feeling frustrated, bored, or isolated, you MUST speak up. Otherwise, your instructor won't be able to help you.

Evaluate your Progress

Set goals for yourself, and look back at them often. Setting your own timelines and deadlines is an excellent way to mark your progress and stay organized during the course. Don't fall behind in the course, as it is often very difficult to catch up again.

Distance Learning Perceptions

During your studies, you may encounter some prejudice or negative opinions, as there are a number of misconceptions concerning distance learning. These may include the belief that distance studies are not as challenging. In October 2000, Vault.com surveyed 239 human resources and hiring professionals about their perceptions of distance learning:

➤ 30% of HR professionals or hiring managers have encountered applicants with online degrees

➤ 77% believe that an online degree earned at an accredited institution (e.g. Duke, Stanford) is more credible than one earned at an Internet-only institution

➤ 26% believe that an online bachelor's degree is as credible as an offline degree

➤ 61% say that the online degree is not as credible, but was acceptable

These numbers may be discouraging, but as more programs become available, beliefs and perceptions about distance studies will continue to shift. Says Dr. John G. Flores, Executive Director of the United States Distance Learning Association, "Resistance to distance learning has been minimal if introduced and implemented [with] a sound educational approach. The challenge," he states, "is to transform as much information as possible into individual knowledge. By doing that, we enable the individual to use knowledge to improve personal productivity and enhance personal growth."

Whether you're interested in supplementing your learning or taking an entire degree, distance studies is a great way to fit education into a busy schedule. Simply choose the program that is right for you and your learning style, and remember that high-quality learning can take place outside a traditional classroom.

United States Distance Learning Association
http://www.uslda.org
http://www.vault.com

Accessed November, 2000

> Because distance learning is mainly self-driven, what you get out of the course depends on what you put into it.

The United States Distance Learning Association

The United States Distance Learning Association (USDLA) is a nonprofit organization formed in 1987. The USDLA has over 3,000 members from higher education, continuing education, Pre-K through grade 12 education, home school education, corporate training, telemedicine, and military and government training. The association's purpose is to promote the development and application of distance learning for education and training.

Toward this purpose, the United States Distance Learning Association has convened National Policy Forums in 1991, 1997, 1999 and 2001 to develop and publish National Policy Recommendations that have been the basis of legislative and administrative proposals in education and telecommunications policy. For example, in 1993 the USDLA Executive Committee was instrumental in establishing an educational technology position in the U.S. Department of Education.

The association has become the leading source of information and recommendations for government agencies, Congress, industry and those entering into the development of distance learning programs.

USDLA began a process in 1993 of establishing state chapters in all fifty states. In addition, USDLA has expanded its global role with annual meetings with leaders of distance learning programs in Europe, the Pacific Rim, Asia and Africa.

The USDLA is constantly working to achieve its goals in the field of distance learning. The association aims to:

➢ Provide national leadership in the field of distance learning

Supporting the development and application of distance learning

➢ Advocate and promote the use of distance learning

➢ Provide current information on distance learning

➢ Represent the distance learning community before government policy and regulatory bodies

➢ Serve and support the state and individual organizations that belong to USDLA

➢ Provide annual recognition and awards of outstanding achievements in distance learning

➢ Serve as a catalyst for the formation of partnerships among education, business, healthcare and government

➢ Achieve a global leadership role through liaisons with international organizations

➢ Promote equity and access to lifelong learning through distance learning

➢ Promote diversity in the organization and its programs

"Distance learning continues to evolve at an exponential rate," says Dr. John G. Flores, Executive Director of the USDLA. "With the Internet fueling our economy and society, more learners are accessing distance learning courses and programs than traditional on-site courses.

There's no question of the vast potential of distance learning to transform education. Knowledge is power and distance learning is the key to that power as we begin the 21st century."

For the leading source of information on distance learning programs and opportunities in the United States, visit the United States Distance Learning Association at www.usdla.org or call 1-800-275-5162.

Take the Next Step!
EI's Reader Response Card Service

**Now that you've begun to explore the range of programs available,
your next step is to determine which school is right for you.**

You can also fax the other side of this card to us at 1-250-658-6285

AIR MAIL

ATTACH
AIR MAIL
POSTAGE

EI ACADEMIC
3873 Airport Way
PO Box 9754
Bellingham WA 98227-9754 USA

ACADEMIC
THE EI GROUP

READER RESPONSE CARD
To find out more about the programs that interest you, circle the name and
page number, complete the form and send the card to the address on the back.

Adams State College ☐	Central Missouri State University ☐	Colorado State University ☐
Bellevue Community College ☐	Champlain College ☐	Community Colleges of Colorado ☐
Bellevue University ☐	Clayton College & State University ☐	Creighton University ☐
Caldwell College ☐	Colorado Electronic Community College ☐	

Last Name_____ First Name_____ Age_____ Sex_____

Address _____

_____ Zip/Postal Code_____ Country _____

Telephone (___)_____ Fax (___)_____ Email_____
Area Code   Area Code

DL-USA 01

ACADEMIC
THE EI GROUP

The Reader Response Cards in this guide provide a quick, convenient way for you to request program information from specific institutions. The following guidelines will help you use the guide's Reader Response Card Service to make an informed, educated decision!

1. As you read the guide, keep a record of schools that interest you.
2. If the school has an institution-specific Reader Response Card, complete it and mail it directly to the school.
3. If the school does not have an institution-specific card, fill out the appropriate general card and mail it to The EI Group. We will forward your request to all the schools you select.

4. Be sure to print clearly and affix proper postage. This will speed up your request for catalogs, brochures, application forms and financial aid.
5. Keep your options open! The purpose of this guide is to help you choose the right program—the more program information you request, the better your chances of finding the perfect program for you.

BELLEVUE UNIVERSITY ONLINE

www.bellevue.edu

Please send information on:

Undergraduate Course Listing
❑ Business Administration of Technical Studies
❑ Business Information Systems
❑ Criminal Justice Administration
❑ E-business
❑ Global Business Management
❑ Health Care Administration
❑ Leadership
❑ Management

❑ Management of Human Resources
❑ Management Information Systems

Graduate Programs
❑ Master of Business Administration
❑ Master of Science in Computer Information Systems
❑ Master of Science in Health Care Administration
❑ Master of Arts in Management
❑ Master of Arts in Leadership

Last Name _____ First Name _____ Age _____ Sex _____

Address _____

City _____ Zip/Postal Code _____ Country _____

Telephone (_____) _____ Fax (_____) _____ Email _____
          Area Code   Area Code

DL-US-01

CREIGHTON UNIVERSITY
School of Pharmacy & Allied Health Professions

Please send information on:
❑ Entry-level Web-based Doctor of Pharmacy
❑ Post-Professional Doctor of Occupational Therapy
❑ Transitional Doctor of Physical Therapy
❑ Non-Traditional Doctor of Pharmacy

Last Name _____ First Name _____ Age _____ Sex _____

Address _____

City _____ State/Province _____ Zip/Postal Code _____ Country _____

Telephone (_____) _____ Fax (_____) _____ Email _____
          Area Code   Area Code

DL-US-01

GEORGIA INSTITUTE OF TECHNOLOGY
Center for Distance Learning
cdl@conted.gatech.edu

Please send information on the following master's degree programs:

❑ Electrical & Computer Engineering
❑ Environmental Engineering
❑ Health Physics/Radiological Engineering

❑ Industrial Engineering
❑ Mechancial Engineering

Last Name _____ First Name _____ Occupation/Title _____

Address _____

City _____ State _____ Zip/Postal Code _____ Country _____

Telephone (_____) _____ Fax (_____) _____ Email _____
          Area Code   Area Code
My undergraduate degree is _____

DL-US-01

You can also fax the other side of this card to us at 402-293-3730

BELLEVUE UNIVERSITY ONLINE
Admissions
1000 Galvin Road South
Bellevue, NE 68005 USA

You can also fax the other side of this card to us at 402-280-5739

CREIGHTON UNIVERSITY
School of Pharmacy & Allied Health Professions
SPAHP Admissions 2500 California Plaza
Omaha, Nebraska 68178
USA

You can also fax the other side of this card to us at 404-385-0322

GEORGIA INSTITUTE OF TECHNOLOGY
Center for Distance Learning
620 Cherry Street, ESM Building - Room G6
Atlanta, Georgia 30332-0240
USA

IWUonline

YES! I am interested in obtaining my Degree.

Please send me information about the online:

- ☐ Bachelor of Science in Management (BSM)
- ☐ Bachelor of Science in Business Information Systems (BSBIS)
- ☐ Master of Business Administration (MBA)
- ☐ Master of Education (MEd)
- ☐ I would like a telephone call from a Representative

Name _____ M ☐ F ☐

Address _____

City _____ State _____ Zip _____

Phone (_____)_____ Email _____

Employer _____

www.IWUonline.com   1-800-895-0036 or 1-765-677-2860

DL-US-01

PENNSTATE
1855

PENN STATE DISTANCE EDUCATION/WORLD CAMPUS

Please send me information on:
- ❏ Bachelor's Degree Completion in Letters, Arts, & Sciences
- ❏ Master's Degree in Adult Education
- ❏ Associate Degree in Dietetic Food Systems Management
- ❏ Associate Degree in Hotel, Restaurant & Institutional Management
- ❏ Antenna Engineering
- ❏ Educational Technology Integration
- ❏ Geographic Information Systems

- ❏ Logistics & Supply Chain Management
- ❏ Management Development
- ❏ Noise Control Engineering
- ❏ Reliability Engineering
- ❏ Turfgrass Management
- ❏ Webmaster

Last Name _____ First Name _____ Age _____ Sex _____

Address _____

City _____ Zip/Postal Code _____ Country _____

Telephone (_____)_____ Fax (_____)_____ Email _____
       Area Code   Area Code

DL-US-01

UNIVERSITY OF WISCONSIN
Whitewater

UNIVERSITY OF WISCONSIN - WHITEWATER
College of Business & Economics

Please provide information on:
- ❏ Master of Business Administration
- ❏ Certificate in Human Resource Management

Last Name _____ First Name _____ Age _____ Sex _____

Address _____

_____ Zip/Postal Code _____ Country _____

Telephone (_____)_____ Fax (_____)_____ Email _____
       Area Code   Area Code

DL-US-01

You can also fax the other side of this card to us at 765-677-2404

ADULT ENROLLMENT SERVICES
INDIANA WESLEYAN UNIVERSITY
4201 South Washington Street
Marion, IN 46953-9906

You can also fax the other side of this card to us at 814-863-4763

PENN STATE DISTANCE EDUCATION/WORLD CAMPUS
The Pennsylvania State University
207 Mitchell Building
University Park, Pennsylvania 16802-3601 USA

You can also fax the other side of this card to us at 262-472-4863

UNIVERSITY OF WISCONSIN - WHITEWATER
College of Business & Economics
800 West Main Street
Whitewater, WI 53190-1790
USA

READER RESPONSE CARD

To find out more about the programs that interest you, circle the name and
page number, complete the form and send the card to the address on the back.

Adams State College ☐
Bellevue Community College ☐
Bellevue University ☐
Caldwell College ☐

Central Missouri State University ☐
Champlain College ☐
Clayton College & State University ☐
Colorado Electronic
Community College ☐

Colorado State University ☐
Community Colleges of Colorado ☐
Creighton University ☐

Last Name _____ First Name _____ Age ___ Sex ___

Address _____

_____ Zip/Postal Code _____ Country _____

Telephone (___) ___ Fax (___) ___ Email _____
Area Code   Area Code

DL-USA 01

ACADEMIC
THE EI GROUP

READER RESPONSE CARD

To find out more about the programs that interest you, circle the name and
page number, complete the form and send the card to the address on the back.

Drexel University ☐
Duquesne University ☐
Eastern Oregon University ☐
Georgia Institute of Technology ☐

Harvard University ☐
Indiana University ☐
Indiana Wesleyan University ☐
Jones International University, Ltd. ☐

Kansas State University ☐
Kentucky Virtual University ☐
Kettering University ☐

Last Name _____ First Name _____ Age ___ Sex ___

Address _____

_____ Zip/Postal Code _____ Country _____

Telephone (___) ___ Fax (___) ___ Email _____
Area Code   Area Code

DL-USA 01

ACADEMIC
THE EI GROUP

READER RESPONSE CARD

To find out more about the programs that interest you, circle the name and
page number, complete the form and send the card to the address on the back.

Lehigh University ☐
Madonna University ☐
Mott Community College ☐
National American University ☐

National Technological University ☐
New Jersey Institute of Technology ☐
Northwest Missouri State University ☐
Northwestern College ☐

Ohio University ☐
Pennsylvania State University ☐
Purdue University ☐

Last Name _____ First Name _____ Age ___ Sex ___

Address _____

_____ Zip/Postal Code _____ Country _____

Telephone (___) ___ Fax (___) ___ Email _____
Area Code   Area Code

DL-USA 01

AIR MAIL		ATTACH AIR MAIL POSTAGE

You can also fax the other side of this card to us at 250-658-6285

EI ACADEMIC
3873 Airport Way
PO Box 9754
Bellingham WA 98227-9754 USA

AIR MAIL		ATTACH AIR MAIL POSTAGE

You can also fax the other side of this card to us at 250-658-6285

EI ACADEMIC
3873 Airport Way
PO Box 9754
Bellingham WA 98227-9754 USA

AIR MAIL		ATTACH AIR MAIL POSTAGE

You can also fax the other side of this card to us at 250-658-6285

EI ACADEMIC
3873 Airport Way
PO Box 9754
Bellingham WA 98227-9754 USA

:: ACADEMIC
THE EI GROUP

READER RESPONSE CARD

To find out more about the programs that interest you, circle the name and
page number, complete the form and send the card to the address on the back.

Rensselaer Polytechnic Institute ☐   Salve Regina University ☐   Southwest Texas State University ☐
Rogers State University ☐   Sinclair Community College ☐   Southwestern Adventist University ☐
Rutgers University ☐   Southern New Hampshire University ☐   Syracuse University ☐
Saint Mary of the Woods College ☐   Southern Oregon University ☐

Last Name _____   First Name _____   Age _____   Sex _____

Address _____

_____   Zip/Postal Code _____   Country _____

Telephone (___)_____   Fax (___)_____   Email _____
Area Code   Area Code

DL-USA 01

:: ACADEMIC
THE EI GROUP

READER RESPONSE CARD

To find out more about the programs that interest you, circle the name and
page number, complete the form and send the card to the address on the back.

Teikyo Post University ☐   University of Colorado   University of Illinois
Thomas Edison State College ☐   at Colorado Springs ☐   at Urbana Champaign ☐
University of Bridgeport ☐   University of Colorado at Denver ☐   University of Maine ☐
University of California ☐   University of Delaware ☐   University of Massachusetts
                                                                                    at Lowell ☐

Last Name _____   First Name _____   Age _____   Sex _____

Address _____

_____   Zip/Postal Code _____   Country _____

Telephone (___)_____   Fax (___)_____   Email _____
Area Code   Area Code

DL-USA 01

:: ACADEMIC
THE EI GROUP

READER RESPONSE CARD

To find out more about the programs that interest you, circle the name and
page number, complete the form and send the card to the address on the back.

University of Nevada at Reno ☐   University of Wyoming ☐   Waukesga County Technical College☐
University of North Texas ☐   Upper Iowa University ☐   Weber State University ☐
University of Tennessee ☐   Vincennes University ☐   Western Oklahoma University ☐
University of Wisconsin, Whitewater ☐   Virginia Polytechnic Institute   Worcester Polytechnic Institute ☐
                                                      & State University ☐

Last Name _____   First Name _____   Age _____   Sex _____

Address _____

_____   Zip/Postal Code _____   Country _____

Telephone (___)_____   Fax (___)_____   Email _____
Area Code   Area Code

DL-USA 01

AIR MAIL	You can also fax the other side of this card to us at 250-658-6285	ATTACH AIR MAIL POSTAGE

EI ACADEMIC
3873 Airport Way
PO Box 9754
Bellingham WA 98227-9754 USA

AIR MAIL	You can also fax the other side of this card to us at 250-658-6285	ATTACH AIR MAIL POSTAGE

EI ACADEMIC
3873 Airport Way
PO Box 9754
Bellingham WA 98227-9754 USA

AIR MAIL	You can also fax the other side of this card to us at 250-658-6285	ATTACH AIR MAIL POSTAGE

EI ACADEMIC
3873 Airport Way
PO Box 9754
Bellingham WA 98227-9754 USA

Financing Your Education

Without a doubt, obtaining an education is a costly endeavour. It is one, however, that offers much in return: personal growth, intellectual maturity, professional preparedness. The expense of a college education should not discourage academically qualified students from reaping these rewards. More than half of all full-time college students in the US receive some form of financial aid.

The following information is intended solely as an introduction to financial assistance possibilities. Applicants must be prepared to research their specific financing options. Keep in mind that some focused financial aid is not available to distance learning students, or students studying less than full-time.

Grants

Grants are the most desirable form of aid as they do not have to be repaid and are distributed based on need. Federal grants are available in two forms: Federal Pell grants, between US$400 and $3,000 annually, are given to those from low to moderate income families. Federal Supplemental Educational Opportunity Grants (SEOG), valued from US$500 to $1,500 per year, are awarded by individual colleges to Federal Pell recipients who demonstrate exceptional need.

Scholarships and Merit-based Awards

Scholarships vary greatly. Typically, they are granted on the basis of academic achievements or accomplishment in areas such as athletics or the arts. Scholarships often require the recipients to meet certain commitments in exchange for the support, such as participating in school athletics, extracurricular activities or maintaining a minimum GPA.

Loans

Loans are an important part of the financial aid system. They offer favourable interest rates and may be either subsidized or unsubsidized. If subsidized, the federal government pays the interest while the student is attending college and the student assumes responsibility for both the loan and interest upon graduation or after leaving school. If unsubsidized, the

---

Some schools offer flexible payment plans that permit students to pay tuition in installments.

---

student can choose either to repay the interest as it accumulates or invest the interest and pay the loan and interest back after graduation. Subsidized loans are subject to income requirements.

Financial Aid Tips

➢ Check with the institution. Some schools offer flexible payment plans that permit students to pay tuition in installments, often without interest. Others have introduced discounts or bonuses for those who prepay. Still others have developed their own low-interest loan programs.

➢ Research all sources of financial aid, including employers and colleges.

➢ International applicants should seek assistance from their own government agencies.

➢ US students should look for assistance at the regional, state and national levels

➢ Maintain organized financial records

➢ Obtain, complete and submit the necessary forms as early as possible

➢ Double-check the information provided on forms for accuracy and clarity

➢ Keep photocopies of all forms sent.

Conclusion

Financial aid is available to help students pursue studies in the US. The majority of full-time students receive assistance in some form. To join their ranks, applicants should conscientiously and thoroughly research all possible funding sources, and apply to as many as possible. While this process will be more difficult for international students, it is time consuming and exhausting for everyone. Most agree, however, that the effort is worth the initial hard work when they obtain the resources needed to finance their education.

The Value of Accreditation

With expanding technology and innovations in distance learning, the availability of distance programs has increased dramatically. Many traditional schools now offer some or all of their courses by distance learning, and more schools are emerging that focus solely on distance learning.

However, in many states there is no regulation of the terms "college" or "university," meaning that almost anyone can declare themselves a college, and begin issuing degrees.

Buyer Beware

How can you protect yourself against fraud and get good value for your money? The number one indicator of a reputable school is accreditation. According to the Distance Education and Training Council, accreditation is "a process that gives public recognition to institutions that meet certain standards. It is a promise that an institution will provide the quality of education it claims to offer." Specifically, "accreditation assures the student that the institution operates on a sound financial basis, has an approved program of study, qualified instructors, adequate facilities and equipment, approved recruitment and admission policies, and advertises its courses truthfully."[1]

The term accredited usually means the institution is accredited by an agency recognized by the US Department of Education. The department's web site (www.ed.gov) provides a list of verified accreditors. There are six regional non-governmental agencies that review

and accredit degree-granting institutions in their respective areas, and at least one agency in each state that reviews higher education. If a student has any concerns about the status of an institution, or its right to award degrees, these agencies can assist in addressing them.

The United States Distance Learning Association (USDLA) is a leading source of information regarding distance learning programs and their accreditation. For more information, students can contact the USDLA

online (www.usdla.org) or call 1-800-275-5162.

The Accreditation Process

To gain recognized accreditation, an institution must have a certain number of years of operating experience and undergo an intensive review process. The process usually includes an evaluation and review of all the courses offered, as well as student and graduate surveys, and an on-site inspection. After accreditation, the institution must submit annual reports, and be re-examined periodically.

Many institutions claim that they are "fully accredited". However, sometimes these institutions are "self-accredited" or accredited only by

unrecognized agencies. These types of schools may also claim that distance learning programs can't receive accreditation because of their non-traditional status – this is, of course, false.

Also, a large gray area exists around schools seeking accreditation, or accreditation "candidates." The DETC reports that only about a quarter of the schools seeking accreditation actually receive it. However, some schools with

> # The number one indicator of a reputable school is accreditation.

questionable credentials have been known to seek accreditation in order to declare candidacy, at least for a little while.

Check it Out

When looking for a distance education program, students are shopping for something that may cost thousands of dollars. They should be informed, and not be afraid to ask questions. As a potential distance learner, be prepared to spend some time on the phone, and on the Internet. Here are some questions to keep in mind:

Does it fit your needs?

Are you looking for a degree for a new job, a raise, or a professional designation? Make sure the program offered will suffice. Most schools will be willing to explain their programs and establish their credentials with employers or state agencies.

Also, remember to check how easily your courses will transfer. If you take a distance course over the summer, will it be accepted for credit elsewhere? Always keep your future goals in mind. Too many people have wasted time and money to complete a course or a degree that was useless to them.

What is the faculty like?

Just because a faculty member is teaching a distance learning course, doesn't mean that he or she is qualified to do so. The nature of distance learning makes it inherently different from teaching a room full of students. Do the instructors have experience teaching distance learning courses? Check if the faculty is comprised mainly of full-time of part-time/adjunct teachers, and where they got their degrees (it's a warning sign if a majority of the faculty earned degrees from their own school).

Your instructor's background (both academic and real-world), level of knowledge, and enthusiasm may make or break the course for you. Be sure you receive credible, high-quality instruction.

How many students are currently enrolled?

Because of the nature of distance learning, and not having to provide a physical space, there is a temptation for schools to pack a class with paying students. However, an over-crowded class means less interaction and personal attention from the instructor, which is often an important necessity of a distance learning course. Make

sure the student-to-instructor ratio is small enough that you will get the deserved time and attention.

What do graduates have to say?

Talk to people who have completed the program, or ask to see some student evaluations. What were their opinions or concerns?

You can also ask to look at work done by former students, which will give you a good idea of the caliber of both the work and the students. Find out where graduates have gone with the degree, and where some are currently employed.

Distance learning is an excellent option for many people, but it is up to you to ensure that you get the appropriate quality of education, and good value for your money.

Sites for further information:

[1] Distance Education and Training Council website http://www.detc.org Accessed March 12, 2001

United States Distance Learning Association website http://www.usdla.org

---

The schools realize you are making a large investment and have a right to know where your money is going.

What kind of support and student service is provided?

If you need it, will there be tech support available? Are there any tutorials you can take to familiarize yourself with the equipment and programs? Some schools also offer academic advising, digital library services, and an assortment of administrative services. Notice how quickly your questions and concerns are addressed. Timeliness is an important feature of distance learning, so pay close attention to turnaround time.

Legitimate schools will want to deal with informed customers, and should be happy to answer these, and other questions. The schools realize that you are making a large investment, and have the right to know where your money is going.

PROFILED

DISTANCE

LEARNING

PROGRAMS

United States of America

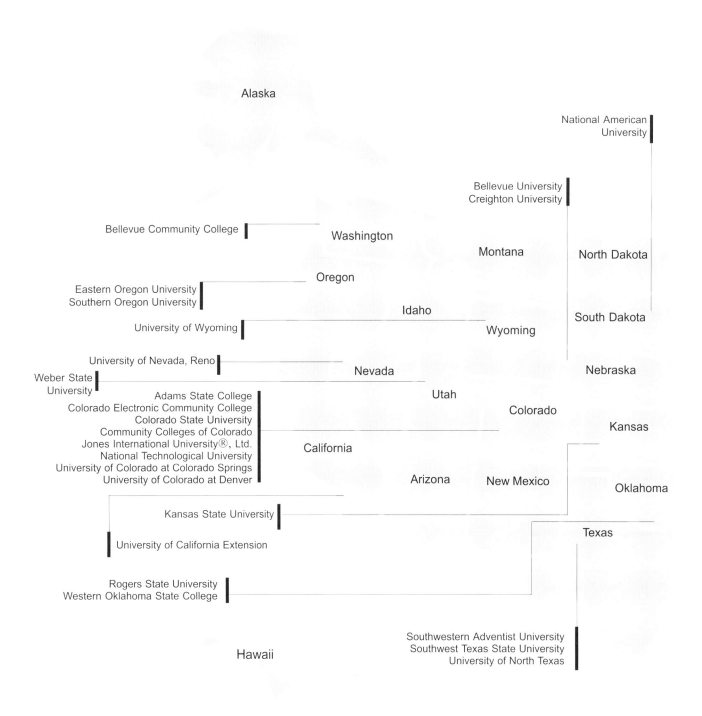

Alaska

National American University

Bellevue University
Creighton University

Bellevue Community College   Washington   Montana   North Dakota

Oregon

Eastern Oregon University
Southern Oregon University   Idaho   South Dakota

University of Wyoming   Wyoming

University of Nevada, Reno   Nevada   Nebraska
Weber State
University   Adams State College   Utah
Colorado Electronic Community College   Colorado
Colorado State University   Kansas
Community Colleges of Colorado
Jones International University®, Ltd.   California
National Technological University
University of Colorado at Colorado Springs   Arizona   New Mexico   Oklahoma
University of Colorado at Denver

Kansas State University   Texas

University of California Extension

Rogers State University
Western Oklahoma State College

Southwestern Adventist University
Southwest Texas State University
Hawaii   University of North Texas

USA

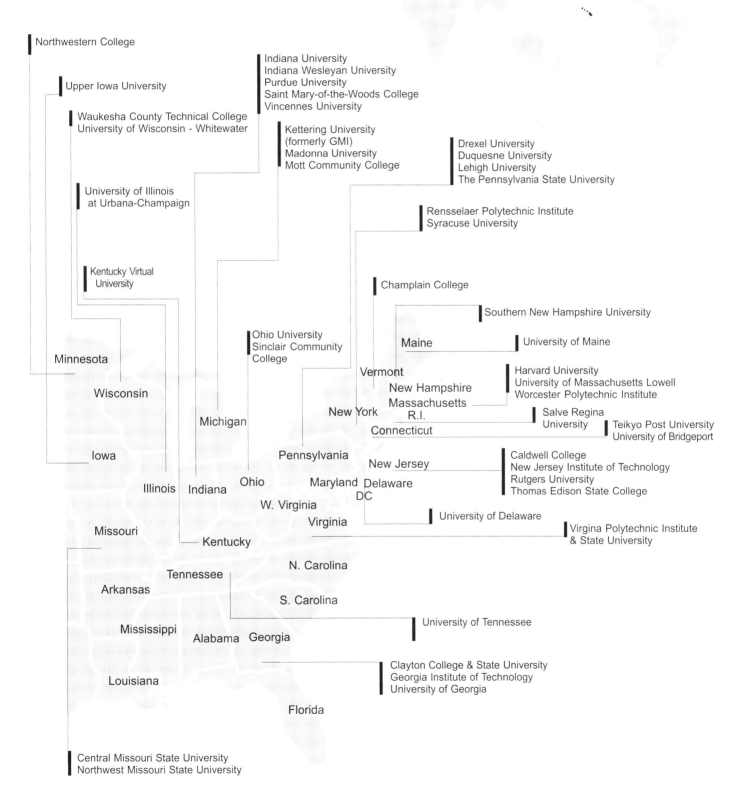

Northwestern College

Upper Iowa University

Waukesha County Technical College
University of Wisconsin - Whitewater

University of Illinois
at Urbana-Champaign

Kentucky Virtual
University

Minnesota

Wisconsin

Iowa

Missouri

Illinois   Indiana

Kentucky

Arkansas

Tennessee

Mississippi

Louisiana

Michigan

Ohio

W. Virginia

Alabama   Georgia

Florida

Indiana University
Indiana Wesleyan University
Purdue University
Saint Mary-of-the-Woods College
Vincennes University

Kettering University
(formerly GMI)
Madonna University
Mott Community College

Drexel University
Duquesne University
Lehigh University
The Pennsylvania State University

Rensselaer Polytechnic Institute
Syracuse University

Champlain College

Southern New Hampshire University

Maine

University of Maine

Vermont

New Hampshire

Massachusetts

R.I.

New York

Connecticut

Harvard University
University of Massachusetts Lowell
Worcester Polytechnic Institute

Salve Regina
University

Teikyo Post University
University of Bridgeport

Ohio University
Sinclair Community
College

Pennsylvania

New Jersey

Caldwell College
New Jersey Institute of Technology
Rutgers University
Thomas Edison State College

Maryland   Delaware

DC

Virginia

University of Delaware

Virgina Polytechnic Institute
& State University

N. Carolina

S. Carolina

University of Tennessee

Clayton College & State University
Georgia Institute of Technology
University of Georgia

Central Missouri State University
Northwest Missouri State University

Program Quick Facts

Institute Name	Page	Programs/Courses						Program Details				Delivery Mode								
		University Transfer	Undergraduate Degree	Graduate Degree	Associate Degree	Certificate/Diploma/Noncredit	Credit Courses	Distance Education Enrollment	Application Fee ($US)	Tuition ($US)	Program Entry Dates	Correspondence/Print	Audio/Videotapes	Internet/Email	Software/CD-ROM	A/V Conferencing	Cable/Satellite TV	Phone/Fax	Discussion Forums/Chat	Other
Adams State College	30						●	18,168	n/a	varies by program	ongoing	●	●				●			
Bellevue Community College	32		●		●		●	6000+	n/a	varies by program	Jun, Sep, Jan, Mar			●			●			
Bellevue University	34		●	●			●	600	–	varies by program	varies			●						
Caldwell College	36		●					–	40	varies by program	fall, spring, summer	●	●	●				●		
Central Missouri State University	38			●			●	1,562	25	varies by program	Jan, May, Aug			●		●				
Champlain College	40		●		●	●		1,500	35	varies by program	Aug, Jan, May			●						
Clayton College & State University	42				●		●	1,670	20	varies by program	fall, winter, spring			●			●			
Colorado Electronic Community College	44				●	●	●	–	n/a	varies by program	Jan, May, Aug			●				●		
Colorado State University	46		●	●	●			1,200	n/a	varies by program	varies	●	●	●		●	●	●		
Community Colleges of Colorado	48				●	●		4,096	n/a	varies by program	six months yearly		●		●				●	●
Creighton University	50			●				268	60	varies by program	Aug	●	●	●	●					
Drexel University	52			●		●		–	n/a	varies by program	three times yearly			●						●

ei's guide to distance and online learning programs in the usa - 2001 edition

Program Quick Facts

Institute Name	Page	Programs/Courses						Program Details				Delivery Mode								
		University Transfer	Undergraduate Degree	Graduate Degree	Associate Degree	Certificate/Diploma/Noncredit	Credit Courses	Distance Education Enrollment	Application Fee ($US)	Tuition ($US)	Program Entry Dates	Correspondence/Print	Audio/Videotapes	Internet/Email	Software/CD-ROM	A/V Conferencing	Cable/Satellite TV	Phone/Fax	Discussion Forums/Chat	Other
Duquesne University	54			●			●	not available	25	varies by program	Sep, Jan, May			●						
Eastern Oregon University	56	●						1,500	50	varies by program	–	●	●	●	●					●
Georgia Institute of Technology	58			●				400–450	50	varies by pr-gram	Aug, Jan, May		●	●	●		●	●	●	●
Harvard University	60						●	13,000	35/term	varies by program	fall, spring			●						
Indiana University	62		●	●	●			18,000+	35	varies by program	fall, spring	●	●	●			●			●
Indiana Wesleyan University	64		●	●				365	20	varies by program	cohort groups	●		●	●				●	
Jones International University®, Ltd.	66		●	●		●		varies	75	varies by program	monthly			●						
Kansas State University	68		●	●		●		5,438	none	varies by program	Jan	●	●	●	●				●	
Kentucky Virtual University	70		●	●	●	●	●	3,105 (spring 2001)	varies	varies by program	fall, spring, summer			●						●
Kettering University (formerly GMI)	72		●	●				700	n/a	varies by program	fall, winter		●	●				●		●
Lehigh University	74			●		●	●	800	–	varies by program	varies		●	●			●	●		

ei's guide to distance and online learning programs in the usa - 2001 edition

Program Quick Facts

Institute Name	Page	University Transfer	Undergraduate Degree	Graduate Degree	Associate Degree	Certificate/Diploma/Noncredit	Credit Courses	Distance Education Enrollment	Application Fee ($US)	Tuition ($US)	Program Entry Dates	Correspondence/Print	Audio/Videotapes	Internet/Email	Software/CD-ROM	A/V Conferencing	Cable/Satellite TV	Phone/Fax	Discussion Forums/Chat	Other
Madonna University	76		•	•				560	25	varies by program	fall		•	•		•				
Mott Community College	78				•			1,880	n/a	varies by program	–	•	•	•	•					
National American University	80		•		•	•		–	25	varies by program	–			•						
National Technological University	82			•		•		1,255	50	varies by program	ongoing		•	•	•		•			
New Jersey Institute of Technology	84		•	•		•		5,000	35	varies by program	Sep, Jan, May		•	•	•				•	
Northwest Missouri State University	86		•					230	15	varies by program	fall			•						
Northwestern College	88		•	•		•	•	700	25	varies by program	continuous	•	•	•						
Ohio University	90		•		•		•	2,500	n/a	varies by program	year round	•	•	•	•			•		
The Pennsylvania State University	92		•	•	•	•		21,566	50	varies by program	year round	•	•	•		•			•	•
Purdue University	94			•			•	1,500	50	varies by program	Aug, Jan	•	•	•	•	•	•			
Rensselaer Polytechnic Institute	96			•		•		1,000	45	varies by program	–		•	•		•	•			

ei's guide to distance and online learning programs in the usa - 2001 edition

Program Quick Facts

Institute Name	Page	Programs/Courses						Program Details				Delivery Mode								
		University Transfer	Undergraduate Degree	Graduate Degree	Associate Degree	Certificate/Diploma/Noncredit	Credit Courses	Distance Education Enrollment	Application Fee ($US)	Tuition ($US)	Program Entry Dates	Correspondence/Print	Audio/Videotapes	Internet/Email	Software/CD-ROM	A/V Conferencing	Cable/Satellite TV	Phone/Fax	Discussion Forums/Chat	Other
Rogers State University	98		●		●		●	1,500	–	varies by program	Jan, Jun, Aug		●	●			●			
Rutgers - The State University of New Jersey	100			●		●		1,000	75	varies by program	Sep, Jan			●	●					
Saint Mary-of-the-Woods College	102		●	●	●	●		1,046	30	varies by program	Sep, Nov, Feb, Apr	●	●	●	●			●		
Salve Regina University	104			●		●		240	50	varies by program	year round	●		●				●		
Sinclair Community College	106				●	●		4,287	10	varies by program	four times yearly	●	●	●	●					
Southern New Hampshire University	108		●	●	●	●		7,000	n/a	varies by program	six times yearly			●					●	●
Southern Oregon University	110						●	150/term	50	varies by program	ongoing			●		●			●	
Southwest Texas State University	112					●	●	2,429	25	varies by program	year round	●	●	●						
Southwestern Adventist University	114		●		●			280	n/a	varies by program	year round	●	●					●		
Syracuse University	116		●	●				1,000	40	varies by program	Jan, May, Aug	●		●				●		●
Teikyo Post University	118		●		●	●		200	40	varies by program	year round			●					●	

ei's guide to distance and online learning programs in the usa - 2001 edition

Program Quick Facts

Institute Name	Page	Programs/Courses						Program Details				Delivery Mode								
		University Transfer	Undergraduate Degree	Graduate Degree	Associate Degree	Certificate/Diploma/Noncredit	Credit Courses	Distance Education Enrollment	Application Fee ($US)	Tuition ($US)	Program Entry Dates	Correspondence/Print	Audio/Videotapes	Internet/Email	Software/CD-ROM	A/V Conferencing	Cable/Satellite TV	Phone/Fax	Discussion Forums/Chat	Other
Thomas Edison State College	120		•	•	•	•		8,137	75	varies by program	year round			•						•
University of Bridgeport	122			•				170	40	varies by program	Sep, Jan			•						•
University of California Extension	124					•	•	5,000	60	varies by program	varies	•		•	•			•	•	
University of Colorado at Colorado Springs	126			•				250 (MBA)	75	varies by program	Aug, Jan, May	•	•	•						
University of Colorado at Denver	128		•	•			•	1,632	varies	varies by program	Aug, Jan			•					•	•
University of Delaware	130		•					1,936	50	varies by program	fall, spring		•	•						
University of Georgia	132						•	4,356	n/a	varies by program	year round	•	•	•						•
University of Illinois at Urbana-Champaign	134			•		•	•	–	40	varies by program	Aug, Jan	•	•	•	•	•				•
University of Maine	136		•			•	•	3,980	25	varies by program	Jan, Sep			•		•				
University of Massachusetts at Lowell	138		•		•	•		4,800	–	varies by program	three times yearly			•				•	•	•
University of Nevada, Reno	140		•					2,500	n/a	varies by program	continuous	•	•	•	•					

ei's guide to distance and online learning programs in the usa - 2001 edition

Program Quick Facts

Institute Name	Page	University Transfer	Undergraduate Degree	Graduate Degree	Associate Degree	Certificate/Diploma/Noncredit	Credit Courses	Distance Education Enrollment	Application Fee ($US)	Tuition ($US)	Program Entry Dates	Correspondence/Print	Audio/Videotapes	Internet/Email	Software/CD-ROM	A/V Conferencing	Cable/Satellite TV	Phone/Fax	Discussion Forums/Chat	Other
University of North Texas	142		●	●		●		varies	25 (dom); 50 (int'l)	varies by program	Aug, Jan, Jun	●		●	●	●				
University of Tennessee	144			●		●		2,600	35	varies by program	–	●	●	●	●			●		
University of Wisconsin - Whitewater	146			●		●		450	45	varies by program	Aug, Jan, May			●	●					●
University of Wyoming	148		●	●		●		1,571	35	varies by program	any semester per year			●		●				●
Upper Iowa University	150		●	●				1,850	50	varies by program	six times yearly			●				●		
Vincennes University	152				●	●		1,700	20	varies by program	year round	●	●	●		●	●			
Virginia Polytechnic Institute & State University	154			●		●		7,300	n/a	varies by program	summer, fall			●	●	●			●	
Waukesha County Technical College	156				●	●	●	675	30	varies by program	fall, spring, summer		●	●		●	●			
Weber State University	158		●		●	●		–	30 + 10 registration	varies by program	varies	●	●	●	●					
Western Oklahoma State College	160						●	211	15	varies by program	Jan, Jun, Aug		●	●		●	●			
Worcester Polytechnic Institute	162			●		●		150	50	varies by program	Sept, Jan, May	●	●	●						

How to Read the Profiles

program descriptions, aims and requirements; may include detailed descriptions of specific programs

unique or important aspects of the distance and/or online learning program

listing of programs leading to degrees, diplomas or certificates; may also include list of credit courses offered by the institution

# of students at all levels of study in full-time enrollment at the institution

# of students enrolled in distance and online learning programs

The Pennsylvania State University

Distance Education Programs

Highlights

- PSU offers more than 150 independent learning credit courses
- PSU establishes distance learning programs with corporate partners
- Money.com has ranked World Campus among the top 10 virtual campuses in the US
- Distance learning alumni include Ben Cohen and Jerry Greenfield of Ben & Jerry's® fame

Programs Offered

Associate Degrees:
  Business Administration
  Dietetic Food Systems Management
  Hotel, Restaurant & Institutional Management
  Human Development & Family Studies
  Letters, Arts & Sciences
Bachelor's Degree Completion:
  Letters, Arts & Sciences
Credit Certificates:
  Postbaccalaureate
  Undergraduate
Dual Degree Program:
  LionHawk
Master's Degree:
  Adult Education

University Statistics

Year Founded:	1855
Total Enrollment:	80,790
Undergraduate Enrollment:	70,796
Graduate Enrollment:	9,994
Distance Education Enrollment:	21,566

Program Overview

Pennsylvania State University is a pioneer in distance learning. PSU's first distance courses in agriculture were offered by correspondence in 1892. More than one hundred years later, PSU still offers distance courses through the World Campus (WC), independent learning (IL) and distributed learning (DL) programs. The Distance Education Report has referred to PSU as a "bellwether institution" in high-technology distance learning and Money.com has ranked World Campus among the country's top 10 virtual campuses.

Penn State Distance Education (PSDE) accepts applications year round. Course length and registration deadlines vary by program, and the campus website contains the most up-to-date program information.

Associate degree program applicants should have a high school diploma, or general education diploma (GED) and acceptable SAT or ACT scores. Other admission options include 18 credits acquired from a regionally accredited institution with a minimum cumulative 2.0 grade point average (GPA), or nine credits acquired from PSU. PSDE also admits high school seniors who expect to receive a 2.0 GPA or higher based on SAT or PSAT results.

The language of instruction of PSDE courses and programs is English. The Test of English as a Foreign Language is therefore required for international degree program applicants, but only recommended for international credit course or certificate program applicants.

Applicants may choose from several credit transfer options. Credit can be applied directly from other regionally accredited institutions, high school advanced placement examinations, college level examinations or military experience. Credit can also be applied through the American Council on Education's College Credit Recommendation Service. Applicants over the age of 60 who are also Pennsylvania residents, PSU alumni or former PSU employees can take credit courses at half tuition.

World Campus Courses and Programs

Initiated in 1998, WC expects to offer between 25 and 30 programs, instruct 300 online credit courses and attain 10,000 enrollments by 2003.

WC enables participants to acquire a master's degree in adult education, in addition to associate degrees in hotel, restaurant, and institutional management and dietetic food

systems management (with health care or school food service emphases). PSU grants a postbaccalaureate certificate in logistics and supply chain management.

Independent Learning Courses and Programs

IL enables students to obtain a bachelor's degree in letters, arts and sciences and associate degrees in business administration, human development and family studies, and letters, arts and sciences. The university grants a certificate in one of ten disciplines: adult development and aging services, business management, dietetics and aging, general business, human resources, marketing management, purchasing management, retail management, writing social commentary, and child, youth and family services. Students can apply credit from more than 150 individual courses toward associate or bachelor's degree requirements.

In cooperation with the University of Iowa (UI), PSU has established the LionHawk program, which permits distance learners to earn an associate degree in letters, arts and science from UI and a bachelor of liberal arts studies from PSU. As well, IL offers a variety of noncredit courses and programs.

details on course delivery methods, specific system/software requirements, along with academic resources available to distance learners

description of the institution, including faculties, departments or disciplines, enrollment figures, history and location

The Pennsylvania State University

Distance Education Programs

contact information details for general or program-specific inquiries

Program Delivery and Student Support

WC students should have access to a 100MHz or higher processor. Other hardware features should include 32MB of RAM, 100MB of free disk space, a 14-inch monitor, graphics-capable (inkjet or laser) printer, and 28.8 kbps or higher-speed modem. WC recommends that participants use operating systems such as Windows 95, Windows 98, Windows NT, or Macintosh System 8.1 or higher, in addition to browser software such as Netscape 4.0 or Internet Explorer 4.0 (or higher).

WC students utilize a selection of online services, including bulletin board discussions, chat rooms, reference materials, learning resources, news updates for adult students, study skills, writing workshops and a calendar of WC events. World Campus 101 is a free online course that familiarizes students with online instruction and procedures. WC students can also access the PSU library via an online catalog ("The Cat") and various online research databases.

University and Location

Pennsylvania State University was founded by private charter in 1855, but the Commonwealth of Pennsylvania recognizes PSU as a "state-related" institution. PSU oversees more than 160 baccalaureate and 150 graduate programs and awards nearly 14,000 degrees each year. During the 1998-99 fiscal year, PSU's research expenditures approached US$393 million.

More than 80,000 undergraduate and graduate students attend classes at PSU's 25 campuses. Slightly more than one half of the student body is enrolled at the University Park campus. During the 1999–2000 academic year, 3,000 international students from more than 100 countries studied at PSU. The university has a student to faculty ratio of 19 to 1.

The PSU library collection houses more than 3.7 million volumes and 31,000 serials and periodicals. Staff handle more than five million transactions each month. Various offices provide services related to audiovisual learning aids, computing and microcomputer purchases, health and wellness, student physical disabilities, hospitality, campus policing and travel.

Centre County, the home of PSU's University Park campus, has a population of approximately 133,000 and is situated at the geographic heart of Pennsylvania. The county's four state parks provide areas for hiking, camping, hunting and fishing.

Contact Information

Distance Education Programs
207 Mitchell Building
University Park Pennsylvania 16802-3601 USA
phone: 1-814-865-5403
fax: 1-814-865-3290
email: psuwd@psu.edu
Internet: http://www.worldcampus.psu.edu

methods and materials used for course instruction & assessment, peer interaction and instructor feedback

Delivery Mode

• World Campus (online instruction, email, chat rooms)
• Independent Learning (textbooks; audio & video tapes; audio, video & computer teleconferences)
• Distributed Learning (classroom instruction, interactive videoconferences)

dates at which students may begin programs

individual program enrollments

course or program costs

entry requirements for specific programs

Program Facts

	Program Entry	Program Length	Total Enrollment	# of Int'l Students	Total Program Costs	Application Fee	Prerequisites
Associate Degree (IL)	year round	varies	566	23	US$130–240 per credit	US$50	high school diploma, GED or 18 credits from a regionally accredited institution with a 2.0 GPA
LionHawk Dual Degree Program	year round	varies	–	–	varies	US$30/UI, $50/PSU	contact LionHawk Program at PSU or UI
Master's Degree in Adult Education (WC)	year round	varies	250	–	US$266 per credit	US$50	bachelor's degree from a regionally accredited institution
Postbaccalaureate Certificate (IL)	year round	varies	244	–	US$130–240 per credit	US$50	bachelor's degree from a regionally accredited institution
Undergraduate Certificate (IL) (WC)	year round	varies	232 IL, 2600 WC	14 IL, 24 WC	US$130–240 per credit	US$50 WC	high school diploma, GED or college credit

PROGRAM
PROFILES

Adams State College

•

Division of Extended Studies

Highlights

- Rated one of 100 Best Buys for Colleges by publication that ranks American colleges and universities
- Professional development programs for educators via StarNet
- Member of Colorado Consortium for Independent Study

Programs Offered

Credit Courses:
  Business
  Economics
  English
  Environmental Science
  Inter-discipline
  Journaling
  Mathematics
  Parenting
  Psychology
  Sociology
  Sports Conditioning
Graduate Credit Courses (Education):
  Anger, Frustration and Low Self-esteem
  Conflict & Confrontation
  Creative Journaling
  Current Issues in Education
  Dealing with Change
  Educational Trends
  Improving Writing Skills (Autobiography)
  Journaling in the Classrooom
  More Navigating the Information Highway
  Navigating the Information Highway
  Positive Classroom Discipline
  Preparing for Today's Students
  Self-care & Renewal
  Time to Read
Graduate Credit Courses (Science):
  Contemporary Topics in Biology

College Statistics

Year Founded:	1921
Total Enrollment:	2,500
Undergraduate Enrollment:	2,000
Graduate Enrollment:	500
Distance Education Enrollment:	18,168

Program Overview

The Division of Extended Studies (DES) at Adams State College (ASC) has two major methods of course delivery that extend instruction across the country and to the world. Courses can be taken for undergraduate or graduate credit as independent paper-based or web-based packages. Professional development courses for educators are delivered through StarNet, which broadcasts interactive instructional programming in the US and beyond.

Courses offered on campus are sometimes produced online. DES also administers credit courses at off campus locations throughout Colorado and New Mexico.

Independent Study

ASC offers approximately 50 paper-based and 15 web-based independent study courses for individuals who wish to upgrade their knowledge, fulfill re-certification requirements, work toward a degree or gain personal satisfaction.

Courses are accessible to a broad base of students through the college's membership in the Colorado Consortium for Independent Study (CCIS). This body comprises seven institutions in the state that offer courses for high school students, undergraduate and graduate credit, and professional development. CCIS brings together independent study course listings from individual institutions under a central calendar and website. Registration is made directly to the college or university offering the course of choice. Registration in independent study courses does not grant students official registration status for regular on-campus courses.

Upon registration, students receive a course package of instructions and a study guide. Assignments can be mailed, e-mailed, faxed or done directly on the web, with most courses requiring supervised examinations. These exams must be taken under the supervision of a school official, principal, guidance counselor, college official, military education officer or clergy person. Exams are ordered directly from the Division of Extended Studies using the Examination Request form provided in the study guide. Grades are sent after all coursework is complete. Any incomplete not changed within a one-year period of time will now revert to an "F" grade. Refund requests must be made within 40 working days from the date of registration and will only constitute 90 percent of tuition paid.

ASC listings include remedial,

undergraduate and graduate courses in business, economics, education, English, environmental science, exercise physiology/leisure science, parenting, journalism, mathematics, psychology, science and sociology.

Professional Development

Seven professional development course areas are broadcast to educators on cable television via StarNet, which offers the largest selection of instructional programming in the US.

StarNet courses are interactive and combine satellite broadcasts, one-way video, 2-way audio, fax or email. The system brings together resources and professionals from 40 states. Courses are frequently composed of several parts and may be broadcast throughout the year.

Normally, interested groups of teachers and other professionals organize themselves around an on-site coordinator, who ensures everyone has sufficient course registration forms. They choose the courses they want to view, and meet together on the broadcast dates. Individuals can also view programs on their own. After viewing, students complete course summaries that include the major concepts covered, examples of how these concepts can be applied to teaching or professional situations, reactions to the topic and new ideas acquired. Summaries must be sent along with registration forms and payment for each course to ASC before the deadline for that school year, usually in June. Fees vary according to semester hour credit.

Grading is completed within three weeks after registrations and summaries are received. Transcripts with grades can be ordered for a fee of US$4.

Program topics include leadership and administration, early childhood development, assessment, curriculum and classroom strategies, alternative education, technical education and special issues. Courses take the form of workshop and seminar series or university credit courses.

Adams State College

●

Division of Extended Studies

Program Delivery and Student Support

Independent study courses are offered through the Extended Studies website or through a link to the Colorado Consortium for Independent Study (CCIS), where general registration forms and catalogs are available. These can be faxed or students can register by phone.

Students can connect with instructors by phone, fax, email or mail. Extended Studies maintains website indices on links to teaching resources, online libraries, technology magazines and distance education sites.

StarNet courses are self-contained within their broadcast format; external support or services are not required. The StarNet website at http://www.starnet.org offers suggestions on how to participate in programs.

College and Location

Founded in 1921, Adams State College enrolls 2,500 students annually in more than 30 areas including pre-professional programs and transfer programs. The college maintains high admission standards, the highest of any non-doctoral institution in the US according to the Colorado Commission on Higher Education (CCHE).

ASC brings together faculty and resources from throughout the state to initiate global instruction. This program is called Connect the DOTS (Delivery of Transparent Systems).

The college is located in the southcentral region of Colorado. It forms part of the Wolf Creek Educational Assistance Region, which is one of the regional components of the Colorado Department of Education.

Contact Information

Division of Extended Studies
Judy Phillips, Director, 208 Edgemont, RH 143
Alamosa Colorado 81102 USA
phone: 1-800-548-6679
fax: 1-719-587-7974
email: ascextend@adams.edu
internet: http://www.adams.edu/exstudies/index.html

Delivery Mode

• Satellite broadcasts
• Video cassettes
• Paper-based course packages

Program Facts

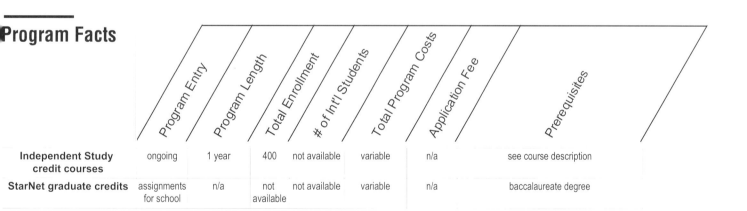

	Program Entry	Program Length	Total Enrollment	# of Int'l Students	Total Program Costs	Application Fee	Prerequisites
Independent Study credit courses	ongoing	1 year	400	not available	variable	n/a	see course description
StarNet graduate credits	assignments for school	n/a	not available	not available	variable	n/a	baccalaureate degree

Bellevue Community College

•

Distance Education

- First two years of university available through transferable credits online, from around the world
- Business administration degree offered in cooperation with two other institutions
- Some online courses tailored to international student interests

Programs Offered

Associate Degrees:
- Arts and Sciences (university transfer)
- General Business (university transfer)
- Media Communication & Technology

Credit Courses:
- Accounting
- Computer Science
- Humanities
- Natural Sciences
- Social Sciences

Degree:
- Business Administration

College Statistics

Year Founded:	1966
Total Enrollment:	20,000+/quarter
Undergraduate Enrollment	20,000+/quarter
Graduate Enrollment:	n/a
Distance Education Enrollment:	6000+

Program Overview

Bellevue Community College (BCC) offers four associate degrees by Distance Learning in arts and sciences, general business, and media communication and technology. Associate degrees require two years of study; two of the degrees offered are transferable to undergraduate degree programs. Distance Learning also offers certificates in media communication and administrative office systems.

Distance Learning (DL) courses for credit are delivered online or by cable television; the course structure is similar to that of on-campus courses. Unlike correspondence courses, DL courses require regular participation and students should expect to spend 10–15 hours studying, five out of seven days per week.

Online courses are available throughout the world. The televised courses often require on-campus attendance for an initial orientation and for material review sessions prior to examinations. All credit courses have specific assignment deadlines and start and end dates.

International Programs maintains a listing of courses not for credit but of particular interest to international students, such as small business, international trade and marketing, or English improvement. Continuing Education delivers non-credit online courses in business and computer skills and for general interest.

Business Administration Degree

Students interested in business administration can pursue either an Associate in Arts & Sciences (AAS) or a Bachelor of Arts (BA) online. Both paths are offered in collaboration with Edmonds Community College and Washington State University.

The undergraduate degree is structured according to curriculum recommendations of the American Association of Collegiate Schools of Business and the International Association for Management Education.

The AAS in General Business is the initial 2-year phase of the BA. Core courses in accounting, business law, mathematics and economics prepare students for further BA studies in finance, management, information systems, marketing and international business.

Students can complete the BA entirely online, or may choose to take on-campus electives at community colleges.

Media Communication & Technology

The Associate in Arts (AA) in Media Communication & Technology (Media) Web Authoring is a non-transferable two-year program designed to fulfill a growing need for skilled workers in media communication resources. A Certificate of Achievement of shorter duration is also available.

The AA degree provides in-depth engagement with all aspects of media production, while the certificate offers exposure to specific media fields for students who possess prior background in media production and computer usage.

To register, all students must either take a core media course, or achieve a high score on a test of knowledge of online techniques, computer platforms and histories, and HTML.

Subjects covered include 2D and 3D animation and graphics, web authoring, and multimedia and video production.

Arts & Sciences

Two programs of study, the Associate in Arts and Sciences (AAS) and the Associate in Arts in General Studies (AAGS) initiate students into general university studies.

The AAS curriculum fulfills the first two years of undergraduate degree requirements at all postsecondary institutions in the state of Washington. Course distribution equally covers the humanities, social sciences, natural sciences and electives, including three distinct disciplines within each area.

The AAGS allows students to explore interests outside of the more structured AAS curriculum. Credit transfer to institutions offering undergraduate degrees may be possible upon consultation. Program prerequisites are high school level math and English.

Recommendations for this associate degree include equal amounts of credit in the humanities, social sciences, natural sciences and physical education.

Bellevue Community College

Distance Education

Program Delivery and Student Support

BCC delivers its own online courses: students must have computer access with a JavaScript-enabled Web browser, an Internet service provider account, and an e-mail account.

Some courses offered online for BCC credit are delivered by WashingtonOnline. These online courses are a compilation offered by instructors throughout Washington and are funded for in-state residents. Non-residents pay regular out-of-state tuition. To take these courses, students need to download the free software, FirstClass.

Television broadcasts of courses depend on the availability of cable television access to BCC's The College Channel on AT&T, centered in the Bellevue area.

Students can order textbooks online from BCC's Online Bookstore, or request the assistance of an academic advisor.

College and Location

Bellevue Community College is accredited by the Northwest Association of Schools and Colleges Commission on Colleges. It offers four associate two-year degrees, with occupational specializations in over 25 areas, and certificates in 30 areas.

The college invites the participation of international students. Students from 60 countries are enrolled at BCC. Through the International Student Services website, students can find assistance ranging from academic counseling to help with homework.

BCC is located in the city of Bellevue in northwest Washington, linked by bridges with Seattle. With a population of 105,700, it is the fifth largest city in the state of Washington.

Contact Information

Distance Education
Rm D261, 3000 Landerholm Cr. SE
Bellevue Washington 98007-6484 USA
phone: 1-425-564-2438
fax: 1-425-564-6186
email: landerso@bcc.ctc.edu
internet: http://distance-ed.bcc.ctc.edu

International Programs Office
Main Campus-House #2
Bellevue Washington 98007-6484 USA
          1-425-564-2409
          1-425-564-0246
          intlprog@bcc.ctc.edu
          http://online.bcc.ctc.edu/intp/

Delivery Mode

• Online via Internet
• Video broadcasts on cable television

Program Facts

	Program Entry	Program Length	Total Enrollment	# of Int'l Students	Total Program Costs	Application Fee	Prerequisites
Associate degrees	Jun, Sep, Jan, Mar	2 years	–	–	US$5,369 in-state	n/a	high school level English and Math
BCC credit courses: in-state	Jun, Sep, Jan, Mar	5 credits = 1 term course	–	–	US$321 per 5 credits	n/a	prerequisites vary
BCC credit courses: out-of-state	Jun, Sep, Jan, Mar	5 credits = 1 term course	–	–	US$340 per 5 credits	n/a	prerequisites vary
BCC/WashingtonOnline courses: in-state	Jun, Sep, Jan, Mar	5 credits = 1 term course	–	–	US$336	n/a	prerequisites vary
BCC/WashingtonOnline courses: out-of-state	Jun, Sep, Jan, Mar	5 credits = 1 term course	–	–	US$1,139	n/a	prerequisites vary

Bellevue University

•

Bellevue University Online

Programs Offered

Bachelor of Arts:
  Leadership
Bachelor of Science:
  Business Admin of Technical Studies
  Business Information Systems
  Criminal Justice Administration
  E-business
  Global Business Management
  Health Care Administration
  Management
  Management Information Systems
  Management of Human Resources
Graduate Courses:
  Variety of courses available
Master of Arts:
  Leadership
  Management
Master of Business Administration:
  Accounting Concentration
  Cyber Law Concentration
  Finance Concentration
  Management Information Systems Concentration
Master of Science:
  Computer Information Systems
  Health Care Administration

University Statistics

Year Founded:	1966
Total Enrollment:	3,445
Undergraduate Enrollment	2,815
Graduate Enrollment:	630
Distance Education Enrollment:	600

Program Overview

Bellevue University Online offers complete degrees accredited by The Higher Learning Commission and is a member of the North Central Association of Colleges and Schools Commission on Institutions of Higher Education (NCA–CIHE). The programs are designed to meet the changing needs of people interested in higher education.

Most online students work full-time and are required to be self-disciplined to handle the added demands of school.

Online programs offered include undergraduate degrees in ten major areas and five graduate degrees. All online degrees are identical on university transcripts to those earned on campus. Students may register online.

The key to Bellevue University Online programs is the use of cyber-active® learning in the online classroom. Through cyber-active® learning, students participate in classroom activities and student forums, which include discussions between students and professors via threaded e-mails. Students have 24-hour access to course sites.

Graduate Degrees Online

Online graduate admissions requirements include a US equivalent undergraduate degree, a GPA of 2.5 or higher in the last 60 credit hours of undergraduate work, completion of the application package and two letters of reference.

Students and faculty in graduate programs work closely together to enhance critical thinking and the generation of ideas. Online communication allows case study analysis and the exchange of ideas applicable to professional work situations.

Master of Business Administration

The Master of Business Administration (MBA) covers the tools and methods required to run a business. The program requires 36 credit hours of coursework. The schedule of course offerings permits an individual working full time to complete all the requirements for the MBA degree in 18 months (two classes per term).

Students who do not have an undergraduate degree in business generally take the Foundation (12 credits) and the Core (24 credits) to complete the degree. MBA concentrations are offered in Accounting, Cyber Law, Finance, International Management and Management Information Systems.

MS in Computer Information Systems

This program has strong elements of both business and computer/telecommunication subjects. Students with business or computer undergraduate preparation will typically finish the program with 36 credits of graduate work.

Students without a computer background are required to complete six additional credits of prerequisites.

MS in Health Care Administration

This program provides clinical health care providers with an opportunity to pursue in depth the various areas of planning, organizing, leading and controlling as they provide administrative guidance to others within their health-related organizations.

MA Programs in Management and Leadership

The MA in Management develops a working knowledge of the application of quantitative techniques, marketing analysis, human resource management, financial analysis, influencing behavior in organizations, and sensitivity to the legal environment in which operations occur.

The MA in Leadership encourages individual thought, synthesis of group contribution, and assimilation of practical and theoretical teachings. Its mission is to combine leadership philosophy, derived from great leaders and their writings, with concepts and theoretical models of organizational leadership.

Undergraduate degrees

Online undergraduate admission requirements include an associate's degree or 60 credit hours from an accredited institution. The majors are offered in an accelerated format of 36 credit hours with about eight to twelve courses. An additional nine hours in the University's Kirkpatrick Signature Series are needed to complete the 45 hours required for the program.

Bellevue University

●

Bellevue University Online

Program Delivery and Student Support

Bellevue University Online is delivered through a web-based course management tool. Students may access the online classroom anytime from anywhere via the Internet. In addition, the University uses the Bellevue Real-time User Information Network (BRUIN). Through the network, students can check progress toward their degree, register for classes, make payments and review class schedules.

Students studying online have full library access. Full-text online journal articles are updated daily, and the library subscribes to 11 research and text databases. The library is connected to nine other institutional libraries.

To access online programs, students need a computer with a minimum 32MB RAM, a modem, Windows 95 or higher, and an Internet provider and e-mail address to access the Web.

University and Location

Bellevue University was founded in 1966 and offers graduate and undergraduate degrees. The University enrolls 3400 students annually, including an international component of students from more than 40 countries.

Bellevue University is actively involved with information technology. It's award-winning website and its online course component provide access to higher education for students worldwide.

The University is located in Bellevue, a suburb of Omaha, Nebraska on the banks of the Missouri River.

Contact Information

Bellevue University Online
Undergraduate Online Admiss., 1000 Galvin Rd S.
Bellevue NB 68005 USA
phone: 1-800-756-7920 ext 3757
fax: 1-402-293-3758
email: online-u@bellevue.edu
internet: http://www.bellevue.edu

Graduate Online Admissions, 1000 Galvin Rd South
Bellevue NB 68005 USA
1-800-756-7920 ext 3757
1-402-293-3758
online-g@bellevue.edu
http://www.bellevue.edu

Delivery Mode

• All distance learning courses offered online

Program Facts

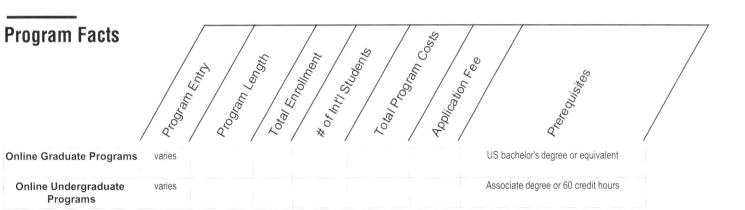

	Program Entry	Program Length	Total Enrollment	# of Int'l Students	Total Program Costs	Application Fee	Prerequisites
Online Graduate Programs	varies						US bachelor's degree or equivalent
Online Undergraduate Programs	varies						Associate degree or 60 credit hours

Caldwell College

•

External Degree Program

Program Overview

For more than 20 years, Caldwell College has supported an External Degree Program (EDP) that enables mature students to complete a bachelor of arts or science through guided independent study. EDP features Saturday and evening classes and seven-week accelerated courses, and EDP students register in one to five courses per semester. The academic year at Caldwell includes five semesters of study; before each semester, students meet with an academic advisor to establish a study plan, and attend an orientation, reception and dinner as well as selected workshops.

External Degrees

External degrees are offered in accounting, business administration, computer information systems, communication arts, criminal justice, English, French, history, international business, management, marketing, political science, psychology, religious studies, sociology, social studies and Spanish. Graduation requirements vary from program to program.

Accounting, business administration, international business, management and marketing majors are encouraged to participate in an internship. Each major consists of 60 credits of liberal arts and sciences core courses, along with credit in major courses and, with the exception of the accounting program, credit in open electives. Students majoring in international business are expected to be competent in a foreign language.

A campus-based cable TV system provides communication arts students who are specializing in broadcast journalism and radio/television performance with a venue to broadcast work to local audiences.

Computer information systems features a major in microcomputer systems, or a certificate with business systems and microcomputer systems options. Majors must complete courses in data structures and algorithms, machine and assembly language, computer organization, operating systems, linear algebra and calculus.

Criminal justice majors are encouraged to select a minor in sociology, psychology, computer science or political science, or a double major with sociology, psychology or history. Students working toward a degree in criminal justice must complete courses in social science research methods, psychological statistics, juvenile justice, community-based corrections, police and law enforcement, the structure and functioning of US courts, and crime and criminal law.

History majors are encouraged to take courses in statistics and computer science; the study of a foreign language is also recommended. Political science majors should include Understanding the Political World (PC 125) as one of the required social science courses in the core curriculum. Majors in psychology must complete PS 325 and PS 402 with a grade of C or better. Religious studies majors may select a minor in philosophy, psychology or sociology. Sociology majors are encouraged to select a minor in business, computer science, psychology, Spanish or communications arts, or a double major with criminal justice or psychology.

Students who are seeking a bachelor of arts in social studies with certification in education must meet all requirements of the Department of Education related to program admission and completion.

RNs who intend to combine a degree program with school nurse certification may receive as many as 30 credits for current RN licensure and 30 credits from an accredited college or university. State certification involves an eight-week field experience in school nursing.

Admission and Registration

Applications for admission are received year round and may be submitted online. Admission criteria include a high school or general education diploma. The application package consists of official transcripts of previous academic work and a copy of the applicant's social security card. Military personnel must submit their DD214 and law enforcement officers are required to include their police training certificate. Registered nurses (RNs) who are applying to the school nurse certificate program must include their RN license number. The US$40 nonrefundable application fee should be sent by mail. EDP applicants must provide evidence of their ability to undertake college-level assignments with little faculty supervision. Students enrolled in undergraduate or graduate distance learning programs at other institutions may enroll as visiting students in EDP.

Tuition for EDP students is US$337 per credit. Applications for institutional financial support can be completed online.

Caldwell College

•

External Degree Program

Program Delivery and Student Support

External degree courses are delivered by mail (including textbooks and course manuals) as well as by facsimile, email and the Internet, and video. The Academic Computing Center supplies computer hardware, software and peripheral equipment for students and faculty.

Several additional centers are available for student support: the Learning Center assists students with academic skill development; the Counseling Office features individual and group counseling; and the Career Development Center sponsors career counseling and career education. Textbooks and optional course materials and software can be purchased at the college bookstore. Jennings Library houses more than 110,000 books and 600 periodicals, as well as CD-ROM databases, video and audio tapes, and compact discs. The library is a member of the Online Computer Library Center.

College and Location

Caldwell College is a Roman Catholic liberal arts college in Caldwell, New Jersey, that was founded by the Sisters of Saint Dominic in 1939 and chartered as an institution of higher learning for women. Full accreditation was granted in 1952 by the Commission on Higher Education of the Middle States Association of Colleges and Schools. The college was last accredited in 1995.

The college campus features six building complexes. An academic building, constructed in 1997, features multimedia equipment, computerized instructional tools, fiber optic communication links and a satellite receiver. Rosary Hall houses administrative offices, classrooms, student residences and Aquinas Hall. The Student Center contains a cafeteria, lounge, snack bar, gymnasium and fitness center, and Visceglia Art Center and Gallery. The Science Building is comprised of Albertus Magnus Hall and Raymond Hall, both of which contain classrooms, laboratories and faculty offices. Jennings Library includes a Center for Continuing Education and theater supported by multimedia and satellite communication. The Mother Joseph Residence Hall houses and feeds most campus residents.

Caldwell is a small community of 11,000 located in northern New Jersey's Essex County.

Contact Information

External Degree Program
Adult Undergraduate Admissions, 9 Ryerson Avenue
Caldwell New Jersey 07006 USA
phone: 1-973-618-3385
fax: 1-973-618-3660
email: agleason@caldwell.edu
internet: http://www.caldwell.edu/adult-admissions

Delivery Mode

- Mail (textbooks and course manuals)
- Facsimile
- Email and Internet
- Videos

Program Facts

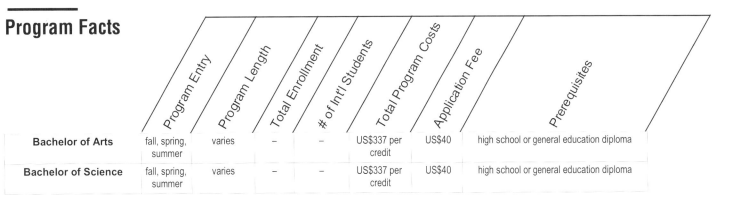

	Program Entry	Program Length	Total Enrollment	# of Int'l Students	Total Program Costs	Application Fee	Prerequisites
Bachelor of Arts	fall, spring, summer	varies	–	–	US$337 per credit	US$40	high school or general education diploma
Bachelor of Science	fall, spring, summer	varies	–	–	US$337 per credit	US$40	high school or general education diploma

Central Missouri State University

•

Office of Extended Campus, Humphreys 403

- Master of Science in Criminal Justice
- Online curriculum for PhD in Technology Management offered through a seven-member consortium
- Professional development for educators

Programs Offered

Graduate Courses:
- Business Education
- Criminal Justice
- Library Information Technology
- Library Science
- Nursing
- Occupational Safety Management
- Physical Education

Graduate Degrees:
- Master of Science in Criminal Justice
- PhD in Technology Management

Graduate Education Courses:
- Curriculum and Instruction
- Education Administration
- Special Education

Undergraduate Courses:
- Child and Family Development
- Communication
- Criminal Justice
- Education
- Electronics Engineering Technology
- History
- Mathematics
- Nutrition
- Physical Education

University Statistics

Year Founded:	1871
Total Enrollment:	11,136
Undergraduate Enrollment	9,013
Graduate Enrollment:	2,123
Distance Education Enrollment:	1,562

Program Overview

The Office of Extended Campus at Central Missouri State University (CMSU) offers distance learning delivery of graduate and postgraduate degree programs, in addition to undergraduate and graduate course work, in several fields of study. Online PhD studies are offered in technology management, and a Master of Science in Criminal Justice is offered via interactive television. Students may enroll in graduate level courses in criminal justice, education, nursing, construction management and occupational safety management. A variety of undergraduate courses are offered, as well as professional development opportunities.

CMSU was designated Missouri's official leader in professional technology in 1996. The university utilizes advanced video teleconferencing technology (interactive television, or I-TV) and the Internet in the delivery of distance education programs. CMSU is a founding member of WeMET, the Western Missouri Educational Technology Consortium, and MOREnet, the Missouri Research and Education Network.

Extended Campus also delivers courses off-site in subjects such as occupational safety management, industrial hygiene, social work, social gerontology, aviation safety, criminal justice and professional development for teachers.

Admission instructions are available by contacting the Office of Admissions or the Graduate School. The application fee for a degree-seeking student is US$25. After admission, students may enroll by telephone or over the Web. Assistance with admission and course enrollment procedures is available through the Office of Extended Campus.

Numerous resources, including modern and technogically available library resources and an experienced and knowledgeable faculty, are available to CMSU's students. Students may tailor their program of study to their personal educational and career needs.

The university's toll-free number, 800-SAY-CMSU, offers distance learning students access to the Office of Extended Campus-Distance Learning, academic advising, admissions, financial aid, revenue, accounts receivable, registrar (student records), university housing, and the Graduate School. All may also be accessed through the Web at the main CMSU homepage (www.cmsu.edu). Extensive course listings and additional information are available on the Extended Campus website, http://www.cmsu.edu/extcamp.

Criminal Justice

The Master of Criminal Justice is designed for professionals active in corrections, juvenile justice and law enforcement at all levels, and for those wishing to find employment in leadership, research, education or specialized careers within the criminal justice field. Courses are delivered online, onsite and via interactive television at various locations throughout Missouri.

Applicants to the program must have an undergraduate degree in criminal justice or a related field. Background courses may otherwise be required. For admission to the degree program, applicants must also submit a GRE score with a total of 1200 or higher and a short statement of purpose. Students choose a thesis or non-thesis option; the latter involves a comprehensive examination following extra coursework.

Education

Graduate coursework toward a Master of Science in Education or toward teacher certification is delivered via I-TV. Courses delivered at pre-arranged sites focus on specific areas within special education, curriculum and instruction, and education administration.

Technology Management

Online courses toward a PhD in Technology Management are offered through a consortium of seven institutions nationwide, with Indiana State University as the degree-granting institution. CMSU offers a core of classes in construction management and manufacturing systems for this degree.

Credit Courses

Distance learning courses allow students to learn and develop professional skills in fields such as nursing, education, child and family development, and nutrition.

Central Missouri State University

•

Office of Extended Campus, Humphreys 403

Program Delivery and Student Support

Online courses require computers with a 4.0 browser, 33.6 kbps modem (a 56K modem or higher connection is suggested) and connection through an Internet service provider.

Interactive television (I-TV) is the synchronous delivery of live courses to prearranged sites. Classrooms are connected by T-1 compressed video lines or by ISDN, the Integrated Services Digital Network. Students in off-campus sites are linked simultaneously via two-way audio and video connections to facilitate teacher-student interaction.

The James C. Kirkpatrick Library provides library resources for distance learning students. Students can borrow books, request interlibrary loans, and call or email staff for reference assistance. Off-campus and distance learning students have full access to the library's electronic databases. An online writing lab provides assistance with writing projects.

University and Location

CMSU is a comprehensive four-year university accredited by the North Central Association of Colleges and Schools. It offers discipline-specific graduate and undergraduate programs in 150 areas of study, including 27 areas of teacher certification and 50 graduate programs. Over 2,000 degrees are conferred annually from the colleges of applied sciences and technology, arts and sciences, business administration, education and human services, and library science. Students come from across the US; four percent of the 11,136 students enrolled are students from 62 foreign countries.

The university is in Warrensburg, central Missouri, one hour's drive southeast of Kansas City. The city has a population of 17,500, for whom CMSU is the main postsecondary institution. CMSU has a long history of providing educational instruction for the area. It originated as a normal school in 1871 and evolved from a teacher's college to its present university status in 1972.

Contact Information

Office of Extended Campus, Humphreys 403
Central Missouri State University
Warrensburg Missouri 64093 USA
phone: 1-660-543-8480
fax: 1-660-543-8333
email: bassore@cmsu1.cmsu.edu
internet: http://www.cmsu.edu/extcamp

Delivery Mode

• Two-way interactive videoconferencing (interactive television)
• Online courses (Web-based learning)

Program Facts

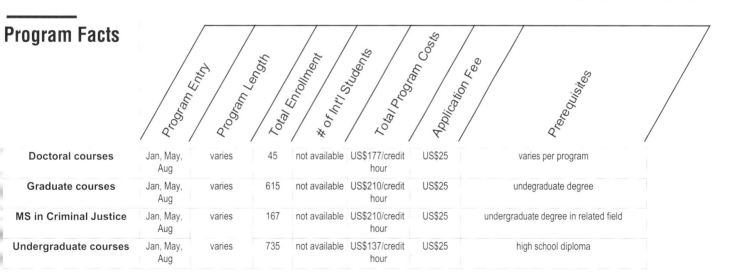

	Program Entry	Program Length	Total Enrollment	# of Int'l Students	Total Program Costs	Application Fee	Prerequisites
Doctoral courses	Jan, May, Aug	varies	45	not available	US$177/credit hour	US$25	varies per program
Graduate courses	Jan, May, Aug	varies	615	not available	US$210/credit hour	US$25	undegraduate degree
MS in Criminal Justice	Jan, May, Aug	varies	167	not available	US$210/credit hour	US$25	undergraduate degree in related field
Undergraduate courses	Jan, May, Aug	varies	735	not available	US$137/credit hour	US$25	high school diploma

Champlain College

•

Champlain College Online Education

Programs Offered

Associate's Degrees:
- Accounting
- Business
- e-Commerce & Business
- Hotel-Restaurant Management
- International Business
- Management
- Software Development
- Telecommunications
- Web Site Development & Management

Bachelor's Degrees:
- Computer Information Systems
- Professional Studies

Professional Certificates:
- Accounting
- Business
- e-Commerce & Business
- Hotel-Restaurant Management
- International Business
- Management
- Software Development
- Telecommunications
- Web Site Development & Management

College Statistics

Year Founded:	1878
Total Enrollment:	1,400
Undergraduate Enrollment:	1,400
Graduate Enrollment:	n/a
Distance Education Enrollment:	1,500

Program Overview

Champlain College OnLine (CCOL) was launched in 1993 and currently enrolls over 1,500 students per year. CCOL's degree programs prepare students for careers in accounting, business, hotel-restaurant management, and technology. Professional Certificates allow students to quickly obtain new skills or update old skills in these fields. Over 100 courses were offered in the 2000-2001 curriculum, with more than 60 courses to choose from each semester. A minimum enrollment of six is necessary for a course to run.

Successful online students are highly motivated and must be comfortable learning and communicating via reading and writing. Basic computer skills, including word processing, are recommended.

Students can obtain an Associate in Science (AS) degree or a professional certificate in accounting, business, e-commerce & business, hotel-restaurant management, international business, management, software development, telecommunications, or web site development and management. Bachelor of Science (BS) degrees are awarded in computer information systems and professional studies.

Online courses operate concurrently with the on-campus semester schedule. They are identical in content, rigor and credit earned to their on-campus counterparts. The World Wide Web and the Internet are used to connect students to the instructors and their classmates, and courses are "asynchronous," meaning students have access to their course(s) twenty-four hours a day, seven days a week. Courses are not self-paced; students are expected to follow a specific schedule of discussions, assignments and exams set forth by the instructor.

The AS degree requires the completion of 60 credits (up to 30 can be transferred) and the BS requires completion of 120 credits (up to 75 can be transferred). Professional certificates require 16–24 core credits from each of the AS programs. Transfer credits are accepted if a course is substantially similar to a required or elective course offered at Champlain, and the student has received a grade of C- or better. Official transcripts are required from the institution where the credit was earned.

Tuition is $330 per credit. Students enrolled in 12 or more credits per semester are considered full-time and are charged accordingly. Full-time students are eligible for federal and state financial aid such as the Pell Grant, Stafford Loan, and Vermont Student Assistance Corporation state grants. Financial

Aid is available for part-time students enrolled in at least six credits per semester. More information is available by calling the Financial Aid Office at 1-800-570-5858.

Online Technology Programs

Software Development trains students in software development and business programming for the personal computer. Telecommunications prepares students to manage high-tech voice- and data-communications systems. Web Site Development & Management students learn how to create web pages and put them to work for an organization engaged in E-commerce. All programs lead into the Computer Information Systems bachelor's degree through which students can develop skills in all three technology areas.

Online Business Programs

The Accounting program prepares students for public, private or governmental accounting careers. The Business program allows students to choose core and elective courses that will help them specialize in an area such as marketing, human resources, e-business or international business, retail or small business management. Hotel-Restaurant Management students obtain skills in hospitality management with the opportunity to specialize in either Food & Beverage or Hotel Operation Management through the certificate option. The Management option, with courses in goal setting, strategy formulation, legal and financial issues and computer applications, is for students interested in business or non-profit organization management. All of these programs lead into the Professional Studies bachelor's degree, which complements the skill-building courses of the associate's degree with a broader understanding of the global economy, while strengthening communication and problem-solving skills.

Special Online Programs

The College has partnered with Mantissa Institute, the educational arm of Fujitsu Systems Business Malaysia, to offer degree programs to the Malaysian public. A five-year old program in Israel has more than 2,000 students studying for Champlain degrees and a three-year-old program in Dubai, United Arab Emirates, has over 350 students. All programs include online learning as part of the partnership. Corporate training partnerships are also available for the purpose of training employees through distance learning technology.

Champlain College

•

Champlain College Online Education

Program Delivery and Student Support

CCOL students should own or have access to an Internet-linked PC with a modem of at least 28.8 baud and a browser that supports JavaScript and uploads. Due to the size of software programs installed and used for Software Development and Web Site Development & Management, it is recommended that students enrolling in these courses have a computer system with a minimum 400 MHz processor, 64 MB RAM, a 6–8 GB hard drive, a CD ROM and Windows 98 or NT 4.0 operating system.

Using e-mail, the telephone or fax, students can work with representatives of the OnLine Office, the Registrar's Office, admissions and academic advising, financial aid, the bookstore, library, career planning or the computer help desk.

College and Location

Founded in 1878, Champlain College is a private, coeducational, non-profit institution accredited by the New England Association of Schools & Colleges. Approximately 1,400 full-time students, from 29 states and 20 countries, and 2,600 part-time students are enrolled. Champlain's 18-acre, 33-building campus is situated in the scenic Hill-section of Burlington, Vermont. Sixteen restored Victorian-era mansions are home to approximately 575 residential students. Over the past eight years, 97% of students seeking employment have found positions within four months of graduating. More than 120 full- and part-time faculty teach at the college.

Supervised computer labs, open every day of the week, contain 200 networked computers with Internet access, an IBM AS/400 system and assorted software. The college library houses 40,000 volumes, as well as PC and Mac workstations, multimedia editing suites and facilities for video conferencing and satellite teleconferencing.

Burlington, home to six colleges and universities, supports lively retail spots such as the outdoor Church Street Marketplace, restaurants, coffee bars and plenty of nightlife. Recreational sites include a movie theater complex, concert venues, a seven-mile recreation path, hiking and climbing in the summer and skiing and snowboarding in the winter.

Contact Information

Champlain College Online Education
163 South Willard Street
Burlington Vermont 05401 USA
phone: 1-802-865-6449 or 1-888-545-3459
fax: 1-802-865-6447
email: online@champlain.edu
internet: http://www.champlain.edu

Admissions Office
163 South Willard Street
Burlington Vermont 05401 USA
          1-802-860-2727 or 1-800-570-5858
          1-802-860-2775
          admission@champlain.edu
          http://www.champlain.edu

Delivery Mode

• Online instruction

Program Facts

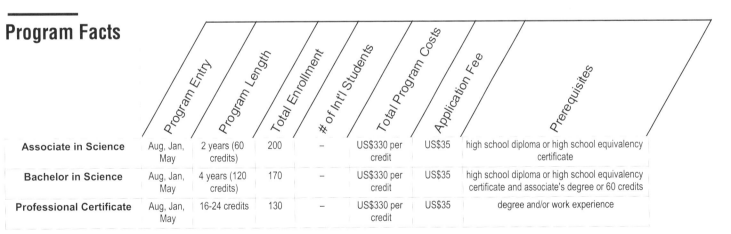

	Program Entry	Program Length	Total Enrollment	# of Int'l Students	Total Program Costs	Application Fee	Prerequisites
Associate in Science	Aug, Jan, May	2 years (60 credits)	200	–	US$330 per credit	US$35	high school diploma or high school equivalency certificate
Bachelor in Science	Aug, Jan, May	4 years (120 credits)	170	–	US$330 per credit	US$35	high school diploma or high school equivalency certificate and associate's degree or 60 credits
Professional Certificate	Aug, Jan, May	16-24 credits	130	–	US$330 per credit	US$35	degree and/or work experience

Clayton College & State University

•

Distance Learning

- Award-winning online degree program
- Integrated studies degree allows freedom to construct curriculum from all disciplines
- Telecourses accessible throughout Georgia
- Internship components

Programs Offered

Associate Degrees:
  Integrative Studies
Credit Couses:
  Business
  Critical Thinking
  Health Sciences
  Humanities
  Information Technology
  Integrative Studies
  Mathematics
  Natural Sciences
  Social Sciences

University Statistics

Year Founded:	1969
Total Enrollment:	4,500
Undergraduate Enrollment	4,500
Graduate Enrollment:	0
Distance Education Enrollment:	1,670

Program Overview

Distance Learning at Clayton College and State University (CCSU) offers an interdisciplinary undergraduate degree and more than 80 courses online, some of which have lectures broadcast on television (telecourses). The university's online degree program was named Best Internet Based Program, and took second place for Best Program in the higher education category, from the United States Distance Learning Association (USDLA) at the 18th Annual TeleCon Conference and Awards in 1999.

The content, structure and delivery of CCSU's distance learning courses are designed to meet the individual interests of students and the advanced technological requirements of the work force. The online degree in integrated studies is coordinated by the School of Arts and Sciences.

The university is working with Georgia Public Broadcasting to further the reach of its distance education telecourses by broadcasting them statewide via satellite.

Integrative Studies

Distance Learning at CCSU offers a two-year associate in arts or science with a major in Integrative Studies (IS). The associate degree comprises half of the four-year Bachelor of Arts or Science (BA or BSC) in Integrative Studies. Currently, only the associate degree is offered online. The degree involves an internship component.

The interdisciplinary IS program fosters critical thinking, creativity and advanced communication skills. Unlike traditional disciplines and structured curriculum, it allows students freedom to construct a program of study that corresponds to their specific career or graduate study goals. Under the guidance of a faculty mentor, students can integrate courses from across the CCSU campus or beyond. They can choose from online courses offered by institutions throughout the Atlanta region.

The non-traditional aspects of the IS program appeal to students with widely different backgrounds. Students are often employed but wish to update their education by earning an undergraduate degree. Studies can be tailored to complement their field of employment

Students applying for integrative studies must apply to both CCSU and the IS program coordinator. Prerequisites include 45 semester hours of postsecondary credits.

Online Courses

Credit courses offered online are taught by CCSU instructors as well as instructors from the southern United States, via the Southern Region Electronic Campus.

Students taking courses online for CCSU credit must register with the university. All CCSU courses require attendance on campus for orientation and examinations.

Subjects covered online include critical thinking, technology and information technology, business, health sciences, integrative studies, mathematics, music and natural sciences.

Telecourses

Lectures for some online courses are broadcast on Georgia Public Television or cable channels in the Atlanta area.

Clayton College & State University

•

Distance Learning

Program Delivery and Student Support

Students from the Atlanta region who take online courses through CCSU are provided with a laptop computer and Internet access as part of the university's Information Technology Project. Students must have Internet access, be familiar with email and Internet techniques, and use software that corresponds with the university's Microsoft Office 97 suite.

Broadcast lectures can be seen on Georgia Public Television, which operates on nine stations throughout Georgia, or through regional cable channels. An extra fee of US$20 covers broadcasting costs. The University System of Georgia provides an online library access catalog called Galileo, which includes full-text journal databases. The new Galileo Interconnected Libraries system (GIL) will facilitate a wide range of services to users throughout Georgia. The CCSU library also provides services to students enrolled in online courses.

University and Location

Clayton College & State University was founded in 1969 to serve the southern Atlanta region. It is accredited by the Commission on Colleges, of the Southern Association of Colleges and Schools, to grant baccalaureate and associate degrees. CCSU college transfer credits can be applied to education at other member institutions of the University System of Georgia.

The university offers study in 40 areas; bachelor's degrees are offered in business administration, nursing and health care management, music, arts, education, applied science, integrative studies, and information technology, with majors in 15 areas.

CCSU is located in the south Atlanta, Georgia suburb of Morrow. Atlanta has a population of 3,650,000, and is known as the cultural capital of the South.

Contact Information

Distance Learning
5900 North Lee Street
Morrow Georgia 30260-0285 USA
phone: 1-770-961-3634
fax: 1-770-961-3630
email: blainecarpenter@mail.clayton.edu
internet: http://distancelearning.clayton.edu

Delivery Mode

• Online via the World Wide Web
• Televised lectures on cable and Georgia Public Television

Program Facts

	Program Entry	Program Length	Total Enrollment	# of Int'l Students	Total Program Costs	Application Fee	Prerequisites
Assoc. in Integrative Studies - in-state	Fall, Winter, Spring	2 years	–	–	US$7,755	US$20	high school diploma; admission to CCSU
Assoc. in Integrative Studies - out-of-state	Fall, Winter, Spring	2 years	–	–	US$20,315	US$20	high school diploma; admission to CCSU
CCSU online credit courses	Fall, Winter, Spring	3 months	–	–	US$675	US$20	high school diploma; admission to CCSU
CCSU online credit courses - out-of-state	Fall, Winter, Spring	3 months	–	–	US$1,353	US$20	high school diploma; admission to CCSU

Colorado Electronic Community College

•

Higher Education & Advanced Technologies Center

Programs Offered

Associate Degrees & Certificates:
- Computer Networking
- Emergency Management & Planning
- Occupational Safety & Health Technology

Associate Degrees:
- Accounting
- Agricultural Business
- Business
- Computer Information Systems
- Construction Technology - Electrician
- General Arts
- Public Administration
- Telecommunication

Credit Courses:
- Art
- Behavioral Sciences
- Communications
- Economics
- English/Literature
- History
- Humanities/Philosophy
- Music
- Photography
- Political Sciences
- Public Administration
- Speech
- Theatre

College Statistics

Year Founded:	1995
Total Enrollment:	4,000
Undergraduate Enrollment	
Graduate Enrollment:	n/a
Distance Education Enrollment:	–

Program Overview

Colorado Electronic Community College, or the Colorado Community College Online (CCCO), is a website consolidating online courses. Thirteen colleges and the Northwest Missouri State University offer certificates and associate degrees for transfer credit through CCCO. From one online location, students can register for and access courses and programs.

The CCCO website is administered by the Higher Education and Advanced Technologies Center at Colorado Community College. All course credits are recognized by each of the institutions participating in the CCCO, and the core credits in business and general education are transferable to most of the postsecondary colleges and universities in Colorado. Online course credits are also usually transferable to distance learning baccalaureate programs throughout the state and beyond. Transfer requirements should be explored early if students plan to take this route.

The associate degree curriculum ensures students graduate with a general education and the critical thinking and communication skills that form the basis of baccalaureate degrees. Associate degrees normally require at least 60 credit hours, or approximately 20 courses. Students can earn an associate degree in arts, business, construction electricity, accounting, agricultural business, computer information systems, public administration, and telecommunication. Associate degrees and certificates are available in emergency management and planning, gerontology, occupational safety and health, and networking.

Students 16 years of age and older are eligible to take CCCO courses, though some courses may require previous academic background.

Registration begins by application on the CCCO website to the institution that offers the program or courses in which a student wishes to begin online studies. A Personal Identification Number (PIN), given at the time of application, directly connects admitted applicants to CCCO online registration.

Courses are delivered in a tri-semester system. Course length can be 10 or 15 weeks starting at different times each semester. Students can drop courses with full tuition refund prior to the last designated drop date, normally one week after the start of classes.

Liberal Arts, Gerontology

An Associate of Arts (AA) degree parallels the first one or two years of a liberal arts baccalaureate degree; students can transfer into four-year undergraduate degree programs at the junior level.

Core courses, equal to half of the degree requirements, ensure students develop research, writing and analytical skills. Course assignments encourage communication, public speaking, critical thinking, and practice in quantitative and qualitative reasoning skills.

Electives and areas of emphasis, comprising the second half of AA credits, can be in art, behavioral sciences, communications, economics, English, history, humanities/philosophy, music, photography, political sciences, speech or theatre. The new public administration concentration has network technician and central office technician options.

Students can also earn an Associate of Arts in gerontology, which offers a practicum component as the program capstone.

Applied Science Major Areas

The Associate of Applied Science (AAS) degrees provides students with a career-oriented education as well as a basic general education. Students must take at least 15 credits in a general education core of English composition, mathematics and speech communication.

The remaining credits can be taken as prescribed curriculum towards applied science areas of business, construction electricity, emergency management and planning, and occupational safety and health. New AAS degrees established in the fall of 2000 include agricultural business, computer information systems, networking and telecommunication. Not all areas of specialty have transferable courses.

Students who have already undergone a recognized apprenticeship training program as construction electricians will have 43 credits granted toward the AAS degree.

Colorado Electronic Community College

•

Higher Education & Advanced Technologies Center

Program Delivery and Student Support

CCC Online Library Services facilitate library research online, and maintain links to library resources, such as databases containing complete books online, and journals online. Links to the libraries of institutions participating in online courses bring students directly to catalogs of libraries in their area.

Courses are delivered online, so students require Internet access via Mac or PC, a Power PC Processor for Mac or a 90MHz Pentium Processor for PC, 32 megabytes of RAM, a 28.8 kbps modem and speakers. RealPlayer software and a Java-capable browser are necessary, as is an internet service provider.

Students who need academic counseling can connect online with an advisor from the college through which they are registered.

College and Location

The Colorado Electronic Community College brings together the faculty and resources of members of the Colorado Community College and Occupational Education System (CCCOES). The system began as the State Board for Community Colleges and Education in 1967 to guide the development of vocational education programs in the state of Colorado. The CCCOES was legislated into being in 1986. As the only such organization in the country, this network of educational institutions, faculty and students serves as a national model. The CCOES now has technical programs in 150 school districts and academic programs in 14 member institutions.

CCC Online continues the process of consolidating vocational and academic education resources, offering education beyond the state's geographic borders. Approximately 2,500 students from across the country and 60 international students are currently enrolled.

The Higher Education and Advanced Technology (HEAT) Center in Denver is the CCOES's showcase. Through HEAT, industry, technology and education bring advanced education and retraining to the workforce in biotechnology, manufacturing and information, and telecommunication technologies.

Contact Information

Higher Education & Advanced Technologies Center
8880 East 10th Place
Denver Colorado 80230 USA
phone: 1-800-801-5040
fax: 1-303-365-7616
email: yen.phillips@heat.cccoes.edu
internet: http://www.ccconline.org

Delivery Mode

- Online via Internet
- Fax, telephone, email connections with instructors

Program Facts

	Program Entry	Program Length	Total Enrollment	# of Int'l Students	Total Program Costs	Application Fee	Prerequisites
3-4 Credit Courses	Jan, May, Aug	10–15 weeks	4,000	75	US$118 per credit hour	n/a	16 years of age; specific course background
Associate of Arts Degree	Jan, May, Aug	60 credit hours	40	5	US$118 per credit hour	n/a	16 years of age; specific course background
Associate of Science Degree	Jan, May, Aug	60 credit hours	80	16	US$118 per credit hour	n/a	16 years of age; specific course background
Certificates	Jan, May, Aug	44 credit hours	150	23	US$118 per credit hour	n/a	16 years of age; specific course background

Colorado State University

•

Division of Educational Outreach

Programs Offered

Baccalaureate Completion Degrees:
　Social Sciences – Online fall 2001

Certificate:
　Child Care Administration
　Educator's Portfolio Builder
　Gerontology
　Postsecondary Teaching

Doctoral:
　Electrical Engineering
　Industrial Engineering
　Mechanical Engineering
　Systems Engineering

Master's:
　Agricultural Science
　Bioresource & Agricultural Engineering
　Business Administration
　Civil Engineering
　Computer Science – Online
　Electrical Engineering
　Engineering Management
　Environmental Engineering
　Human Resource Development
　Industrial Engineering
　Mechanical Engineering
　Statistics
　Systems Engineering
　Telecommunications – Online

University Statistics

Year Founded:	1870
Total Enrollment:	22,523
Undergraduate Enrollment	18,607
Graduate Enrollment:	3,380
Distance Education Enrollment:	1,200

Program Overview

The Colorado State University Network for Learning (CSUN), part of Colorado State University's Division of Educational Outreach, offers a broad range of distance education programs and courses through a network of learning media and 57 statewide Cooperative Extension offices. CSU is a member of the National Universities Degree Consortium and the Colorado Consortium for Independent Study. More than 2,000 students from around the world enroll in courses offered by CSUN each year.

Distance Degree Program

Since 1967, Colorado State University (CSU) has developed high-quality distance education degree programs. CSUN's distance degree program offers 20 degree programs in areas such as business, agricultural sciences and engineering. Each semester, the program delivers more than 80 courses representing 17 departments in eight colleges at CSU.

Many programs can be completed entirely through distance education. The Master of Business Administration (MBA) program has been recognized as one of the 20 best "cyber" programs in the nation by Forbes magazine. As with many distance degree programs, the MBA program combines video and computer technology with intensive coursework. All of CSUN's distance degree programs emphasize independent study, close interaction with faculty members and instructors, and access to modern technological resources and comprehensive support services through CSUN.

There are three study options for distance master's programs. Beyond required courses, students can choose to complete a thesis under the supervision of a faculty member or complete additional advanced coursework. MBA students may also decide to forego additional coursework and complete a comprehensive examination.

Applicants to master's and doctoral programs must submit a completed graduate application, three letters of recommendation and official academic transcripts to CSU's Admissions Office. International students must also submit proof of adequate finances for an entire academic year. In addition, international students who are not native speakers of English must submit a TOEFL score of 550 or higher.

Beginning in the fall of 2001, a baccalaureate degree in Liberal Arts, a Master's in Computer Science and an ME/EE (emphasis in telecommunications) will be offered online.

Certificates & Other Programs

In addition to the degree programs, CSUN offers several distance certificate and professional programs. The Gerontology Certificate program is an interdisciplinary program for individuals interested in a career working with the elderly. The Postsecondary Teaching Certificate program enables new instructors to acquire a practical overview of a range of effective teaching models. The Educator's Portfolio Builder program is an individualized program that allows current and former teachers to gain the credits needed for relicensure or career advancement. A Child Care Administration Certificate program is also available. CSU is one of the few schools in the US offering a distance Seed Analyst training program, which includes four courses developed by the National Seed Storage Laboratory and CSU.

CSUN's Denver Center offers distance degree programs, certificate programs and workshops in a face-to-face format for the convenience of local employees and employers.

Independent Study Program

CSU students and other individuals looking to supplement their on-campus education can select from more than 70 independent study program courses offered through CSUN. Potential students do not need to be enrolled at CSU to take these courses.

Colorado State University

•

Division of Educational Outreach

Program Delivery and Student Support

CSU's distance education programs and courses are delivered through many technologies, including two-way videoconferencing, online environments, satellite broadcasts, correspondence and videotapes. Some of the distance degree courses taught on campus are videotaped in specially equipped classrooms and distributed through CSUN. Students reside nationally, live in Canada or are part of the US military. Online courses are available to all international students. CSU's online campus features course information, advising, and library and bookstore access. Online library resources available to distance education students include over 400 extensive databases and an electronic journal collection.

Faculty and students interact through email, fax, mail and Internet communications. On-campus advisers are available to students for academic advising, curriculum planning and career counseling.

University and Location

Colorado State University was founded in 1870 as the Agricultural College of Colorado, assumed its present name and status in 1957, and has doubled in size since 1974. CSU is the largest of the three institutional members of the Colorado State University System and has been ranked by the Carnegie Commission and the Association of Research Libraries as one of the top 100 research universities in the US. The university comprises six campuses; the 200-hectare central area of the main campus houses nearly 100 buildings, including classrooms, laboratories, residence halls, student facilities, a bookstore, restaurants and offices.

CSU is located in Fort Collins, Colorado. Fort Collins is a community of 103,000, located in the foothills of the Rocky Mountains, less than 104 kilometers from Denver and 56 kilometers from Cheyenne, Wyoming.

Contact Information

Division of Educational Outreach
Colorado State University
Fort Collins Colorado 80523-1040 USA
phone: 1-877-491-4336 toll free
fax: 1-970-491-7885
email: info@learn.colostate.edu
internet: http://www.csu2learn.colostate.edu

Undergraduate Admissions Office
Fort Collins Colorado 80523-0015 USA
        1-970-491-6909
        1-970-491-7799
        admissions@colostate.edu
        http://www.admissions.colostate.edu

Delivery Mode

- Two-way videoconference (Colorado)
- Online courses and degrees
- Satellite broadcast
- Correspondence
- Email, fax and Internet correspondence with faculty
- Videotapes

Program Facts

	Program Entry	Program Length	Total Enrollment	# of Int'l Students	Total Program Costs	Application Fee	Prerequisites
Certificates	varies	varies	–	n/a	varies	n/a	work experience (for Postsecondary Teaching Certificate: Bed)
Doctoral	Aug, Jan	3–6 years	35	n/a	US$18,000 –32,000	US$30	baccalaureate or master's (or additional course credits required for program completion)
Master's	Aug, Jan	2–5 years	1,218	40 (in North America)	US$10,800 –18,000	US$30	baccalaureate in related field; some require work experience
Online baccalaureate (Social Sciences)	Aug, Jan	2–4 years	begin fall 2001	n/a	US$15,600	US$30	associate degree

47

Community Colleges of Colorado

CCCOnline

- AAS and AA degrees can be completed online through 16 member colleges
- Construction Technology programs apply completed apprenticeships to AAS degree
- Certificate-level study, including Microsoft certification, can be undertaken online
- Application and course registration can be completed concurrently

Programs Offered

Associate of Applied Science:
- Business
- Construction Technology (two streams)
- Convergent Technology
- Emergency Management & Planning
- Library Technician
- Occupational Health & Safety

Associate of Arts:
- Degree coursework at member colleges
- Public Administration (emphasis)

Coursework Leading to Certificates:
- Agricultural Business
- Computer Networking
- Convergent Technologies
- Emergency Management & Planning
- Library Technician
- Microsoft Certified System Engineer (MCSE)
- Occupational Safety & Health Technology

College Statistics

Year Founded:	1997
Total Enrollment:	–
Undergraduate Enrollment	–
Graduate Enrollment:	–
Distance Education Enrollment:	4,096

Program Overview

Formed by the Community Colleges of Colorado in 1997, CCCOnline is a college consortium that offers full online degree and certificate programs to distance learning students. CCCOnline offers coursework leading to Associate of Applied Science and Associate of Arts degrees as well as a number of certificates. The consortium's website is regularly updated to reflect ongoing program changes and developments; students should visit http://www.ccconline.org to review the latest degree and course offerings.

Associate of Applied Science (AAS)

AAS degrees prepare students for immediate employment in a full-time and/or para-professional occupation. Each AAS degree comprises at least 60 semester credits of approved coursework; 15 credits are earned in general education courses, and the remaining 45 credits are earned in specific career courses.

All partner colleges offer the AAS in Business. Degree coursework covers topics such as accounting, business law, management and human resources, as well as general education requirements.

Red Rocks Community College (Red Rocks) offers the AAS in Construction Technology in either Construction Electrician or Power Technology. After completing a specified apprenticeship, the degree requires the completion of six general education courses. Red Rocks also offer the AAS in Emergency Management and Planning, with coursework in areas such as emergency exercise design & evaluation, operations center and communications, leadership & influence, and volunteer resources.

The AAS in Convergent Technology can be earned online through Arapahoe Community College.

Pueblo Community College offers the Library Technician Certificate program, which includes the completion of seven core courses in areas such as library services, cataloging and classification, selection & acquisitions and management & public relations.

Trinidad State Junior College offers the Occupational Safety & Health Technology degree, comprising 69 credit hours including course areas such as Fire Protection & Analysis, Safety Program Planning, Accident Prevention and Safety Training Methods.

For all AAS degree programs, articulation agreements have been created with four-year universities and colleges.

Associate of Arts (AA)

The AA in General Education is offered by all consortial college members, and features lower-level coursework in the liberal arts. Students graduating with the AA degree may transfer into liberal arts programs in public baccalaureate colleges and universities with junior standing. The AA with emphasis in Public Administration comprises 60–61 required credits in areas such as accouting, HR management, public administration, state & local government, public finance and community development planning as well as general education and elective courses in humanities and social science. All CCCOnline member colleges offer this degree.

Certificates

Students can undertake certificate-level study in several areas including Agricultural Business, Computer Networking and Microsoft Certified System Engineer (MCSE). The Agri-Business certificate comprises 30–32 credits plus an internship, and covers agricultural economics, marketing, management and science as well as applicable general studies. Students in the Computer Networking certificate program complete eight courses that provide a fundamental grounding in local and wide area network components. The MCSE certificate comprises seven Computer Networking courses, covering topics such as Local and Wide Area Networks, Network Analysis & Design, TCP/IP & Network Architectures, and Internet Technologies. Certificates are also offered in Convergent Technologies, Emergency Management & Planning, Library Technician, and Occupational Health & Safety, and students enrolled in these programs fulfill partial requirements from the AAS degree program curricula.

Admission and Registration

Students can apply online (http://ccconline.org/Apply/index.cfm), and must be admitted to one of the partner colleges in order to register for courses. For those certificate or degree programs offered by a specific college, students choose that college as their college of record at the time of application. For certificate or degree programs offered by all colleges, students may choose from any of the college partners listed. Once the application is complete, students can register for courses by returning to the Application & Registration page (http://ccconline.org/registration/index.cfm).

Community Colleges of Colorado

CCCOnline

Program Delivery and Student Support

CCCOnline students should have access to a 90 MHZ Pentium PC running Windows 95, 98 or NT or a MAC 604 PowerPC running MacOS 8.1 or later. In addition, systems should have the following specifications: 32MB RAM, 28.8 kbps modem, sound card, speakers, RealPlayer Basic, Java-capable browser (4.0 or better). Before enrolling, students should arrange Internet and email accounts through a service provider. Up-to-date technical requirements are available online at http://ccconline.org/studentinfo/index.cfm.

An online student handbook (http://ccconline.org/studentinfo/handbk.cfm) is available to guide students through questions and issues related to study at CCCOnline. Students can access numerous online library resources while enrolled, and course materials may be acquired through the CCCOnline Bookstore (http://ccconline.org/bookstore/index.cfm).

College and Location

CCCOnline is a single location website where students can earn certificates and Associate degrees from any of the CCCOnline Partner Colleges. Partners include the 14 colleges in the Community Colleges of Colorado (CC of C), Dawson Community College and Northwest Missouri State University. Depending on their program of study, students may choose online at which college they wish to be registered.

CCCOnline is an initiative of the Community Colleges of Colorado (CC of C) System, the largest system of higher education in Colorado. The CC of C serves more than 247,000 students annually. Students from 18 countries, 47 states & the District of Columbia and 182 Colorado communities have participated in CCCOnline programs and courses.

CCCOnline colleges are accredited by the Higher Learning Commission of the North Central Association of Colleges and Schools (formerly called the North Central Association of Colleges and Secondary Schools).

Contact Information

CCCOnline
Student Services, 8880 East 10th Place
Denver Colorado 80230 USA
phone: 1-303-365-8807
fax: 1-303-365-7616
email: john.schmahl@heat.cccoes.edu
internet: www.ccconline.org

Delivery Mode

- Threaded discussions
- Webliographies
- Online testing
- Chats
- Virtual labs
- Videotapes (select courses only)
- CD-ROM (select courses only)

Program Facts

	Program Entry	Program Length	Total Enrollment	# of Int'l Students	Total Program Costs	Application Fee	Prerequisites
AA Degree Coursework	6 months out of year	2 yrs	unlimited	–	US$7564 (approx)	n/a	–
AA Public Administration (Emphasis)	6 months out of year	2 yrs	unlimited	–	US$7564 (approx)	n/a	–
AAS in Business	6 months out of year	2 yrs	unlimited	–	US$7564 (approx)	n/a	–
AAS in Construction Technology (two streams)	6 months out of year	2 yrs	unlimited	–	US$7564 (approx)	n/a	–
AAS in Convergent Technology	6 months out of year	2 yrs	unlimited	–	US$7564 (approx)	n/a	–
AAS in Emergency Management & Planning	6 months out of year	2 yrs	unlimited	–	US$7564 (approx)	n/a	–
AAS in Library Technician	6 months out of year	2 yrs	unlimited	–	US$7564 (approx)	n/a	–
AAS in Occup. Safety & Health Technology	6 months out of year	2 yrs	unlimited	–	US$7564 (approx)	n/a	–

Creighton University

•

School of Pharmacy & Allied Health Professions

Highlights

- Academic studies can be arranged around work and personal schedules
- On-campus components range from four days to two weeks, once per year
- Professional practice, rotations or clerkships are integral to the programs
- All programs are fully accredited

Programs Offered

Entry-level Doctoral Programs:
  Doctor of Pharmacy (Web-based)

Post-professional Doctoral Programs:
  Doctor of Occupational Therapy
  Doctor of Pharmacy (Non- traditional)
  Doctor of Physical Therapy (Transitional)

University Statistics

Year Founded:	1878
Total Enrollment:	6,158
Undergraduate Enrollment	3,765
Graduate Enrollment:	2,472
Distance Education Enrollment:	268

Program Overview

The School of Pharmacy and Allied Health Professions (SPAHP) at Creighton University (Creighton) offers the post-professional Doctor of Occupational Therapy, transitional Doctor of Physical Therapy, and non traditional and web-based Doctor of Pharmacy degrees through distance education.

Doctor of Occupational Therapy

The post-professional Doctor of Occupational Therapy (OTD) program is designed to strengthen occupational therapists' professional, practice management, teaching and administrative skills, and prepare graduates for positions in a range of practice environments. OTD program curriculum comprises 61 credit hours, in addition to two advanced professional rotations. Three curriculum courses involve one-week on-campus intensive instruction. The program offers basic and applied courses in occupational science theory, occupation-based practice, neuro-occupation and critical analysis of OT practice, as well as courses addressing legal, ethical, employee, third-party reimbursement, and quality review issues.

Doctor of Pharmacy

The Doctor of Pharmacy is offered in entry level web-based and post-professional non-traditional streams.

The full-time, entry level Doctor of Pharmacy degree requires the completion of 215 semester hours, including 63 pre-professional credit hours. The clinical component of the Pharm.D. program consists of 10 four-week rotations, six of which are required and four of which are elective. The entry-level, web-based program involves several innovative approaches to education. First, all didactic courses in the program are taught by distance mediums that use Internet and CD-ROM. Interactions with faculty and mentors occur via Internet chat rooms, email, fax and telephone. Students need to be on campus for several laboratory courses, annual assessments and some clinical rotations. Second, the entry-level, web-based distance education pathway is taught on a trimester basis (year-round), which allows students to complete the program by taking the laboratory courses in a condensed manner through the summers. The third innovation is the development of a mentoring system of practicing pharmacists, whereby participating students are assigned to mentors within the program.

The non-traditional Doctor of Pharmacy combines coursework and clinical clerkship in a 57 credit hour program. The program allows pharmacists with their BS in Pharmacy to acquire Doctor of Pharmacy certification, and emphasizes pharmaceutical care through a focus on therapeutics, patient assessment, patient counseling, pharmacokinetics and immunopharmacology. Course delivery, comprising 33 credit hours, includes print, videotape and computer/Internet methods, and students have four months to complete each course. Clinical clerkships, comprising the remaining credit hours, can be undertaken in the candidate's geographic location.

Doctor of Physical Therapy

The transitional post-professional Doctor of Physical Therapy program is designed for field practitioners who have a certificate, bachelor's degree or master's degree in physical therapy and wish to attain the doctoral credential. Prospective students must have a license to practice physical therapy in the US and have at least two years of clinical experience. The program is primarily delivered through distance methods including print, videotape, CD-ROM, computer/internet, online discussion groups and teleconferencing. Completion requirements include 41 to 50 semester credit hours, depending on the level of previous study. Two on-campus four-day intensives are required during summer sessions, and a professional practice component must be scheduled.

Admission Requirements

For acceptance to the post-professional Doctor of Occupational Therapy program, applicants must have a Bachelor of Science or master's degree in Occupational Therapy and have successfully qualified for or completed the certification examination. Entry-level Doctor of Pharmacy applicants must have completed all pre-pharmacy credit hours to be admitted to the full-time doctoral program. Applicants to the non-traditional post-professional Doctor of Pharmacy must have a degree from an accredited School or College of Pharmacy, a current license and two years of practice experience. Doctor of Physical Therapy applicants should have a physical therapy degree from a CAPTE-accredited program, a current state license and two years of licensed practice. All applications should include an application form, $60 application fee, current resume, statement of purpose & practice, official transcripts of applicable education and notarized copy of the appropriate license.

Creighton University

●

School of Pharmacy & Allied Health Professions

Program Delivery and Student Support

Distance doctoral students should have access to a Pentium or PowerPC (Macintosh platforms are not supported) running Windows 95, 98, NT, 2000 or ME, and with the following specifications: at least 32MB of RAM (48MB recommended); a 15" color monitor (minimum 800x600 resolution); a 56 kbps modem; a CD-ROM drive; a sound card; sufficient hard disk space to store course materials; an inkjet, bubblejet or laser printer; Microsoft Internet Explorer 4.0 or higher; RealPlayer plug-in software for audio and video clips; and Adobe Acrobat Reader for viewing PDF files.

Via the Creighton University web site (www.creighton.edu), Creighton distance students enjoy the same access to campus resources including admissions, registration, advising and library services, as on-campus students.

University and Location

Creighton University, named after transcontinental telegraph pioneers John and Edward Creighton, was founded in 1878 as a Jesuit college by Right Reverend James O'Connor, D.D. One year later, Bishop O'Connor surrendered his trust to a new corporation, The Creighton University.

In its early history, the university and its endowment grew through the benefactions of the Creighton family. In 1968, the Board of Directors was expanded to include both Jesuits and laypersons. Today, Creighton is a Catholic and Jesuit comprehensive university with several colleges and professional schools directed to the intellectual, social, spiritual, physical and recreational aspects of students' lives.

Located in Omaha, Nebraska, Creighton enjoys proximity to the cultural and recreational attractions of a bustling city of 350,000. Omaha is a major urban area located between Chicago and Denver, and Kansas City and Minneapolis, and is home to the NCAA College World Series as well as the Omaha Symphony, Opera Omaha and Ballet Omaha.

Contact Information

School of Pharmacy & Allied Health Professions
SPAHP Admissions 2500 California Plaza
Omaha Nebraska 68132 USA
phone: 1-402-282-2662
fax: 1-402-280-5739
email: phaaadmis@creighton.edu
internet: http://spahp.creighton.edu

Delivery Mode

- Audiotapes
- Videotapes
- Course Manuals
- CD-ROM
- Internet

Program Facts

	Program Entry	Program Length	Total Enrollment	# of Int'l Students	Total Program Costs	Application Fee	Prerequisites
Doctor of Occupational Therapy (post-prof)	Sep, Jan	61 cr hrs + 2 prof rotations	not avail	n/a	US$300/cr hr	US$60	BS/MS in Occupational Therapy
Doctor of Pharmacy (entry)	Aug	4 years incl rotations	50	n/a	US$7834/sem	US$60	63 sem hrs of pre-pharmacy courses
Doctor of Pharmacy (post-prof)	Sep, Jan, May	57 cr hrs incl clerkship	180	n/a	US$300/cr hr	US$60	BS Pharmacy, license, 2 yrs professional exp
Doctor of Physical Therapy	Sep, Jan, May	41–50 cr hrs + practice comp	38	n/a	US$300/cr hr	US$60	CAPTE-accredited BS/MS in Physical Therapy, license, 2 yrs professional exp

Drexel University

•

Master of Science in Information Systems

Program Overview

The College of Information Science and Technology at Drexel University (DU) offers three online programs: a master of science in information systems (MSIS), a master of science with a concentration in management of digital information (MS/MDI), and a non-degree Certificate of Competitive Intelligence (CI). The programs are designed for professionals who hold a bachelor's degree and are serious about broadening and formalizing their knowledge about information science and technology. Classes are conducted online, providing an intensive learning experience with the same content and quality as the degrees available through the university's traditionally delivered, campus-based master's degree programs.

Applicant Profile

A diverse mixture of student backgrounds enriches the Drexel online experience. Some students enroll in a program soon after completing an undergraduate degree, while others have career experience. The curriculum accommodates many professional objectives in a wide range of settings. Many who enroll in DU online programs are pursuing a degree in order to change careers.

Prerequisites and Admission Procedures

Students holding undergraduate degrees in any field of study may be admitted to the MS or MSIS programs. Applicants must take the Graduate Record Examination and have their scores sent to the Graduate Office. Applicants who have at least a 3.2 grade point average in the last half of their undergraduate program may be eligible for admission without taking the GRE. This decision is made by the associate dean of the college after review of the application. A basic knowledge of operating systems, hardware and common applications such as word processing, spreadsheets, presentation, internet access and file management or database packages is expected. In addition, applicants for the MSIS program must demonstrate competency in basic descriptive and inferential statistics, and a third generation programming language (Pascal, C, Cobol, Ada, Fortran etc.) or object-oriented language (C++, Smalltalk, Java). Deficiencies may be satisfied by completing approved courses through DU or other institutions.

Students interested in taking the CI certificate should have experience working

with information in business decision-making and an understanding of the strategic use of information. There is no GRE requirement for admission. The certificate program consists of three ten-week modules and students usually progress through the program by taking one module per term.

DU has established a career integrated education program that helps students secure jobs. Recent MSIS and MS graduates work for the IBM Corporation, Lockheed Martin Corporation, Merck & Co., Bell Atlantic, Princeton University, E.I. DuPont Co. Inc. and the Franklin Mint.

Curriculum and Graduation Requirements

A candidate for the MS degree must complete sixty (60) credits of graduate study. The program includes required courses in information science as well as information systems, giving the student a balanced curriculum of information content, information management practices and information technology. In addition to these courses, students choose a specialization through electives in areas such as competitive intelligence and web content management.

A candidate for the MSIS degree must also complete sixty (60) credits of graduate study. The MSIS program includes required and distribution courses and free electives as well as a strong focus on the design, implementation and evaluation of software-intensive information systems.

Drexel operates on a quarter system, offering four 11-week terms per calendar year. The college recommends that students devote between 15 and 24 months to the program.

Drexel University

Master of Science in Information Systems

Program Delivery and Student Support

MSIS classes are delivered through an asynchronous learning network (ALN) integrating Lotus Notes and the Internet.

Participants should have access to a Pentium PC, 16 MB RAM, 14-inch monitor at 640x480, 28.8 baud modem and Windows 95, 98, NT or OS 3.x. Those preferring Macintosh components should have access to a PPC, 16 MB RAM, 14-inch monitor at 640x480, 28.8 baud modem and Macintosh OS 7.x or 8.x. Program coordinators recommend browser software such as Netscape Communicator 4.x or Microsoft Internet Explorer 4.x.

The microcomputer and mainframe platforms at the college's computing resource center are available to MSIS students. As well, they can also utilize the science and technology collections at DU's W.W. Hagerty Library.

University and Location

The College of Information Science and Technology (IST) at DU is an internationally recognized center for education and research in all facets of information science and information systems. The college enrolls over 1,300 students in its bachelor's, master's and doctoral degree programs. Its faculty consists of individuals who not only hold PhD degrees, but also have extensive experience in the work place. Drexel's MS program is ranked among the top ten in the US, according to US News & World Report, and ranked first for specialized programs in information systems.

Contact Information

Master of Science in Information Systems
3141 Chesnut Street
Philadelphia Pennsylvania 19104-2875 USA
phone: 1-215-895-2474
fax: 1-215-895-2494
email: info@cis.drexel.edu.
internet: http://www.cis.drexel.edu

Delivery Mode

• Asynchronous Learning Network (Lotus Notes and Internet)

Program Facts

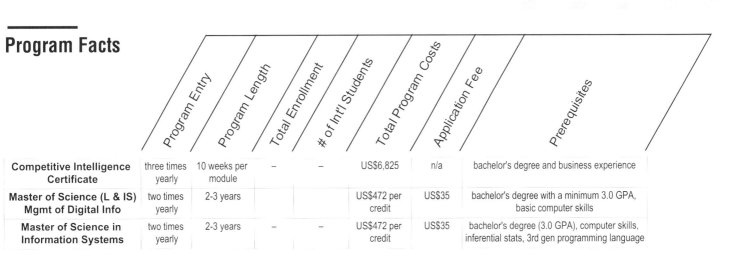

	Program Entry	Program Length	Total Enrollment	# of Int'l Students	Total Program Costs	Application Fee	Prerequisites
Competitive Intelligence Certificate	three times yearly	10 weeks per module	–	–	US$6,825	n/a	bachelor's degree and business experience
Master of Science (L & IS) Mgmt of Digital Info	two times yearly	2-3 years			US$472 per credit	US$35	bachelor's degree with a minimum 3.0 GPA, basic computer skills
Master of Science in Information Systems	two times yearly	2-3 years	–	–	US$472 per credit	US$35	bachelor's degree (3.0 GPA), computer skills, inferential stats, 3rd gen programming language

Duquesne University

•

School of Leadership and Professional Advancement

Programs Offered

Graduate Courses: Leadership/Liberal Studies
- Colloquium
- Conflict Resolution
- Decision Making & Problem Solving
- Ethical & Spiritual Dimensions
- Human & Financial Resources
- Info. Technologies for Modern Organizations
- Leader's Role in a Diverse Workforce
- Legal Issues for Leaders
- Organizational Communication
- Science, Technology & Society
- Social, Political & Economic Issues
- The Humanistic Perspective

Graduate Degrees:
- MA in Leadership and Liberal Studies

University Statistics

Year Founded:	1878
Total Enrollment:	9,500
Undergraduate Enrollment	5,600
Graduate Enrollment:	4,000
Distance Education Enrollment:	not available

Program Overview

The School of Leadership and Professional Advancement at Duquesne University (DU) administers a Master of Arts in Leadership and Liberal Studies (MLLS). The degree has won two national awards: the Distinguished Credit Program Award from the Association for Continuing Higher Education, and the Outstanding Leadership Program for 1999 award from the Association for Leadership Educators.

The MLLS program enhances the leadership skills of students who are already leaders and builds skills for those who have career goals in this area. Graduates of this program develop a clear idea of their own leadership values and how to affect decisions within changing environments. In the words of graduate Graduate Michael Fostyk, Vice President of American Eagle Outfitters, the MLLS program "prepares you for the real issues of today's dynamic, changing workplace where traditional techniques are losing their effectiveness. The curriculum helps the student awaken and develop the critical thinking necessary for many leadership situations regardless of the student's position within an organization. Ultimately, the program not only educates the individual to be better prepared as a leader, but . . . translates into tangible benefits for . . . organization(s)."

Program participants gain a comprehensive background in the social sciences and liberal arts. This interdisciplinary focus is designed to hone the critical thinking and problem solving skills needed to motivate others and to communicate effectively. The study of great thinkers of the past provides insight into different styles and philosophies of leadership and how these affected contemporary environments. Electives explore the development of world events related to the functions of leaders in different aspects of society.

Online Curriculum

Classes for the online MLLS program are small and interactive. Courses reflect the content of, and have the same instructors as, the program's on-campus format, in which classes are taught on Saturdays at DU.

The 12-credit core in liberal studies is designed for the MLLS by the Graduate School of Liberal Arts. The four required courses include an investigaton of the human perspective in leadership; social, political and economic issues; ethical and spiritual issues; and a colloquium to further explore and integrate these ideas in the context of contemporary problems.

The leadership course component requires students to take 15 credits, or five courses, that form the foundation for studies in leadership. These include organizational communication for leaders, decision making and problem solving, conflict resolution, the leader's role in a diverse workforce, and legal issues.

Nine elective credits, or three courses, help students identify leadership issues and roles in different contexts and disciplines. Electives are chosen according to students' specific interests.

Applicant Information

Admission to the MLLS degree program is based on a combination of at least two years professional experience, transcripts, a personal statement and an interview.

Transcripts of undergraduate degrees and other study from accredited colleges or universities should be sent to the MLLS Admissions Committee, along with a 500-word personal statement outlining reasons for applying to leadership studies, along with the complete application form and the US$25 application fee. After application, prospective students must schedule an interview, which can be carried out over the telephone or in person.

Duquesne University

School of Leadership and Professional Advancement

Program Delivery and Student Support

Six schools at DU, including nursing, pharmacy, education, music and the School of Leadership and Professional Advancement, offer undergraduate and graduate courses online.

Students who wish to enroll in online classes need access to an Internet service provider; DU offers connection through Stargate at a discount for its students. Online students have access to courses, as well as to library services including 100 online databases and 1,950 electronic publications. The library, which includes over 466,000 volumes, has an advanced integrated online system.

Online students have academic advisors who can assist with course selection, registration and other issues. Academic advisors in the MLLS program have expertise in dealing with online and adult students.

University and Location

Duquesne University is a comprehensive, private co-educational university with a Catholic affiliation, and is sponsored by the Congregation of the Holy Spirit. Duquesne has been ranked as one of the top 10 Catholic universities in the US by the US News and World Report survey.

The student body of the university's nine schools comprises approximately 9,500 students, including international students from 100 nations and diverse faiths. An Office of International Student Affairs offers services and assistance to international students. Duquesne University's programs are recognized around the world.

Contact Information

School of Leadership and Professional Advancement
210 Rockwell Hall
Pittsburgh Pennsylvania 15282 USA
phone: 1-800-283-3853
fax: 1-412-396-5072
email: coned@duq.edu
internet: http://coned.duq.edu/mlls/mllsmain.html

Delivery Mode

• Online via Internet

Program Facts

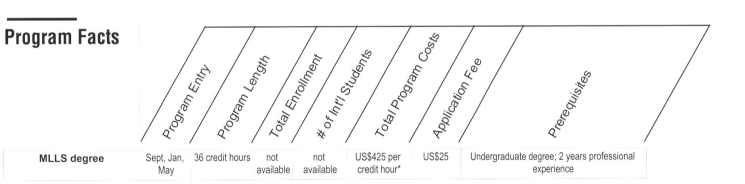

	Program Entry	Program Length	Total Enrollment	# of Int'l Students	Total Program Costs	Application Fee	Prerequisites
MLLS degree	Sept, Jan, May	36 credit hours	not available	not available	US$425 per credit hour*	US$25	Undergraduate degree; 2 years professional experience

Eastern Oregon University

•

Division of Distance Education

Program Overview

Eastern Oregon University (EOU) offers bachelor of arts/bachelor of science (BA/BS) distance degrees to resident and out-of-state students at the same tuition rate. BA/BS distance degrees can be obtained in the following areas: business administration; business and economics; fire services administration; liberal studies; philosophy, politics and economics; and physical education and health.

BA/BS Distance Degrees

Liberal studies combines two fields of study into an interdisciplinary degree program that leads to a BA or BS. Available combinations include one of several preapproved liberal studies programs, two minors from EOU, one minor from EOU with one minor from a second accredited institution, and two disciplines in an individualized program. Liberal studies programs are supervised by faculty and participating students access resources in both disciplines. General education and degree requirements must be completed in a timely fashion. By integrating various fields of study, liberal studies is designed to fulfill unique personal objectives.

The BS in business administration is a professional program that features concentrations in marketing, international business, accounting & leadership, organization and management. Graduates are qualified to pursue advanced studies in business administration or assume entry-level management, marketing, accounting and finance positions. To be eligible for graduation in this field, business administration students must maintain a grade of C- or higher in mandatory business and economics courses. This degree program can be completed on the EOU campus or through the Division of Distance Education, Eastern Oregon Community College Consortium or Portland Metro Center.

The BS in business and economics is a liberal arts program that features specializations in administration, accounting and economics. Graduates obtain a solid background in business and economics theory. As a result, they are qualified to pursue advanced studies in business and economics or a career in management, accounting, finance or economics. To be eligible for graduation in this field, business administration students must maintain a grade of C- or higher in mandatory business and economics courses. This degree program can be completed on the

EOU campus or through the Division of Distance Education.

The BA/BS program in philosophy, politics and economics (PPE) combines study of these fields in the analyis of social problems and policies. Graduates pursue careers in teaching, banking and finance, journalism, resource management, social services, criminal justice and other areas of public service. This program also lays the academic groundwork for the study of law and advanced studies in economics, political science and philosophy. To be eligible for graduation, PPE students must maintain a grade of C - or higher in required courses and a cumulative grade point average (CGPA) of 2.00 or higher. Those who intend to graduate with a BS must complete STAT 315/316 or a college-level statistics course.

The BA/BS program in health and physical education prepares graduates for careers in wellness, sport, recreation and the exercise sciences. To be eligible for graduation, health and physical education students must meet the following requirements: maintain a minimum CGPA of 2.00; pass the Writing Proficiency Examination; complete a standard fitness test in the 65th percentile or above; demonstrate competency in a selected field of sport by completing PEH 180 or a skills test, or participating in intramural or intercollegiate competition; demonstrate competency in First Aid and CPR; and complete all PEH coursework with a grade of C or higher. Those who intend to graduate with a BS must complete MATH 111, 112, 113, 211, 212 or 213.

The university's bachelor's degree program in fire services administration is offered in cooperation with Western Oregon University, Chemeketa Community College and Portland Community College. Graduates are qualified to work for fire departments and private agencies as administrators and supervisors. This program is designed for fire service professionals who wish to pursue both liberal studies and technical education. Modes of delivery include on-site Fire Services Administrators Institutes or Open Learning correspondence courses. The FSA program consists of 24 credits in lower division professional courses, 21 credits in upper division professional courses and 27 credits in upper division social science and business courses.

Eastern Oregon University

•

Division of Distance Education

Program Delivery and Student Support

EOU's distance degree programs utilize six modes of delivery: individualized study, which normally spans one or two terms and employs print and video materials; computer conferencing courses, which are normally one term in duration; regional courses at various sites; NET 2 interactive television; web-based courses, which are normally one term in duration; and weekend college throughout Oregon. Students submit assignments and communicate with instructors via email. All distance students in degree programs must provide evidence of computer literacy.

Through the Oregon Network for Education, students register in distance education courses from member colleges, but receive support services and maintain their academic record at a specified "home" campus.

University and Location

Eastern Oregon University awards a master of teacher education, associate degrees in office administration and general studies, and preprofessional degrees. In addition to the distance degree fields, a bachelor's degree can be obtained in agricultural business management, agriculture and resource economics, anthropology/sociology, art, biology, chemistry, crop science, education, English, history, liberal studies, mathematics, music, nursing, psychology, physics, rangeland resources and theater arts. EOU students enjoy high acceptance rates into professional schools, including 70 percent for medical students, 95 percent for dental students and 92 percent for veterinary students. EOU freshmen may apply for one or more of 75 available scholarships, such as Eastern Scholar/Oregon Laurels Program and Presidential scholarships.

The university operates three residence halls, each featuring a study emphasis floor, recreation center and laundry facilities. EOU supports venues for a symphony orchestra, music performances, theater productions and art exhibits. La Grande, the home of EOU, is situated in the Wallowa Mountains and Eaglecap Wilderness. Here, outdoor enthusiasts can downhill and cross country ski, raft, hunt and fish, backpack and water ski.

Contact Information

Division of Distance Education
One University Boulevard
La Grande Oregon 47850 USA
phone: 1-800-544-2195
fax: 1-541-962-3627
email: dde@eou.edu or djones@eou.edu
internet: http://www.eou.edu/dde

Delivery Mode

• Print
• Audiotapes
• Compact discs
• Internet
• IPTU

Program Facts

	Program Entry	Program Length	Total Enrollment	# of Int'l Students	Total Program Costs	Application Fee	Prerequisites
Business & Economics	–	varies	150	n/a	US$95/credit	US$50	high school graduation
Business Administration	–	varies	100	n/a	US$95/credit	US$50	high school graduation
Fire Services Administration	–	varies	80	n/a	US$95/credit	US$50	high school graduation
Liberal Studies	–	varies	900	n/a	US$95/credit	US$50	high school graduation
Philosophy, Politics & Economics	–	varies	35	n/a	US$95/credit	US$50	high school graduation
Physical Education & Health	–	varies	35	n/a	US$95/credit	US$50	high school graduation

ei's guide to distance and online learning programs in the usa - 2001 edition

Georgia Institute of Technology

•

Center for Distance Learning

Programs Offered

Master's Degrees:
   Electrical & Computer Engineering
   Environmental Engineering
   Health Physics/Radiological Engineering
   Industrial Engineering
   Mechanical Engineering

Institute Statistics

Year Founded:	1888
Total Enrollment:	14,804
Undergraduate Enrollment	10,745
Graduate Enrollment:	4,059
Distance Education Enrollment:	400–450

Program Overview

Georgia Institute of Technology's (Georgia Tech's) Center for Distance Learning (CDL) offers individual engineering courses and graduate study leading to the MS degree in five engineering disciplines. Students admitted to the Graduate School can enroll in the Registered Graduate Option (RGO) for academic degree credit, and professionals interested in further development can enroll in individual courses through the Professional Development Option (PDO). Courses and MS degrees are offered in the following areas: Electrical & Computer Engineering, Environmental Engineering, Health Physics/Radiological Engineering, Industrial Engineering and Mechanical Engineering. The MS in Electrical & Computer Engineering program also offers specialization in computer engineering, telecommunications & digital signal processing, and electric power, systems & controls.

Using several distance delivery systems, Georgia Tech extends its classroom walls to serve students who cannot attend campus classes. Working professionals have the opportunity to earn an advanced degree or undertake a sequence of courses via distance education, and enrolled students can view classroom lectures asynchronously, at times that meet their personal schedules. Live classes are recorded and provided on videotape to students in the US and abroad.

US students usually receive class materials within two to three days of the original class, and international students can receive materials within three to four days. Select courses in mechanical, electrical and environmental engineering are also offered via the Internet and CD-ROM, and the CDL website can be consulted for Internet course offerings each semester. The majority of courses are offered during the fall and spring semesters; select courses are available during the May–July summer session.

MS in Engineering, Registered Graduate Option (RGO)

Students who wish to pursue a master's degree through distance study, and who have been accepted to Georgia Tech's Graduate School, can enroll as RGO students. Program participants meet the same admission standards, assignment requirements and examination obligations as on-campus students; grades and transcripts form part of their permanent record at Georgia Tech. Students are encouraged to take two to four courses per academic year to make steady progress toward their degree. Faculty advisors are available to assist students with program planning and special problems.

Engineering Professional Development Option (PDO)

Professional engineers who wish to take graduate level coursework in engineering can enroll as PDO students. Courses are offered on a non-credit basis, and students can choose to have a grade assigned to their coursework. Students who choose the grade option must complete all homework and assignments, while those who audit courses are not required to fulfill coursework requirements. On request students can receive a letter listing the Continuing Education Units (CEUs) they have earned through the program. The PDO option is intended to assist engineers in furthering their professional development. As courses are non-credit, they cannot be applied to the graduate degree program.

Admission Requirements

Students applying to an MS program should submit the following materials: Application for Admission form; US$50 application fee; three letters of recommendation (from professors, colleagues and/or supervisors); a biographical sketch; and two official transcripts of all previous college coursework. Graduate Record Exmination (GRE) General Test scores are required from all applicants. All admission materials must be received by June 1 for the fall semester, November 1 for the spring semester and March 1 for the summer semester, and should be addressed to "Graduate Academic and Enrollment Services" at Georgia Tech.

International students who are graduates of non-US institutions must hold a degree equivalent to a bachelor's degree from an accredited US institution, and demonstrate advanced proficiency in English. This can be provided through a minimum TOEFL score of 550 (paper-based test) or 213 (computer-based test).

Applicants to the PDO option must complete a one-time application form and a registration form. There is no application fee associated with enrollment. PDO application forms are available on the Center for Distance Learning web site (http://www.cdl.gatech. edu/distance) by clicking on "Professional Development," or can be obtained by calling or faxing the CDL office (telephone: 404-894-3378; toll free: 800-225-4656; fax: 404-894-8924).

Georgia Institute of Technology

·

Center for Distance Learning

Program Delivery and Student Support

Georgia Tech uses several distance learning systems including videotape, CD-ROM and the Internet to deliver its graduate engineering courses. All students enrolled in the Distance Learning program must have access to the following resources: a computer with an Internet connection, CD-ROM drive and valid email account; a fax machine; a VCR; a business or home address where UPS package deliveries can be received. Students residing outside the continental US pay extra shipping costs for tapes to arrive within three to four working days. These costs usually range between US$300 and $600 per course.

RGO and PDO students participate in classes by reviewing class tapes on video monitors at work, at home or at a designated location. Students regularly communicate with faculty and CDL staff through fax and email correspondence.

Institute and Location

Since offering its first technology courses in 1888, Georgia Tech has developed as a prominent technology- and research-based institution. US News & World Report lists Georgia Tech among the 50 best universities in the nation; its College of Engineering is ranked fourth in the US, and seven of the 11 programs within engineering are ranked in the top 10 of their respective areas.

Georgia Tech benefits from major industry and research support. The Ford Motor Company has committed $10 million toward the construction of the new Environmental Science and Technology Building, which will house research into sustainable technologies. The institute also enjoys a working partnership with NASA on the production of clean propulsion engines, and has received a contract worth $9 million over the next five years to work with NASA's Ultra Efficient Engine Technology program.

More than 90 percent of Georgia Tech faculty hold PhD degrees and more than 55 faculty members have received Presidential, National Science Foundation Young Investigator, or National Science Foundation CAREER awards. Georgia Tech is located in Atlanta, Georgia, site of the 1996 summer Olympics and home to numerous sports and artistic venues.

Contact Information

Center for Distance Learning
620 Cherry St. ESM Building – Room G6
Atlanta Georgia 30332-0240 USA
phone: 1-404-894-8572
fax: 1-404-385-0322
email: cdl@conted.gatech.edu
internet: http://www.cdl.gatech.edu/distance

Delivery Mode

- Videotape, CD-ROM, Internet, Satellite, ITFS (micro wave), Cable TV
- Course assessment via Proctor System
- Course interaction via email, fax, 800 number, online chat

Program Facts

	Program Entry	Program Length	Total Enrollment	# of Int'l Students	Total Program Costs	Application Fee	Prerequisites
MS in Electrical & Computer Eng	Aug, Jan, May	varies	150	not available	US$17,000 –20,000	US$50	Varies – typically a BS in Electrical & Computer Engineering
MS in Environmental Engineering	Aug, Jan	varies	25	not available	US$17,000 –20,000	US$50	Varies – typically a BS in Env or Civil Eng or science program with related coursework
MS in Health Physics/ Radiological Eng	Aug, Jan	varies	20	not available	US$17,000 –20,000	US$50	Varies – contact department for specific details
MS in Industrial Engineering	Aug, Jan	varies	50	not available	US$17,000 –20,000	US$50	Industrial systems/eng, mech or electrical eng, or math or computer science background
MS in Mechanical Engineering	Aug, Jan	varies	125	not available	US$17,000 –20,000	US$50	Varies – contact department for specific details
MS in Operations Research	Aug, Jan	varies	25	not available	US$17,000 –20,000	US$50	Industrial systems/eng, mech or electrical eng, or math or computer science background

Harvard University

•

Harvard Extension School

Program Overview

The Harvard University Extension School offers a number of courses via the Internet using streaming video and multimedia technology. When enrolled via distance education, Harvard Extension School students can attend some lectures on campus or view them via the Internet anywhere in the world. Distance students can also participate in classroom discussions and assignments as would on-campus students.

Prospective distance students must view the sample online lectures before they register. Sample lectures and technical information are available on the Distance Education Program website (http://distanceEd.dce.harvard.edu).

Courses

The Extension School currently offers courses in biology, the classics, computer science, government, museum studies, natural sciences and philosophy by distance education. Over 20 computer science courses, including programming (C++, Perl, Java), Internet technology (Web programming, communication protocols) and theory were available in the most recent academic session. Courses offered in other disciplines include Introduction to Greek Literature, Information Technology for Museums & Nonprofits, Genomics & Computational Biology and Environmental Management. Complete course syllabi are available through the Extension website (http://www.extension.harvard.edu).

Students cannot currently complete a Harvard program through distance education. However, individual distance courses can be used to fulfill some requirements for degree and certificate programs including the certificate in applied sciences, master of liberal arts in information technology and master of liberal arts in liberal studies.

Course prerequisites vary and allow prospective students to judge if the course will be appropriate to their needs; students should have the equivalent knowledge and experience, whether through coursework, on-the-job experience or individual study. Students can preview course prequisities through the individual online course descriptions.

Some courses have limited enrollment and students should register early in these cases. Admission is offered on a first-come, first-served basis and special requests for admission, either from students or instructors, do not apply. Students applying to limited-enrollment courses with placement tests are admitted in the order in which they register and pass the tests. Those who do not attend the first class meeting may forfeit their seat in the course.

Depending on the course, distance education offers three possible levels of credit: non-credit (NC), undergraduate (UN) and graduate (GR). If students take a course for non-credit, they are not graded on their work and cannot use the course to fulfill requirements of an academic program. In some cases, non-credit courses can apply for those who wish to brush up on prerequisites.

Once they have selected their credit status, students taking courses via distance education earn academic credit and are graded in the same way as students attending on-campus classes.

Admissions

Distance education courses follow the same calendar, policies, and procedures as other Harvard Extension School courses. Courses offer open enrollment, enabling anyone to register provided seats are still available in a course. To register, students must complete and submit the online registration form (http://www.extension.harvard.edu) by the applicable deadline, along with full payment including a US$35 registration fee each term. Students may also download printed registration forms and mail, fax (with credit card payment only), or deliver them with full payment to Student Financial Services.

Extension School students must be enrolled in at least 14 units of credit per term to qualify for full-time status. One unit of credit is equivalent to one semester hour. Distance students must be enrolled in at least eight units of credit per term to qualify as half-time students.

Where distance education courses have in-class examinations, students in the New England area must take the examination on campus as scheduled. Students who cannot travel to the Harvard Campus must submit Distance Education Course Proctored Examination forms two weeks before the scheduled examination date.

Harvard University

•

Harvard Extension School

Program Delivery and Student Support

Videotaped lectures are available for online viewing approximately 48 hours after a scheduled on-campus lecture. For the balance of the course, most communication between teaching staff and students takes place via email and on the course website. The format of each course varies, but most courses have a bulletin board or chat room to foster dialogue among students and instructors. Distance education and local students follow the same schedule for assignments and exams.

Students pursuing a distance education course must have access to a computer system that is capable of streaming the video lectures. Once the link for a class is posted, students can view a lecture video at any time.

Contact Information

Harvard Extension School
51 Brattle Street
Cambridge Massachusetts 02138 USA
phone: 1-617-495-4024
fax: –
email: dce-distance-ed@harvard.edu
internet: http://www.extension.harvard.edu

University and Location

Harvard University, which celebrated its 350th anniversary in 1986, is the oldest institution of higher learning in the US. Founded 16 years after the arrival of the Pilgrims at Plymouth, the University has grown from nine students with a single master to an enrollment of more than 18,000 degree candidates, including undergraduates and students in 10 graduate and professional schools. An additional 13,000 students are enrolled in one or more courses in the Harvard Extension School.

The Extension School offers part-time study through distance education that attracts students from all walks of life, academic backgrounds and level of academic experience—from those with their doctorate to those with no degree at all. Most students at the Extension School enroll in individual courses for personal or professional enrichment. Extension School faculty include Harvard instructors, instructors from other academic institutions and industry professionals.

With a population of approximately 95,800, Cambridge, Massachusetts is the state's seventh-largest city. It is the site of the Harvard University campus, which includes Harvard College, the Radcliffe Institute for Advanced Study, the Graduate School of Arts and Sciences, the Divinity School, the Design School, the Law School, the Kennedy School of Government, the School of Education and the Extension School.

Delivery Mode

• All distance education courses are available via Internet streaming video and other multimedia technology.

Program Facts

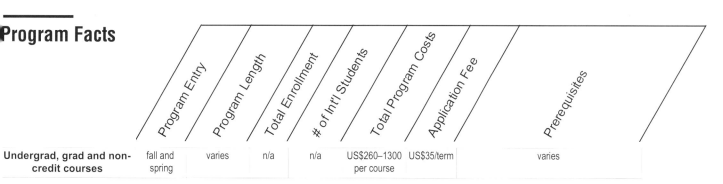

	Program Entry	Program Length	Total Enrollment	# of Int'l Students	Total Program Costs	Application Fee	Prerequisites
Undergrad, grad and non-credit courses	fall and spring	varies	n/a	n/a	US$260–1300 per course	US$35/term	varies

Indiana University

●

Office of Distributed Education

- High school diploma, 2-year associate degree and 4-year bachelor's degree programs available through Continuing Studies
- MBA and five Master of Science degrees can be completed primarily at a distance
- Ranked among the nation's leading hi-tech institutions by Yahoo! Internet Life and PC Week

Programs Offered

(*)Some on-campus meetings are required
 for degree completion

Associate Degrees:
 Associate of General Studies
 Associate of Science in Histotechnology
 Associate of Science in Labor Studies

Bachelor's Degrees:
 Bachelor of General Studies
 Bachelor of Science in Labor Studies

Master's Degrees:
 Master of Business Administration
 Master of Science in Adult Education*
 Master of Science in Language Education
 Master of Science in Music Technology
 Master of Science in Therapeutic Recreation
 MS in Instructional Systems Technology

University Statistics

Year Founded:	1820
Total Enrollment:	93,775
Undergraduate Enrollment:	
Graduate Enrollment:	
Distance Education Enrollment:	18,000+

Program Overview

Indiana University (IU) offers associate, bachelor's and master's level study through distance education. Through the IU School of Continuing Studies students can also pursue the fully-accredited Indiana University High School Diploma. Courses are delivered through a variety of systems including correspondence, the Internet, interactive video, television and videotape. As course and degree offerings are updated frequently, students should visit the IU Office of Distributed Education website (www.indiana.edu/~iude) to gain up-to-date course information.

Associate and Bachelor's Study

Through its General Studies Degree Program, the School of Continuing Studies offers the Associate of General Studies (60 hours) and the Bachelor of General Studies (120 hours). General studies students pursue an interdisciplinary plan of study in arts & humanities, social & behavioral sciences and mathematics & natural sciences. Degree information is available from the School of Continuing Studies website (http://scs. indiana.edu).

Through the IU-Purdue University Indianapolis campus, IU offers the Associate of Science in Histotechnology. Applicants should have one year (24 credit hours) of full-time certificate level coursework, or prior certification by the Board of Registry of the American Society of Clinical Pathologists. The program comprises professional courses through distance education. Degree requirements and information are outlined on the program website (http://www.sahs.iupui. edu/histo/histodegree.shtml)

IU's Division of Labor Studies (http://www.indiana.edu/~labor00/) offers correspondence study toward the Associate and Bachelor of Labor Studies degrees. Students complete a minimum total of 12 credit hours (associate) or 24 credit hours (bachelor) in labor studies, as well as required area and elective courses.

Bachelor and associate degree admission, course and exam requirements vary for each program. Students are encouraged to visit program websites for details.

Master's Study

The Master of Science in Adult Education (http://scs.indiana.edu) requires the completion of 36 credit hours. A six credit thesis option is offered. Students who complete the degree are eligible to pursue a variety of adult education

and training opportunities in both the private and public sectors.

The Indiana University Kelley Direct Online MBA Program (http://kelley.iupui. edu/graduate/omba/default.cfm) is one of the first MBA degrees available online from a nationally-ranked business school. The two-year, 48 credit hour program centers around web-based courses and one week residential experiences at the beginning of each academic year. Students can access course materials and participate in class discussion through a number of technologies; all course requirements can be completed at a distance.

The MS in Instructional Systems Technology (http://www.indiana.edu/~ist/ programs/masters/masters.html) is a 36-credit program offered primarily through web-based instruction. The program focuses on the use of technology in training and education and requires a four-day on-campus orientation and four-day on-campus capstone experience. Students must complete at least three units per semester and the degree can be completed in three years.

The MS in Language Education (http:// education.indiana.edu/~disted/lemasters.html) is delivered through a combination of online, interactive TV and on-campus courses. Emphases are available in Elementary or Secondary Reading, TESL or Adult Literacy. The degree requires the completion of 36 credit hours of study, plus the completion of seven additional courses if an emphasis is undertaken.

The Master of Science in Music Technology (MSMT) offers graduate students a background in digital music production, instructional design and multimedia development. The degree comprises 30 credit hours of instruction, and current graduates have found employment in a wide range of business and educational settings. Complete degree information is available on the program website (http://www.music.iupui.edu/).

IU's Department of Recreation and Park Administration offers the MS in Therapeutic Recreation by closed-circuit interactive TV. The 35 semester-credit program can be completed in three years on a part-time basis; most classes are offered in the evening or during early morning hours, and comprise live classroom instruction and participation. Students can consult the program website (http://www.indiana.edu/~distance/ther.html) for curriculum details.

Master's degree admission, course and exam requirements vary for each program. Students should consult websites for individual program requirements.

Indiana University

•

Office of Distributed Education

Program Delivery and Student Support

IU distance courses are delivered through a variety of media including correspondence, the Internet, IU's two-way interactive Virtual Indiana Classroom (VIC) network, Indiana Higher Education Telecommunication System (IHETS), television and videotape. Select programs may require on-campus attendance. Course delivery requirements are outlined on individual program websites and can be accessed through the Office of Distributed Education website (http://www.indiana.edu~iude).

IU's "insite" service provides students with access to university admissions, advising, course, financial aid, transcript and scheduling information via the World Wide Web. During their degree, students can regularly access updated advising reports online to plan their current or proposed course of study.

University and Location

Founded in 1820, Indiana University (IU) is one of the largest institutions of higher education in the US, enrolling more than 93,000 students at eight campuses. IU has had 116 of its degree programs ranked among the nation's top 20 by the Gourman Report, US News & World Report and the National Research Council. The university's largest campus, IU Bloomington, has been named among the nation's top 10 "wired" campuses by Yahoo! Internet Life magazine and PC Week has ranked IU among the top public institutions for information technology innovation.

IU Bloomington is home to the schools of Business, Education, Health, Physical Education and Recreation, Informatics, Library and Information Sciences, Journalism, Music, Optometry, and Public and Environmental Affairs, as well as 39 disciplines offered by the College of Arts and Sciences. Indiana University-Purdue University Indianapolis (IUPUI) is the university's second largest campus, and is home to the schools of Medicine, Allied Health Sciences, Nursing, Dentistry and Social Work, as well as programs in the Liberal Arts & Sciences and Engineering. IU's additional campuses reside in Fort Wayne, Gary, Kokomo, New Albany, Richmond and Southbend.

Contact Information

Office of Distributed Education
Ms. Carol Kegeris, PO Box 1345
Bloomington Indiana 47402 USA
phone: 1-800-334-1011
fax: 1-317-274-4513
email: scs@indiana.edu
internet: http://www.indiana.edu/~iude/

Delivery Mode

• Courses are offered through a variety of delivery systems: correspondence, the Internet, the university's two-way interactive Virtual Indiana Classroom (VIC) Network, Indiana Higher Education Telecommunication System (IHETS), television and videotape

Program Facts

	Program Entry	Program Length	Total Enrollment	# of Int'l Students	Total Program Costs	Application Fee	Prerequisites
AS (Histotechnology)	fall, spr	up to 5 yrs	10	0	varies	US$35	biology, chemistry, math
Cert (Histotechnology)	fall	1 yr	31	0	US$3,600	US$35	same
AS (Labor Studies)	year-round	2 yrs	n/a	n/a	US$5,976	US$35	
BS (Labor Studies)	year-round	4 yrs	n/a	n/a	US$11,952	US$35	
Associate of General Studies	year-round	2 yrs	1,745	n/a	US$5,976	US$35	
Bachelor of General Studies	year-round	4 yrs	4,168	n/a	US$11,952	US$35	
MS (Instructional Systems Technology)	fall	up to 3 yrs	12	0	US$6,070 IS US$17,680 OS	US$35	bachelor's degree
MS (Language Education)	fall, spr, sum	up to 7 yrs	700	100	US$5,465	US$35	bachelor's degree, GRE scores of 1300+
MS (Music Technology)	year-round	3 yrs	6	0	US$4,728 IS US$13,640 OS	US$35	bachelor's degree, literate musician
MS (Therapeutic Recreation)	year-round	3–4 yrs	12	1	US$6,800	US$45	none

Indiana Wesleyan University

•

IWUonline

Programs Offered

Bachelor of Science:
  Business Information Systems
  Management
Master's Degree:
  Business Administration
  Education

University Statistics

Year Founded:	1920
Total Enrollment:	7,095
Undergraduate Enrollment	5,227
Graduate Enrollment:	1,868
Distance Education Enrollment:	365

Program Overview

Indiana Wesleyan University (IWU) coordinates four distance degree programs through IWUonline: a bachelor of science in management (BSM), bachelor of science in business information systems (BSBIS), master of education (MEd) and master of business administration (MBA). IWUonline degree programs are organized into cohorts, or groups of 14 to 18 students. These degree programs can be completed completely online; there are no residency requirements for any of IWUonline's degree programs. Tuition, which varies between degree programs, may be paid in installments throughout the course of a program. Financial aid in the form of scholarships, employer reimbursement programs and loans is available to distance students. In most cases, international students are ineligible to receive financial support from the federal government.

Bachelor of Science in Management

The BSM completion program (40 credit hours/20 months) is a series of core courses that span from four to six weeks in a lock-step sequential format. Students take one subject at a time in weeklong online tutorials and interact with fellow students and facilitators on discussion sites. Additional credits may be fulfilled through transfer credits from other accredited institutions, CLEP examinations, IWU online elective courses and/or a prior learning portfolio. Admission requirements include a minimum cumulative grade point average of 2.0 in previous undergraduate work, no less than 60 credit hours, and two years of full-time work experience. The total cost of the core program is US$11,656 ($250/credit hr) for domestic students and US$12,146 for international students; this includes tuition, books and fees.

BS in Business Information Systems

The BSBIS completion program (52 credit hours/28 months) enables graduates to assist and lead in the planning, development and operation of information systems. Graduates develop aptitude in analytical thinking, communication, programming and systems design and will use their skills in database administration, systems analysis, computer support analysis or programming/analysis. Admission requirements include no less than 60 credit hours of previous undergraduate work (with a cumulative grade point average of 2.0) and two years of full-time work experience. Graduation (at 124 credit hours)

requires completion of the BSBIS core through IWU, with 72 additional credit hours filled through transfer credits from other accredited institutions, CLEP examinations, online elective courses and/or a prior learning portfolio. The total cost of the core program is US$17,360 ($295/credit hr) for domestic students and US$17,972 for international students; this includes tuition, books and fees.

Master of Education

The MEd program is tailored to professional teachers who wish to obtain an advanced degree that focuses on curriculum, instruction and teaching strategies. Five areas of teacher education are considered: implementing instructional effectiveness, leading curricular change, managing classroom learning, practicing reflective assessment and building learning networks. To fulfill graduation requirements of the MEd program, students complete 30 credits of core courses and six credits of elective courses. No thesis is required, but students must present a portfolio Admission criteria include a bachelor's degree in education from a regionally accredited institution, a 2.75 CGPA in previous undergraduate work, valid teacher's license and minimum of one year of K–12 teaching experience. The total cost of the online MEd program is US$9,812 for domestic students and US$10,134 for international students. These figures include tuition, books and fees.

Master of Business Administration

The MBA program prepares graduates to apply practical skills in accounting, economics, finance and operations to business decision-making. Program graduation requirements consist of 41 credits in economics, finance and accounting, marketing management and business law. In addition, students must maintain a minimum 3.00 CGPA and a grade of C in each course, and complete an applied management project.

It takes approximately 20 months to complete the core program. Admission criteria include a bachelor's degree from a regionally accredited institution with a 2.50 CGPA in previous college work, and at least three years of full-time professional experience in business administration. The total cost of the online MBA program is US$17,645 for domestic students and $18,812 for international students. These figures include tuition, books and fees. International students require a TOEFL score of 550 (CBT=213) plus a course-by-course evaluation by Educational Credential Evaluators.

Indiana Wesleyan University

IWUonline

Program Delivery and Student Support

IWUonline students learn in a "virtual classroom" forum, enabling them to interact with faculty and fellow students on a broad range of issues. Each student interacts online with fellow classmates and professors, which allows for group learning. The user-friendly interface combines web page discussion forums, live chats, collaborative software, and e-mail to facilitate interaction.

All textbooks and other study materials are mailed to students prior to each class. IWUonline offers off-campus library services to all students completing online degree programs. Students may request copies of articles and other items by e-mail or through a toll-free number. Academic advising is also provided. Before starting their program, students receive technical assistance that includes startup documents, e-mail addresses, usernames and technical support.

University and Location

Indiana Wesleyan University is an evangelical Christian liberal arts college affiliated with the Wesleyan Church, whose international headquarters are located in Indianapolis. IWU prepares students for careers in business, industry, education, health care, social work and public service. The university also supports preprofessional programs.

More than 2,000 students attend classes at IWU's Marion Campus, while nearly 5,000 are registered in the Adult and Professional Studies Division. The student body represents 45 states and 25 countries. Several venues exist for students to showcase their talents. Beard Arts Center features art studios, galleries and shops, as well as audio and video studios. A performing arts center houses a 1,200-seat auditorium and recital hall. IWU student athletes participates in the Mid-Central Conference, National Association of Intercollegiate Athletics and National Christian College Athletic Association.

Marion is a small Indiana city situated between Chicago, St. Louis, Cincinnati and Detroit; Ft. Wayne and Indianapolis are located 50 to 60 miles away. Marion residents work in the financial, retail, service manufacturing, distribution, automotive and agricultural industries.

Contact Information

IWUonline
Adult Enrollment Services, 4301 S. Washington Stree
Marion Indiana 46953 USA
phone: 1-765-677-2860 or 1-800-895-0036
fax: 1-765-677-2404
email: info@IWUonline.com
internet: http://www.IWUonline.com

Delivery Mode

- Course manual
- CD-ROMs
- Internet
- Discussion forums
- Live chats
- Collaborative software

Program Facts

	Program Entry	Program Length	Total Enrollment	# of Int'l Students	Total Program Costs	Application Fee	Prerequisites
Bachelor of Science in Management	cohort groups	20 months	n/a	n/a	US$11,656	US$20	60 sem hrs. of transferable credit; 2 years of relevant work experience
BS in Business Information Systems	cohort groups	2.5 years	n/a	n/a	US$17,360	US$20	60 sem hrs of transferable credit; 2 years of relevant work exp.; 1 sem. of math or statistics
Master of Business Administration	cohort groups	2 years	n/a	n/a	US$18,990	US$20	bachelor's degree; 3 yrs. of relevant work exp.; credit in math, econ., finance & accounting
Master of Education	cohort groups	20 months	n/a	n/a	US$9,812	US$20	bachelor's degree in education; 1 year of teaching exp.; valid teaching license

Jones International University®, Ltd.

Programs Offered

A word on programs offered:

    100 courses, 45 certificates & 15 degrees

    Courses are 100% online

Degree Programs:

    Bachelor of Arts in Business Communication

    Master of Arts in Business Communication

    Master's of Business Administration (7 areas)

    Master's of Education in e-Learning (6 areas)

Executive Certificates (a sample):

    Entrepreneurship: How Start-Ups Succeed

    Exploring E-Commerce

    Health Care Management

    Management Conflict, Negotiating Success

    Managing a Global Enterprise

    Managing Info. Tech. Today & Tomorrow

    Project Management

Professional Certificates (a sample):

    Global Communication

    Leadership/Communication Skills for Managers and Executives

    New Communications Technologies

    Public Relations and Marketing

    Using the Internet in Corporate Training

    Using the Internet in Higher Education

    Using the Internet in K–12 Education

University Statistics

Year Founded:	1993
Total Enrollment:	varies
Undergraduate Enrollment	varies
Graduate Enrollment:	varies
Distance Education Enrollment:	varies

Program Overview

Jones International University®, Ltd. (JIU), the first fully online accredited university, offers over 100 credit and non-credit courses, as well as 45 certificate and 15 undergraduate and graduate degree programs. JIU's online programs provide adult learners with the opportunity to earn a bachelor's or master's degree, or explore new fields of interest.

JIU courses are offered in accelerated 8-week and 12 week terms, and courses start every month. Each three-credit course is designed to be content-rich and interactive and to be offered in weekly modules with clearly defined learning outcomes.

In addition to a US$75 non-refundable application fee, degree applicants must submit an application, official transcripts, a writing sample, three letters of reference and a resume. Those applicants, whose native language is not English, must attain a score of 500 on the paper-based Test of English as a foreign language. The university grants credit for prior learning and for successful completion of standardized examinations.

Online Learning Environment

For each course, JIU degree students are assigned a faculty member with whom they interact in a web-based forum with up to 25 other classmates. This interactive community allows students and faculty to exchange ideas in a collaborative learning environment.

BA in Business Communication

JIU's Bachelor of Arts in Business Communication curriculum blends theory and practice toward the effective management of communication. The program focuses on the knowledge and communication skills, which help develop creativity, innovation, entrepreneurship, and leadership in the management of communication services or new communication technologies.

JIU's BA degree is designed for students who have successfully completed 60 credit hours of undergraduate studies or an associate's degree from a regionally accredited college or university and have earned a minimum cumulative grade point average of 2.5. JIU will consider admitting students with 35 credits of undergraduate work on a provisional basis.

MA in Business Communication

Master of Arts in Business Communication degree students gain valuable knowledge in human communication, current and emerging communication technologies and oral and written communication skills.

Admission to the 35-credit-hour Master of Arts in Business Communications Degree (MABC) program requires a bachelor's degree from a regionally accredited college or university (2.5 grade point average or above) and successful completion of undergraduate courses in speaking and writing.

Masters of Business Administration

JIU offers seven MBA Programs. Through a unique combination of academic learning and practical skills, students learn the critical fundamentals and expertise of conducting business globally and e-business. Flexibility is a hallmark of the JIU MBA Program. A choice of seven specialized degrees allows students to tailor a degree to their career and learning goals.

Admission to the MBA program requires a bachelor's degree from a regionally accredited college or university (2.5 grade point average or above), at least one year of professional work experience, three letters of reference, a current resume, and a statement of managerial achievements and professional goals in addition to the application form.

Masters of Education in e-Learning

JIU offers six M.Ed. in e-Learning Degree Programs. Students can select the program area that best matches their professional interests. M.Ed. in e-Learning degree candidates acquire a wide range of professional and practical skills and strategies.

Admission as an M.Ed. in e-Learning degree student requires proof of a Bachelor's Degree from a regionally accredited college or university, a minimum of a 2.5 cumulative grade point average, at least one year of professional work experience, three professional letters of reference, a current resume and a statement of professional accomplishments as well as professional goals. Applicants must also submit a JIU application form.

Certificate Programs

JIU Executive and Professional Certificate Programs allow students to develop the skills, depth of understanding and credentials needed to succeed in a particular field. The programs can be custom-tailored to suit organizations. Credits earned in one or more of JIU's Certificate Programs can also be applied towards a number of degree programs.

Jones International University®, Ltd.

Program Delivery and Student Support

Jones International University®, Ltd. courses are delivered completely on the Internet. To prepare for attendance at JIU's online campus, students must have access to a Pentium (or equivalent) Processor with at least 240 MHz, 16MB of RAM, a 13–15 inch VGA 256 color monitor and a 33.6 modem. Software should include an Internet browser such as Netscape Navigator 4.08, Netscape Communicator 6.0 or Internet Explorer 5.0+. JIU offers technical assistance for issues relating to using the JIU website and online courses 24 hours a day, 7 days a week. Once students log in, help is readily available.

JIU students may purchase textbooks through the online bookstore and use the e-global library™, Inc. a web-based library, to access information on reference resources through the Internet and World Wide Web. A reference librarian is available to assist JIU students with research.

University and Location

Founded in 1993 and launched online in 1995, JIU's learning model represents a true best practice in online education. The JIU curriculum is designed by recognized content experts at such schools as the London School of Economics, Columbia University, Michigan State University and Rutgers University.

JIU's administrative offices are located in Englewood, Colorado. Its campus is located 100% on the web at http://www.jonesinternational.edu. JIU has students from over 57 countries. Administrative policy follows that of most traditional universities in issues related to academic integrity, availability of records, online privacy, affirmative action and grievance procedures.

In recognition of its high program quality, JIU became the first 100% online educational institution accredited by The Higher Learning Commission, a member of the North Central Association of Colleges and Schools (NCA).

Contact Information

9697 E. Mineral Avenue
Englewood Colorado 80112 USA
phone: +1-303-784-8045 or 1-800-811-5663 (US)
fax: +1-303-811-8547
email: info@international.edu
internet: http://www.jonesinternational.edu

Delivery Mode

- Internet (email, online instruction, streaming audio and video)

Program Facts

	Program Entry	Program Length	Total Enrollment	# of Int'l Students	Total Program Costs	Application Fee	Prerequisites
BA in Business Communication	monthly	8 or 12 wks per course	–	–	US$695 per 3 credit course	US$75	60 credit hours AA, AAS; 35 credit hours for provisional admission
Continuing Education Certificates	monthly	4 wks per course	–	–	US$300-500 per course	n/a	experience teaching K-12, or college- or university-level courses
Executive Certificates	monthly	8 or 12 wks per course	–	–	US$825 per course	n/a	n/a
MA in Business Communication	monthly	8 or 12 wks per course	–	–	US$825 per 3 credit course	n/a	bachelor's degree; public speaking or writing
Master in Business Administration	monthly	8 or 12 wks per course	–	–	US$825 per 3 credit course	n/a	bachelor's degree; 1 year professional experience
Masters of Education in e-Learning	monthly	8 or 12 wks per course	–	–	US$825 per 3 credit course	US$75	bachelor's degree
Professional Certificates	monthly	8 or 12 wks per course	–	–	US$825 per course	US$75	n/a

Kansas State University

•

Division of Continuing Education, Distance Education

Highlights

- Variety of choices in degrees, courses and delivery methods
- Student services especially designed for students at a distance
- More than 250 courses offered each year
- Financial aid available for degree-seeking students

Programs Offered

Bachelor's Degree Completion Programs:
- Animal Science & Industry: Animal Products
- Coursework toward Dietetics
- Food Science & Industry: Food Bus & Operations
- General Business
- Interdisciplinary Social Science

Certificate, Endorsement & Specialty Programs:
- Food Science Certificate Program

Engineering Master's Degrees:
- Chemical Engineering
- Civil Engineering
- Electrical Engineering
- Engineering Management
- Software Engineering

Master's Degrees:
- Agribusiness
- Family Financial Planning
- Industrial/Organizational Psychology

University Statistics

Year Founded:	1863
Total Enrollment:	21,500
Undergraduate Enrollment	18,000
Graduate Enrollment:	3,500
Distance Education Enrollment:	5,438

Program Overview

Kansas State University's (K-State's) Division of Continuing Education offers master's-level, bachelor completion and certificate programs through a combination of multimedia, distance, web and guided study technologies. K-State students can pursue one of five Master of Engineering (MEng) degrees, as well as master's degrees in Agribusiness, Family Financial Planning or Industrial/Organizational Psychology.

Through distance education, K-State also offers bachelor's completion programs in the following disciplines: Animal Science & Industry (Animal Products Option), Food Science & Industry (Foods Business & Operations Management Option), General Business and Interdisciplinary Social Science. Students enrolled in K-State distance education can also pursue coursework toward the bachelor's degree in Dietetics.

K-State distance courses follow the semester schedule, and are taught by the same faculty who instruct on-campus courses.

Master's Degrees

The master's in Industrial/Organizational Psychology enables students to develop the skills and knowledge necessary to solve current problems in the human resources sector. Curriculum emphases include concepts and behavioral science methodologies. The 21/2-year program consists of 38 credits hours, 16 of which must be taken in each of the first two years. Students are required to attend an on-campus component of six credits for each of two summers, and complete the remaining 10 credit hours via web instruction. A guided six-credit practicum completes the program.

The master's degree in Agribusiness is an advanced degree for working professionals in the industry. The program focuses on mid-level managers who must make informed decisions based on a thorough understanding of current industry issues. The course can be completed within 21/2 years, including two one-week on-campus components per year. The balance of the program is undertaken through Internet instruction.

A master's degree in Family Financial Planning is offered in collaboration with the Great Plains Interactive Distance Education Alliance. The program provides participants with the skills necessary to counsel families on income, asset and debt management.

Through K-State, distance students can undertake one of five Master of Engineering

degrees in Electrical, Civil, Chemical, or Software Engineering, or Engineering Management. MEng programs are delivered through a combination of distance technologies, including videotaped, multimedia and web courses. K-State's MEng in Engineering Management enables participants to study engineering management and its application to business and industry problems. All programs range from 30 to 36 credit hours or ten to twelve courses.

Bachelor's Completion & Certificate Programs

Bachelor's degree completion programs are available for mature students with at least 60 credit hours of college coursework who wish to complete their undergraduate studies. The completion stream is offered in the following disciplines: Animal Science, Food Science, General Business, Interdisciplinary Social Science and Dietetics. The course of study requires the completion of at least 30 semester hours of coursework, of which 20 must be earned through K-State. The average student can complete the requirements for a baccalaureate degree within two to six years, and can take their studies through a number of methods, including the following: on-campus courses (evening, summer, intersession, short, or at partner universities), community outreach courses, TELENET 2 courses, video courses, Internet and web-based courses, and independent, guided or correspondence study.

The Food Science Certificate program comprises undergraduate credit courses delivered on video- and audiotape, and is designed for professionals in the food industry. The certificate is awarded at the completion of 20 hours of coursework.

Admission Procedures

Master's applicants should have a bachelor's degree; the relevant undergraduate degree, coursework or work experience; and be computer literate. Most programs require GRE scores in lieu of appropriate degrees or minimum GPA requirements. All MEng programs require a GPA of 3.0 in the last 60 credit hours of coursework. International applicants may be required to submit TOEFL scores.

Requirements for bachelor's completion programs and certificates vary; students should consult K-State directly for full details on admission requirements and procedures. Master's, bachelor's and certificate programs offer rolling admission and most are aligned with the semester schedule.

ei's guide to distance and online learning programs in the usa - 2001 edition

Kansas State University

•

Division of Continuing Education, Distance Education

Program Delivery and Student Support

Students should have access to a Pentium II PC or higher running Windows 95, 98 or NT, with the following components: 56 kbps or higher modem, sound card & speakers, 8X CD-ROM drive or higher, 64 megabytes of RAM, and a super VGA videocard supporting a minimum 24-bit color resolution of 800x600. Macintosh system requirements include a Quadra 700 (040 processor) or better running System 7.5, with double-speed or better CD-ROM drive, at least 16 megabytes of RAM, and a 28.8 kbps modem or direct network connection.

K-State offers a technical support help desk for distance education students that provides a variety of technical support services.

University and Location

K-State was established in 1863 as a land-grant institution on the former grounds of Bluemont Central College, chartered in 1858. The university moved to its present location in 1875.

The main K-State Manhattan campus comprises 664 acres in the rolling Flint Hills of northeast Kansas, 125 miles west of Kansas City. The K-State campus network consists of the Manhattan and Salina campuses, four branch locations of the Agricultural Experiment Station (Hays, Garden City, Colby and Parsons) and the Konza Prairie Research Natural Area, jointly operated by the Agricultural Experiment Station and the K-State Division of Biology.

A city of 45,000, Manhattan is home to Kansas State University and the Fort Riley Military Reservation, and is located 50 miles west of the state capitol of Topeka.

Contact Information

Division of Continuing Education, Distance Education
Public Information Office 21 College Court Building
Manhattan Kansas 66506 USA
phone: 1-785-532-5566
fax: 1-785-532-5637
email: info@dce.ksu.edu
internet: www.dce.ksu.edu

Delivery Mode

- Audiotape
- CD-Rom
- Guided Study
- Listservs/Message Boards/
  Chat Rooms/E-mail
- Multimedia & Web Technology
- Videotape

Program Facts

	Program Entry	Program Length	Total Enrollment	# of Int'l Students	Total Program Costs	Application Fee	Prerequisites
Agribusiness	Jan	3 years	25	varies	US$13,500	none	bachelor's degree & coursework, 3.0 GPA, 2 yrs experience, computer skills
Animal Science	varies	varies	varies	varies	varies	US$30	60 hours of college credit
Family Financial Planning	varies	3 years	varies	varies	varies	none	BS
Food Science; Dietetics	varies; "	varies; "	varies; "	varies; "	varies; "	US$30; "	60 hours of college credit; "
General Business	varies	varies	varies	varies	varies	US$30	60 hours of college credit
Industrial/Organizational Psychology	Jul	2.5 years	25	varies	US$13,000	none	bachelor's degree, 3.0 GPA in last 2 yrs, computer skills, coursework/experience
Interdisciplinary Social Science	varies	varies	varies	varies	varies	US$30	60 hours of college credit
MEng	varies	varies	varies	none	varies	none	BS

Kentucky Virtual University

•

Program Overview

Kentucky Virtual University (KYVU) is a program of the Kentucky Council on Postsecondary Education created by the Kentucky General Assembly in 1997. The KYVU is a partnership among Kentucky's public and independent institutions of postsecondary education, as well as other educational providers. All KYVU courses and programs are offered by existing, fully accredited institutions that confer diplomas, certificates or degrees.

KYVU is student-centered, technology-based system for coordinating delivery of postsecondary education that meets the needs of citizens and employers. A clearinghouse for distance learning opportunities, KYVU provides a single point of access to student, library and academic support services. Most courses and programs offered through KYVU are delivered through asynchronous web-based technologies.

The KYVU features both college credit and professional development programs. College credit programs include the following: Associate in Applied Science (Network and Information System Technology), Associate in Arts (Business Transfer Framework), Bachelor of Independent Studies in Human Services or Applied Science/Agriculture, Bachelor of Science in Business Administration (Hospitality Management) or Human Resources Leadership, Master of Business Administration (through Morehead State or Sullivan universities), Master of Science Managing Information Technology (MSMIT), Master of Science (Communication Disorders), Master of Public Administration (through University of Louisville, for military personnel or civil servants), Certificate in Office Systems Technology, Teaching Certificate (Special Education: Moderate and Severe Disabilities), Library Science and a TESOL Program (ESL Certificate).

KYVU also offers more than 210 accredited courses in a variety of disciplines, all of which are applicable to graduate and undergraduate degrees. All KYVU instructors are faculty members of accredited institutions awarding credit for their courses.

All courses are fully transferable to applicable degree or certificate programs at partnering institutions. Since all KYVU courses bearing academic credit are offered by accredited postsecondary institutions, they are transferable to Kentucky institutions and should be transferable to most other institutions.

Professional training programs are offered in Certified Public Accounting, Firefighters Certificate, Paralegal and Legal Assistant, Public Safety Communications and Travel & Tourism. In addition, KYVU offers programs in Information Technology, including the following: Certified Internet Webmaster (CIW), Cisco Certified Network Associate (CCNA) 2.0, CompTIA Certifications, End User Training in Lotus Notes and Lotus Domino R5, SAIR Linux Certification, and Windows 2000 MCSE (Microsoft Certified Systems Engineer or Systems Engineer Upgrade).

KYVU is charged with offering place- and time-bound students, employers and employees in business, government and industry and P-12 students, teachers and administrators with increased access to and attainment of postsecondary educational experiences. However, the nature of electronic delivery systems is such that potential users/clients are essentially unlimited and will include traditional residential students as well as students in other states and countries. All are welcome.

Kentucky Virtual Library

The Kentucky Virtual Library (KYVL) is a fundamental and vital component of KYVU. While associated with KYVU, the KYVL serves all citizens of Kentucky. KYVL services include access to a wide range of electronic databases, thousands of full-text articles, journals and other publications, inter-library document delivery service, Internet/fax/e-mail transmission of journal articles, a single point of service for technical and reference assistance and an information literacy tutorial program. Prospective students can visit the virtual library at www.kyvl.org.

Admissions

Students can apply online through KYVU for admission to all 57 Kentucky public & private colleges and universities and pay only one fee. Final admission decisions are made by the individual institutions. KYVU facilitates this process. Tuition and fees are set by the participating institutions. Financial aid for KYVU students is governed by the rules of the institutions offering the course or courses.

Students and prospective students are encouraged to visit the KYVU website at www.kyvu.org. Students may also contact the KYVU Call Center toll-free at 877-740-4357.

Kentucky Virtual University

Program Delivery and Student Support

At the heart of KYVU is a wide range of services to students, faculty and the public. Through its Call Center and website, KYVU provides course schedules, general advising and referrals for students, toll-free phone-in and online registration, an online bookstore and 24X7 technical assistance.

Students also have unlimited access to the new Kentucky Virtual Library at www.kyvl.org. The bookstore website (ecampus.com) can be used to sell or trade books or purchase merchandise online.

KYVU students will need a computer, an Internet connection, a modem of 28.8 kbps or higher, an email account and Netscape Navigator or Microsoft Internet Explorer browser software. Any further requirements are listed in course descriptions on the KYVU website.

University and Location

Headquartered in Frankfort, Kentucky, KYVU was created by the 1997 Kentucky General Assembly and launched in 1999. It combines programs from public and private postsecondary institutions.

Eighty-seven percent of students surveyed during the first semester of courses in the fall of 1999 said their expectations were met or exceeded by courses they took, and 82 percent said they would enroll in further classes.

KYVU is committed to exploring all aspects of technology-enhanced education. Programs are expanded and developed continually as this new virtual university assesses its current offerings and explores student interests and needs.

Contact Information

1024 Capital Center Drive, Ste. 320
Frankfort Kentucky 40601 USA
phone: 1-877-740-4357
fax: 1-502-573-0222
email: KYVU@kyvu.org
internet: http://www.kyvu.org

Delivery Mode

- Online via Internet
- Other web-based distance learning technologies

Program Facts

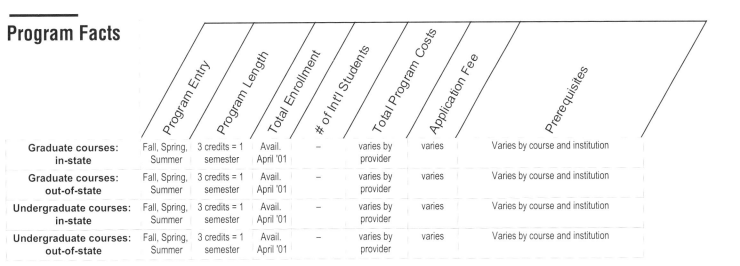

	Program Entry	Program Length	Total Enrollment	# of Int'l Students	Total Program Costs	Application Fee	Prerequisites
Graduate courses: in-state	Fall, Spring, Summer	3 credits = 1 semester	Avail. April '01	–	varies by provider	varies	Varies by course and institution
Graduate courses: out-of-state	Fall, Spring, Summer	3 credits = 1 semester	Avail. April '01	–	varies by provider	varies	Varies by course and institution
Undergraduate courses: in-state	Fall, Spring, Summer	3 credits = 1 semester	Avail. April '01	–	varies by provider	varies	Varies by course and institution
Undergraduate courses: out-of-state	Fall, Spring, Summer	3 credits = 1 semester	Avail. April '01	–	varies by provider	varies	Varies by course and institution

Kettering University (formerly GMI)

●

Extension Learning

Highlights

- Part-time distance learners can earn an MS in one of three disciplines
- Specializations offered in automotive systems, mechanical design and manufacturing systems engineering
- Cooperative education liaisons with over 500 companies worldwide
- Distance learners eligible for loans or employer assistance

Programs Offered

Dual Degree Program:
    BS & MS in Engineering
Graduate Degrees:
    MS in Engineering
    MS in Manufacturing Management
    MS in Operations Management

University Statistics

Year Founded:	1919
Total Enrollment:	not available
Undergraduate Enrollment	not available
Graduate Enrollment:	700
Distance Education Enrollment:	700

Program Overview

For nearly 80 years, Kettering University has been devoted to the production of highly trained managers and engineers for the automotive and other high-technology industries. At present, Kettering's graduate programs are delivered by distance education technologies and tailored for students whose jobs only permit part-time study. The university awards a master of science (MS) in engineering in three concentrations, an MS in manufacturing management, and an MS in operations management.

Off-campus courses at Kettering are identical to on-campus ones in terms of tuition, credit, content, instructors and evaluation. The delivery mode for off-campus courses consists of videotaped presentations of lectures at off-campus sites, telephone contact between students and instructors, and evaluation of student performance. Learning sites are established as needed at various corporate locations. Many instructors employ online teaching methods.

The academic schedule varies from program to program. Applications for the fall term must be received by July 15, and for the winter term, by November 1. Cooperative education and international students must submit applications by April 15. Application packages can be requested online.

MS in Engineering

The university offers an MS in engineering in one of three concentrations: automotive systems, manufacturing engineering systems or mechanical design. Each concentration consists of 15 three-credit courses, including one or two electives, and an optional thesis.

Full-time students take four courses per term and complete the program within one year. Those who opt for a cooperative education plan will take twice as long to complete the program. Part-time students take one or two courses per term and finish the program within two years. A maximum of five years is permitted for any student to fulfill degree requirements. The academic year for each concentration has four 12-week terms.

Applicants should hold a bachelor's degree in engineering from a program approved by the Accreditation Board for Engineering and Technology (ABET). Those considering the automotive systems concentration must have taken the Kettering course ME-521 (vehicle performance and transmission design), or equivalent. Graduates of engineering programs not accredited by ABET may be considered

for probationary admission. Engineering technology graduates are ineligible for admission. All applicants must submit Graduate Record Examinations (GRE) scores, while international applicants must submit Test of English as a Foreign Language scores.

The university awards a dual degree at the culmination of a five-and-one-quarter-year integrated bachelor of science and master of science engineering program. Under this option, graduate courses replace undergraduate courses during the last term of the bachelor's degree program and a graduate thesis replaces the undergraduate thesis.

MS in Manufacturing Management

Kettering University awards an MS in manufacturing management, a part-time 18-course program designed for managers in any profession. Subjects addressed include finance and economics, quantitative skills and computer applications, management and administration, and manufacturing engineering. No thesis is required. A regular course load consists of one or two courses per term, enabling most students to complete the program within three years. A maximum of six years is permitted to fulfill degree requirements. The academic year for manufacturing management students has three 12-week terms.

Applicants should possess a bachelor's degree from a regionally accredited college or university. Consideration for admission is also based on the applicant's management potential

MS in Operations Management

The university grants an MS in operations management, a part-time 16-course program designed for managers in any industry. The course load per term and duration of this program are identical to the manufacturing management program. The academic year for operations management students consists of four 12-week terms.

Applicants should hold a bachelor's degree from a regionally accredited institution. Consideration for admission is also based on the candidate's management potential.

Kettering University (formerly GMI)

●

Extension Learning

Program Delivery and Student Support

Students enrolled in online courses should have access to an MPEG-capable processor, preferably Pentium class, SVGA monitor configured for at least 800 x 600 pixels and 16-bit color, 36.6 baud modem and browser software, such as Netscape Navigator 4.0 or Microsoft Internet Explorer.

The Kettering library collection houses 100,000 print and nonprint items and more than 500 periodicals. Along with three local colleges and two public libraries, KU is a member of the Flint Area Library Cooperative Online Network. The university's academic support center is staffed by student tutors 60 hours per week.

University and Location

Founded as the School of Automotive Trades in 1919, Kettering University was subsequently known as the Flint Institute of Technology in 1923 and then the General Motors Institute (GMI) in 1926. In 1982, General Motors Corporation (MacEwan) relinquished control of GMI and, in 1998, the institute honored American industrialist Charles F. "Boss" Kettering by assuming his name. The US News and World Report has ranked Kettering among the top 15 technical institutes in the country.

All undergraduate programs have cooperative education options, while graduate programs are largely administered at a distance. During the 1990s, nearly 900 students received master's degrees from Kettering, while 800 are currently enrolled in master's programs. Corporate partners have included Ford, Xerox, General Motors, Harley-Davidson, Mack Truck, United Technologies, Pratt and Whitney, Johnson and Johnson, Hamilton Sunstrand, Federal Mogul, Allied Signal, Texas Instruments, Honda, Whirlpool, General Electric, Toyota and Sun Microsystems.

The university is located in the city of Flint, a major motor vehicle assembly center in southeast Michigan. Regional historical attractions include the Alfred P. Sloan Museum, Buick Gallery and Research Center, and Crossroads Village.

Contact Information

Extension Learning
1700 West Third Avenue
Flint Michigan 48504-4898 USA
phone: 1-810-762-7479
fax: 1-810-762-9935
email: gradoff@kettering.edu
internet: http://www.kettering.edu

Delivery Mode

- Internet (email, online instruction)
- On-campus classes
- Telephone contact between instructor and students
- Videotape classes at sites provided by corporate partners

Program Facts

	Program Entry	Program Length	Total Enrollment	# of Int'l Students	Total Program Costs	Application Fee	Prerequisites
BS & MS in Engineering	fall, winter	5¼ years	–	–	--	n/a	–
MS in Engineering	fall, winter	1–2 years	–	–	US$20,400*	n/a	bachelor of engineering in appropriate concentration, GRE
MS in Manufacturing Management	fall, winter	3 years	–	–	US$22,950*	n/a	bachelor's degree, GMAT
MS in Operations Management	fall, winter	1–2 years	–	–	US$19,125*	n/a	bachelor's degree, GMAT

Lehigh University

●

Office of Distance Education

Program Overview

The Office of Distance Education (ODE) at Lehigh University (Lehigh) offers distance education programs to individual students and corporate employees using distance learning technologies such as satellite broadcasting and Internet streaming video.

Satellite-based programs are delivered through the Lehigh Educational Satellite Network (LESN) to work sites in corporations or other organizations to provide educational opportunities for their employees. Satellite access is limited to certain geographic areas.

Lehigh has recently begun to present educational programming on the Internet through LESN-Online.

Distance education is targeted at technical, administrative and professional men and women interested in enhancing their career options, mid-career professionals who need to review, upgrade or expand knowledge within their particular fields and personnel requiring new expertise for use within their companies or organizations. Programs offered via LESN and LESN-Online share the same high academic standards as all of Lehigh's programs and offer convenient access to a variety of credit and noncredit programming. Distance education is a cost-effective option for individual and corporate clients and students can rely upon delivery through dependable technology and the assistance of expert technical support staff.

Satellite-Based Programs

LESN offers seven master's degrees by satellite as well as occasional noncredit short courses. Students can earn a Master of Science (MS) degree in chemistry, quality engineering, molecular biology, polymer engineering and science and pharmaceutical chemistry; a Master of Engineering (ME) degree in chemical engineering or polymer engineering & science; and a Master of Business Administration (MBA) degree.

Students can earn the MS in chemistry with a concentration in analytical, organic or bio-organic chemistry through a 30-credit program that includes three to six credits of experimental research or through a 33-credit program that includes a literature review paper. The MS in pharmaceutical chemistry is a 30-credit interdisciplinary degree. The molecular biology degree can be earned through a thesis or nonthesis option, both of which require completion of 30 credits. Students in the chemical engineering or quality engineering programs earn their

degrees through 30-credit nonthesis programs and MBA students complete 36 credits. The polymer engineering and science program includes six credits of research based on a preapproved laboratory problem, and can lead to the MS degree, or to the ME degree through a nonthesis program (for students who do not work in a laboratory setting, or for whom thesis research is inconvenient).

LESN classes enable students to pursue graduate and continuing education at work. Students attend classes in a conference room or classroom at their workplace, where they watch a video monitor carrying a live broadcast of a class being held on Lehigh's campus. During class, corporate students interact with the instructor and other students by phone, fax or computer.

LESN offers a package of downlink equipment intended to be affordable for most organizations, and provides technical information and assistance to any firm interested in receiving satellite-based programs.

Internet-Based Programs

Distance education via the Internet is a relatively new program at Lehigh but it shares the standards of excellence and focus on students common to all of the university's programs. An MS degree in Pharmaceutical Chemistry is now available, in addition to a certificate program in Supply Chain Management. Other selected courses in business, science and engineering are available for anytime, anywhere student access. LESN-Online delivers instruction through streaming video technology, so students can simultaneously view the instructor and online course material.

To register for LESN-Online credit courses, students must complete the LESN-Online graduate registration form and submit it via fax or email, along with payment of all course fees. Students must be officially admitted in order to register for courses for academic credit. Prospective students seeking admission should contact Lehigh's ODE.

Noncredit courses are currently being offered in the areas of business, chemistry, chemical engineering and manufacturing systems engineering. To register for noncredit courses, students should submit the LESN-Online noncredit registration form and all required fees. Students are advised not to register until they have confirmed that their computers meet the system requirements.

Lehigh University

•

Office of Distance Education

Program Delivery and Student Support

The method of delivery for LESN programs is synchronous satellite transmission. LESN-Online delivers programs asynchronously to students via Internet streaming video.

To receive LESN satellite programs, corporate sites require a Ku-Band downlink and an NDS digital receiver. Each worksite classroom must be equipped with a video monitor, phone, fax machine, VCR and interactive computer system.

The minimum system requirements needed for LESN-Online courses include a Pentium 133 computer with 32 megabytes of RAM, connection to a local area network or a 56K modem, a 16-bit sound card and speakers, a 65,000-color video display card, a printer, Windows 95 or 98 or NT 4.0 operating system with Service Pack 3, Netscape Navigator 4.6 or 4.7 or Internet Explorer 5.5, Real G2 Player or higher and Adobe Acrobat Reader 4.05.

University and Location

Lehigh University was founded in 1865 by Asa Packer, an entrepreneur and railway builder. The university believes in providing the opportunity for individual interaction between students and professors, as well as academic flexibility and opportunities for interdisciplinary study. The university is accredited by the Middle States Association of Colleges and Schools.

Lehigh University is located in Bethlehem, Pennsylvania. The city of Bethlehem, founded in 1741, is a historic town popular for its quaint buildings and shops, as well as for special events such as a Bach music festival, the Celtic Classic and First Night. The natural beauty of the Pocono Mountains is only a 30-minute drive away, and the attractions of New York city are less than a two-hour drive from Bethlehem.

Contact Information

Office of Distance Education
205 Johnson Hall, 36 University Drive
Bethlehem Pennsylvania 18015-3062 USA
phone: 1-610-758-5794
fax: 1-610-758-6269
email: mak5@lehigh.edu
internet: http://www.distance.lehigh.edu/index.htm

Delivery Mode

- Synchronous satellite broadcast
- Online courses using asynchronous video streaming
- Telephone interaction during live classes
- Email, fax and Internet correspondence with faculty and classmates
- Videotape backup

Program Facts

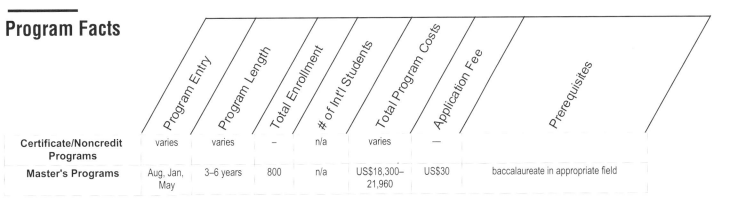

	Program Entry	Program Length	Total Enrollment	# of Int'l Students	Total Program Costs	Application Fee	Prerequisites
Certificate/Noncredit Programs	varies	varies	–	n/a	varies	—	
Master's Programs	Aug, Jan, May	3–6 years	800	n/a	US$18,300–21,960	US$30	baccalaureate in appropriate field

Madonna University

•

Distance Learning Programs

- OMNIBUS business program leads to three degrees within four years
- COP business students need only visit the campus twice during their studies
- Executive Fellows Program designed for practicing physicians and dentists
- Distance version of BSW accredited by Council on Social Work Education

Programs Offered

Graduate Programs:

    Master of Business Administration

    Master of Science in Business Administration

Undergraduate Programs:

    Bachelor of General Studies

    Bachelor of Social Work

University Statistics

Year Founded:	1947
Total Enrollment:	4,000
Undergraduate Enrollment	3,500
Graduate Enrollment:	500
Distance Education Enrollment:	560

Program Overview

Madonna University offers a variety of undergraduate and graduate programs via distance learning technologies.

OMNIBUS

In cooperation with Schoolcraft College, Madonna coordinates Online Multidegrees in National and International Business (OMNIBUS). This is a four-year program that leads to the acquisition of an associate of arts, bachelor of science in business and master of science in business administration.

The OMNIBUS curriculum focuses on four areas of business administration. Effective decision making entails learning how to communicate in written and oral form, apply critical reasoning skills and use information technology to address business problems. Global citizenship and diversity for international development involves developing a global awareness of international cultural and economic issues. Paradigms for organizational change refers to the use of qualitative and quantitative techniques for the analysis of business problems and the consequences of business decisions, including financial forecasting, operational administration and organizational development. Future trends in leadership for world organization emphasizes professional standards and leadership roles.

Cohort Online Program

Madonna's School of Business offers a graduate business degree at a distance through the Cohort Online Program (COP), in which students progress as a unit through the curriculum. COP is 23 months in duration and features 36 semester hours of coursework, as well as two prerequisite semesters each of undergraduate accounting and statistics. Weekly assignments require students to access their email and the Internet three to four hours each week and complete six to eight semester hours per term. Students visit the campus twice during the program. On the first weekend they attend an orientation and on the final weekend they present the results of a research project. Registration occurs automatically each semester.

Executive Fellows Program

The 20-month Executive Fellows Program (EFP) enables physicians and dentists to develop skills in private practice leadership and obtain a master of science in business administration. Executive Fellows was devised by Madonna faculty in consultation with an advisory council comprised of physicians and dentists who practice in the surrounding areas. EFP is characterized by many occasions for practitioners to network with colleagues and specialists through team projects and class interaction. Graduation requirements consist of 30 semester hours of coursework, including weekly class meetings and occasional weekend sessions.

The curriculum features seminars in computer applications, health care community leadership, patient satisfaction and quality service management, the legal and risk aspects of business, and ethical and strategic growth management.

To be considered for admission, applicants must have the following qualifications: an MD, DO, DMD or DDS from an accredited institution with internship and residency; at least two years in private practice as a licensed professional; and a score of 650 or higher on the Test of English as a Foreign Language for students whose native language is other than English.

Bachelor of Social Work

The bachelor of social work (BSW) equips graduates for careers as generalist social workers or for advanced study leading to a master of social work. This program is ideally suited for transfer students who are pursuing their studies on a part-time basis. The distance learning component of the BSW is known as the Gaylord Social Work Distance Learning Program and was accredited by the Council on Social Work Education in 1997.

Bachelor of General Studies

The bachelor of general studies (BGS) program emphasizes personal development, broad academic exploration and applied research in interdisciplinary projects. Graduation requirements include topics and senior seminars, and courses in advanced composition and research strategies. Experiential learning credits can be obtained through CLEP, DANTES, apprenticeship and noncollegiate training. Students must formulate a plan of study in consultation with the BGS Faculty Advisory Board; 45 hours of upper-division courses are required. Students may select online, face-to-face or telecourses. The program is ideally suited to adult transfer students. Up to 74 hours may be transferred from two-year institutions; a minimum of 30 hours must be earned through Madonna University.

ei's guide to distance and online learning programs in the usa - 2001 edition

Madonna University

•

Distance Learning Programs

Program Delivery and Student Support

COP students have access to syllabi, lectures and assignments through the university's website, email, and video- and audiotapes. Textbooks are mailed to students before the beginning of each term. EFP uses email discussions, videotapes, classroom instruction and individualized learning. Northern Michigan students participate in the BSW program through interactive television at University Center in Gaylord. Madonna supports a dial-in service for library database searches. Students seeking career counseling may visit the campus and access the System of Interactive Guidance and Information Plus More. This computer-based career counseling program features a step-by-step self assessment, occupation search and career information review.

University and Location

Madonna University was founded in 1947 by the Felician Sisters of Livonia and is one of the largest independent Franciscan institutions in the United States. The university offers undergraduate degree programs in more than 50 majors, graduate degrees and cooperative education programs with nearly100 employers. The student body totals 4,000 and is approximately 50 percent Roman Catholic, although religious affiliation is not a criterion for admission. The student-faculty ratio is 15 to one.

The university's residence hall accommodates 200 men and women in separate areas and sponsors dances and floor parties. The athletic department holds membership in the Wolverine Hoosier Athletic Conference and is recognized by the National Association of Intercollegiate Athletics. Various student organizations operate on campus. These include the Accounting Club, Music Club, Nursing Student Association, Project Earth, Psychology Club, Residence Hall Council, International Student Organization and Student Government Association.

Madonna's 49-acre campus and Schoolcraft College are located in Livonia, Michigan. Other cities such as Ann Arbor, Detroit, Lansing, Toledo and Windsor (Canada) are within an easy commute.

Contact Information

Distance Learning Programs
Undergraduate Admissions, 36600 Schoolcraft Road
Livonia Michigan 48150-1173 USA
phone: 1-734-432-5339 or 1-800-852-4951
fax: 1-734-432-5393
email: novak@smtp.munet.edu
internet: http://www.munet.edu

Office of Graduate Studies
36600 Schoolcraft Road
Livonia Michigan 48150-1173 USA
       1-734-432-5667
       1-734-432-5862
       kellums@smtp.munet.edu
       ww3.munet.edu/gradstdy/admission.htm

Delivery Mode

• Internet and email
• Video- and audiotapes
• Interactive television

Program Facts

	Program Entry	Program Length	Total Enrollment	# of Int'l Students	Total Program Costs	Application Fee	Prerequisites
Bachelor of General Studies	open	30+ sem hrs	50	0	US$252/ sem hr	n/a	Associate degree or equivalent
Bachelor of Social Work	fall	28 months	22	0	US$252/ sem hr	n/a	Associate degree or equivalent
Cohort Online Program	fall	23 months	25	0	US$310/ sem hr	US$25	Bachelor's degree
Executive Fellows Program	fall	20 months	25	0	US$310/ sem hr	US$25	MD, DO, DMD or DDS; 2 years of private practice; TOEFL 650 (pbt)
OMNIBUS	fall	4 years	25	0	varies	US$25	High school diploma

ei's guide to distance and online learning programs in the usa - 2001 edition

Mott Community College

•

College in the Workplace

Highlights

- CWP features courses with full college credit, instructor guidance and evaluation
- CWP courses follow campus-based schedule
- Credit earned in freshman- and sophomore-level courses at accredited institutions is transferable to MCC
- Distance learning staff collaborate with various companies and businesses

Programs Offered

Associate Degrees:
- Applied Science–COT
- Applied Science–General Business
- Arts
- General Studies
- Science

College Statistics

Year Founded:	1923
Total Enrollment:	9,000
Undergraduate Enrollment	9,000
Graduate Enrollment:	–
Distance Education Enrollment:	1,880

Program Overview

Mott Community College (MCC) offers five associate degree programs through College in the Workplace (CWP). No residency or campus activities are required since these "campus-free" programs are tailored for adult learners employed by manufacturers throughout the United States. Course content, registration, orientation, placement, academic advising and various support services are delivered entirely at a distance. CWP is also characterized by courses with full college credit, instructor guidance and evaluation, and a 15-week semester schedule that follows campus-based courses. Three courses must be completed in each program to fulfill writing across the curriculum, computer use and multicultural requirements.

Students who work full time normally complete an associate degree within four years. Each associate degree consists of approximately 20 courses worth a total of 62 credits. Distance learning staff at the college collaborate with staff at various companies and businesses to enhance the employee's learning experience.

Credit earned with a grade of C or better in freshman- and sophomore-level at other accredited institutions is transferable. This provision excludes religion and military science courses. The college's graduation policy obligates students to complete at least 30 credits of acceptable work through MCC. Placement tests are sometimes required and scores determine course placement, rather than college admission. Tuition for distance students is US$450 per course in addition to a US$35 per semester registration fee.

Associate of Arts

Students who undertake the associate of arts (AA) program complete 62 credit hours of coursework; at least 30 of the last 45 credits are earned at MCC. Furthermore, students must earn eight credits in humanities, eight credits in natural sciences and mathematics, four credits in social sciences, six credits in English, four credits in political science and four credits in natural/technical laboratory science. Additional credit is needed in mathematics and occupational sciences. AA students must maintain a cumulative grade point average (CGPA) of no less than 2.00.

Associate of Science

Students who undertake the associate of science (AS) program complete 62 credit hours of coursework; at least 30 of the last 45 credits are earned at MCC. Furthermore, students must earn six credits in English, four credits in occupational sciences and additional credit in mathematics and humanities/social sciences. AS students must maintain a CGPA of no less than 2.00.

Associate of General Studies

Students who undertake the associate of general studies (AGS) program complete 62 credit hours of coursework; at least 30 of the last 45 credits are earned at MCC. One course in humanities/social sciences is required, as are six credits in English, four credits in political science, four credits in natural/technical laboratory science, four credits in occupational sciences and additional credit in mathematics. General studies students must maintain a CGPA of no less than 2.00.

Associate of Applied Science–General Business

Students who undertake the associate of applied science in general business (AAS–GB) program must complete 62 credit hours of coursework; at least 30 of the last 45 credits are earned at MCC. Students must earn four credits each in social sciences, political science and natural/technical laboratory science, six credits each in computer information systems, office information systems, marketing and management, a total of 22 credits in their occupational specialty and additional credit in mathematics. General business students must maintain a CGPA of no less than 2.00.

Associate of Applied Science–COT

Students who undertake the associate of applied science in computer occupations technology (AAS–COT) program must complete 62 credit hours of coursework; at least 30 of the last 45 credits are earned at MCC. The curriculum is designed to increase students' proficiency in using software such as Microsoft Office, and knowledge of operating systems, programming and information systems. Computer operations technology students must maintain a CGPA of no less than 2.00.

Mott Community College

●

College in the Workplace

Program Delivery and Student Support

Mott Community College delivers distance courses through telecourses, modules and the Internet. An MCC college instructor supervises each course, issues assignments, assesses student performance and communicates with students by way of a toll-free telephone number, facsimile and email. CWP students sit for tests at their worksite under the guidance of an employer-supplied proctor. MCC coordinates distance education through the Distance Learning Office; student resources include library services, counseling and tutoring services.

MCC distance students need the following computer hardware and operating systems: Pentium 133 with 16MB RAM, Windows 95/98 and 28.8 baud modem.

College and Location

Mott Community College's main campus is located in Flint, Michigan, and enrolls between 9,000 and 10,000 students each semester. MCC is accredited by the Commission on Institutions of Higher Education of the North Central Association of Colleges and Schools. The college also holds membership in the Michigan Community College Association, American Association of Community Colleges, American Council on Education and Council of North Central Community and Junior Colleges. MCC's nursing, dental hygiene, dental assisting, physical and occupational therapy assisting, and respiratory therapy programs are individually approved for licensure.

Flint is the third largest city in Michigan and was first settled in 1825 by Jacob Stevens, a pioneer from New York State. The city's economic development is inextricably connected to the automobile industry. Local attractions include the Flint Cultural Center, which features the Alfred P. Sloan Museum, Buick Gallery & Research Center, Flint Institutes of Arts and Music, Flint Symphony Orchestra and Longway Planetarium. The Sloan Museum chronicles the history of General Motors.

Contact Information

College in the Workplace
1401 East Court Street
Flint Michigan 48403 USA
phone: 1-810-762-5686 or 1-800-398-2715
fax: 1-810-762-0282
email: lfrance@mcc.edu
internet: http://cwp.mcc.edu

Delivery Mode

• Videotape
• Internet
• CD-ROM
• Print (textbooks and study guides)

Program Facts

	Program Entry	Program Length	Total Enrollment	# of Int'l Students	Total Program Costs	Application Fee	Prerequisites
Associate of Applied Science-COT	–	2 years	–	–	US$450/course + US$35 reg	n/a	none
Associate of Applied Science-General Business	–	2 years	–	–	US$450/course + US$35 reg	n/a	none
Associate of Arts	–	2 years	–	–	US$450/course + US$35 reg	n/a	none
Associate of General Studies	–	2 years	–	–	US$450/course + US$35 reg	n/a	none
Associate of Science	–	2 years	–	–	US$450/course + US$35 reg	n/a	none

National American University

●

- AAS and BS degrees in Business Administration and Applied Management
- BS in Information Technology offers MIS/Networking and Webmaster emphases
- Degree and diploma programs can be completed online
- Best of Both Worlds-IDP™ program lets international students earn an accredited degree from their home country

Programs Offered

Bachelor of Science:
  Applied Management
  Business Administration
  Information Technology
  Information Technology (MIS/Networking)
  Information Technology (Webmaster)
Computer Industry Certificate Programs:
  Variety of courses leading to certification
Diploma Programs:
  E-Commerce
  Network Management/Microsoft
  Webmaster

University Statistics

Year Founded:

Total Enrollment:

Undergraduate Enrollment

Graduate Enrollment:

Distance Education Enrollment:

Program Overview

National American University (NAU) offers associate and bachelor's degrees, diplomas and computer certification courses through its distance learning program. NAU's accredited programs provide working adults with the opportunity to complete their education through a supportive and flexible online program.

International students can undertake NAU degree programs from their home country through a variety of options including NAU's Best of Both Worlds-IDP™ program (http://www.national.edu/distance/international_students.html). This program allows students to study at international affiliates of NAU and work toward an accredited US college degree.

Business Administration: AAS and BS Degrees

NAU distance learning students can undertake the Associate of Applied Science (AAS) or Bachelor of Science (BS) degree in Business Administration. The AAS in Business Administration provides an understanding of business and introduces students to the use of computers in business. Students who pursue the AAS may continue in the BS degree program.

BS in Business Administration students can undertake a general degree or concentrate coursework in one of several emphases including Computer Technology, Financial Management, International Business, E-Commerce, Management and Marketing. Emphases are designed to prepare students for technical and managerial positions within appropriate business sectors.

Applied Management: AAS and BS Degrees

NAU offers the AAS and BS degrees in Applied Management through online study. The AAS degree program is designed for individuals who have acquired occupationally-related training at community colleges, technical institutes, military service schools or industry-related schools in business, health or a technical field, and who wish to apply their earned credit to an undergraduate degree.

The BS program is designed for individuals with degrees, diplomas or certificates in specialty areas such as merchandising, dental hygiene, electronics, medical assisting, drafting, welding or other vocations. The degree prepares graduates for advancement in management areas associated with their specialty field.

Information Technology: BS Degree

NAU offers Bachelor of Science in Information Technology degree with Network Management/Microsoft and Web Developer emphases. The general BS degree provides background in the application of computer technology to solving information technology needs. The Network Management/Microsoft option focuses on Microsoft Networking and prepares students for the Microsoft Certified Systems Engineer (MCSE) exams. Graduates of this program are prepared to manage and provide technical support for a computer network. The four-year Web Developer program prepares students for the responsibility of developing and maintaining web pages to represent their company to the outside world.

Diploma and Certificate Programs

NAU offers Webmaster, MCSE and E-Commerce Professional diploma programs. The one-year Webmaster program prepares students for website development, programming and administration, and comprises 55 credit hours of online coursework. The 61 credit-hour E-Commerce Professional Diploma program provides graduates with experience in a variety of e-business topics including databases, electronic marketing, e-commerce software and e-commerce business practices. Students enrolled in the Webmaster and E-Commerce programs must demonstrate a working knowledge of Internet software and technologies. The one-year Microsoft Networking diploma provides computer professionals with training leading to Microsoft Certified Systems Engineer (MCSE certification and comprises 55 credit hours. NAU also offers computer certification courses to assist students in achieving a variety of industry certifications including MCP, Cisco CCNA, Red Hat Linux, CompTIA Network + and CompTIA A+.

Admissions Requirements

Students undertaking online learning should be highly motivated and dedicated to furthering their personal and professional goals. NAU students should expect to spend several hours each week on class readings, discussion, assignments, and projects.

Students can apply online through NAU's distance learning website. A complete admission materials checklist is available online (http://www.national.edu/distance/).

National American University

●

Program Delivery and Student Support

To participate in online courses, NAU students should have access to a Pentium PC with 100 MHz processor or better and the following components: 16 MB RAM (minimum), Windows 95, 98 or NT operating system, Internet Explorer 4 or 5 or Netscape Communicator 4.5. Students undertaking MCSE certification will need access to two computers after their first course; a home network will be constructed for use in later courses. MCSE students should consult NAU online (http://www.national.edu/distance/hardware.html) for required system specifications.

A dedicated technical team is in place to assist NAU distance learning students during their online studies. Technical support can be accessed by telephone or email 24 hours a day, seven days a week.

University and Location

The university first opened in 1941 under the name of the National School of Business, offering secretarial and accounting classes and programs. During the 1960s, NAU moved to its current location and expanded offerings to include a Business Administration curriculum for post-war veterans and greater demand for business programming. NAU has established campuses in Denver and Colorado Springs, Colorado; Albuquerque and Rio Rancho, New Mexico; Kansas City, Missouri; Mall of America, Bloomington and St. Paul, Minnesota; and Sioux Falls, South Dakota. There are also extension locations at Ellsworth Air Force Base, South Dakota and Brooklyn Center, Minnesota.

Since 1996, NAU has developed online courses offered on the Web and has established a virtual campus offering degree programs and courses to students on an international basis. NAU curriculum encompasses online business and technical degree, diploma and certificate programs as well as on-campus specialized program areas such as Therapeutic Massage, Athletic Training, Organizational Leadership and Veterinary Technology. NAU is regionally accredited by North Central Association of Colleges and Schools.

Contact Information

Rapid City South Dakota 57701 USA
phone: 1-605-394-4934 or 1-800-843-8892 (US)
fax: 1-605-394-4871
email: tfaulkner@national.edu
internet: http://www.national.edu/distance/

Delivery Mode

• Internet

Program Facts

	Program Entry	Program Length	Total Enrollment	# of Int'l Students	Total Program Costs	Application Fee	Prerequisites
AAS in Applied Management	–	–	–	–	US$200 per cr hr	US$25	Occupationally-related training
AAS in Business Administration	–	–	–	–	US$200 per cr hr	US$25	
BS in Applied Management	–	–	–	–	US$200 per cr hr	US$25	Degree, diploma or certificate in specialty area
BS in Business Administration	–	–	–	–	US$200 per cr hr	US$25	
BS in Information Technology	–	–	–	–	US$200 per cr hr	US$25	
Diploma in E-Commerce	–	–	–	–	US$200 per cr hr	US$25	Working knowledge of Internet software & technologies
Diploma in Network Mgmt/Microsoft	–	1 yr	–	–	US$200 per cr hr	US$25	Working knowledge of operation/support of hardware & software in standalone PCs
Diploma in Webmaster	–	1 yr	–	–	US$200 per cr hr	US$25	Working knowledge of Internet software & technologies

ei's guide to distance and online learning programs in the usa - 2001 edition

National Technological University

•

Master's Degree Programs

Program Overview

National Technological University (NTU) awards 19 master's degrees and various certificates of completion via four delivery methods, including satellite, online, CD-ROM and videotape. Since its inception in 1984, NTU has granted more than 1,600 master's degrees to individuals who have completed their programs of study while working as full-time technical professionals and managers.

NTU's master's degree programs offer curricula instructed by faculty from more than 50 universities and no disruption for part-time students whose jobs require travel. Under the Independent Student Program, professionals who are not currently associated with an NTU instructional site may register for courses and apply for admission to a master's program.

Master's Degree Programs

Master's degree program applicants must have the prerequisites listed below. A cumulative grade point average (CGPA) of no less than 2.90 on a 4.00 scale is needed for each program. Special major applicants, however, need a CGPA of no less than 3.00.

Applicants to the Chemical, Computer, Electrical and Mechanical Engineering or Engineering Management programs need a BS in their field from an ABET-accredited US program, CEAB-accredited Canadian program or the equivalent from a foreign institution. The Computer Engineering program is also available online. Engineering Management applicants must provide proof of two years of professional engineering experience.

Computer Science applicants must have a BS in their field. This program is also available online. Fast Track in Computer Science applicants should have knowledge of a high level programming language; Pascal, C or C++ are recommended.

Environmental Systems Management applicants must have a BS in engineering, biology, chemistry, physics or geology from an accredited institution. Their competence in mathematics must include differential equations.

Management of Technology applicants need a BS in engineering from an ABET-accredited program at a US institution, CEAB-accredited program at a Canadian institution or the equivalent from an overseas institution. Proof of two years of work experience in a technical environment, management sponsorship and undergraduate courses in calculus, economics, and statistics are required.

Manufacturing Systems Engineering

applicants must hold a BS in engineering from an ABET-accredited program at a US institution, CEAB-accredited program at a Canadian institution or the equivalent from an overseas institution.

Master's in Business Administration (MBA) applicants need a four-year BS and proof of two years of professional managerial experience. They should also be competent in basic business skills, such as accounting, economics and mathematics. A letter of recommendation from a supervisor is necessary.

Materials Science and Engineering applicants need a BS in Materials Science, the Physical Sciences, or in Engineering from an ABET-accredited engineering program at a US institution, CEAB-accredited program at a Canadian institution or the equivalent from an overseas institution.

Applicants to the Microelectronics and Semiconductor Engineering program need a BS in Computer, Chemical or Electrical Engineering or in Materials Science from an ABET-accredited engineering program at a US institution, CEAB-accredited program at a Canadian institution or the equivalent from an overseas institution.

Software Engineering applicants need a BS in computer engineering or computer science or ABET-accredited engineering program with a minor in computing systems. In order to be considered for admission, they should also provide evidence of knowledge of important software engineering topics. This program is also available online.

Systems Engineering applicants must hold a BS in an engineering discipline from an ABET-accredited program at a US institution, CEAB-accredited program at a Canadian institution or the equivalent from an overseas institution. This program is also available online.

Special majors applicants must hold a BS in an appropriate science or engineering area. In order to be considered for admission, they must submit a Proposed Program of Study Plan and statement of purpose, goals and objectives.

Certificate Programs

In cooperation with the Massachusetts Institute of Technology, NTU awards a certificate in E-Business. NTU also grants a certificate in E-Commerce in conjunction with the Walden Institute. Other certificate programs include Internet Applications Development, Information Systems Design & Development and a Webmaster 2001 Webmaster's Fundamentals Certificate (with NJIT).

National Technological University

•

Master's Degree Programs

Program Delivery and Student Support

Courses originate on the campuses of NTU member universities and are delivered directly to participants via the NTU satellite network, as well as online, by CD-ROM and by videotape. Faculty and students interact through email, telephone, facsimile, teleconferencing and express and regular mail. On occasion, NTU contracts with partner institutions and faculty to create new curricula and courses.

NTU has established Total Information, Inc. of Rochester, New York as the sole distributor of textbooks for NTU credit courses. Corporate customers order textbooks directly from the Total Information website or by fax or email. Tuition payment can be made online or by telephone or facsimile.

University and Location

National Technological University, a part of Stratys Learning Solutions, is based in Fort Collins, Colorado. Stratys Learning Solutions is the for-profit affiliate of National Technological University. NTU was founded in 1984 by Lionel Baldwin, then Dean of Engineering at Colorado State University.

NTU offers over 1300 academic courses from a partnership of over 50 of the leading US universities. Thirteen of the top 25 graduate engineering programs in the country as ranked by US News & World Report are included in this partnership. The NTU customer base consists of 200 major corporations and government departments and agencies, including IBM, Lucent, Hewlett-Packard, Motorola and the Department of Defense. NTU is accredited by The Higher Learning Commission and holds membership in the North Central Association of Colleges and Schools.

In 1999, NTU acquired the Public Broadcasting Service's The Business Channel to form PBS The Business & Technology Network, offering a broad portfolio of professional development courses in business, management and technical training. Programming is divided into three channels including the Business and Management Channel, the NTU Information Technology Channel and the NTU Engineering Channel.

Contact Information

Master's Degree Programs
700 Centre Avenue
Fort Collins Colorado 80526-1842 USA
phone: 1-970-495-6400 or 1-800-582-9976
fax: 1-970-484-0668
email: Admissions@mail.ntu.edu
internet: http://www.ntu.edu

Alexandria Office
1330 Braddock Place, Suite 201
Alexandria Virginia 22314 USA
1- 888-822-8229
1-703-837-1211
_
_

Delivery Mode

• Satellite
• Internet
• CD-ROM
• Videotape

Program Facts

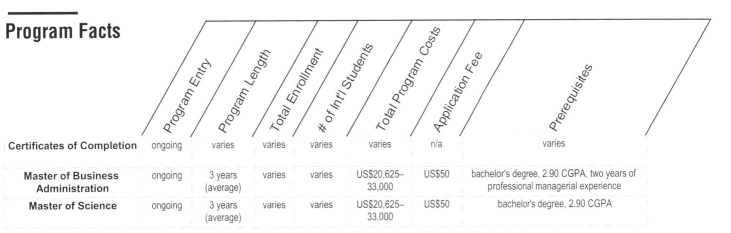

	Program Entry	Program Length	Total Enrollment	# of Int'l Students	Total Program Costs	Application Fee	Prerequisites
Certificates of Completion	ongoing	varies	varies	varies	varies	n/a	varies
Master of Business Administration	ongoing	3 years (average)	varies	varies	US$20,625–33,000	US$50	bachelor's degree, 2.90 CGPA, two years of professional managerial experience
Master of Science	ongoing	3 years (average)	varies	varies	US$20,625–33,000	US$50	bachelor's degree, 2.90 CGPA

New Jersey Institute of Technology

●

Distance Learning Programs

Program Overview

The New Jersey Institute of Technology has been committed to distance learning since 1982, when it began producing and airing videotaped courses in calculus, computer science and physics. NJIT Distance Learning coordinates the institute's current distance learning curriculum of 120 undergraduate and graduate courses.

Mentored NJIT Distance Learning courses are available during the fall (14 weeks), spring (14 weeks) and summer (10 weeks) semesters. Resident tuition is US$206 per undergraduate credit and US$388 per graduate credit; out-of-state students pay US$424 per undergraduate credit and US$534 per graduate credit. Fees are extra. Upon admission, students download a course syllabus that lists assignments and projects; the mentor's contact information; online registration procedures; and instructions for viewing lectures and ordering textbooks.

Application Procedures

First-time nondegree, first-time graduate certificate students and students returning to their studies after at least one semester's absence (with no more than nine graduate credits or 15 undergraduate credits, including credits to be earned after enrollment), use the nonmatriculated application for enrollment.

Continuing nondegree students and continuing graduate certificate students who have not missed a semester need only register for courses. Similarly, continuing nondegree students who have acquired no more than nine graduate credits or 15 undergraduate credits, including credits to be earned after re-enrollment, need only register for courses.

Students who have obtained a graduate certificate and intend to complete an NJIT master's degree program, as well as nondegree students who have acquired more than nine graduate credits or 15 graduate credits use the matriculated studies application.

Nondegree students must reapply each semester and may do so no more than three times for undergraduate studies. Moreover, they cannot take more than nine credits of graduate coursework at NJIT. Normal procedures apply for students who wish to move from nonmatriculated to matriculated status.

Prerequisites for entry to undergraduate courses are a high school, or general equivalency, diploma. Those for entry to graduate courses are a bachelor's degree from an accredited college or university and a minimum 2.8 grade point average.

Bachelor's Degrees

NJIT Distance Learning permits students to obtain a bachelor of arts in information systems (BAIS) and a bachelor of science in computer science (BSCS). The BAIS is a 129-credit program that enables students to apply computing and information systems principles to real-life problems in business and industry. BAIS graduates enter careers in accounting, environmental science, finance, manufacturing science and marketing. The BSCS is a 134-credit program that equips students with the theoretical and practical elements of computer science. The core curriculum consists of 51 credits in computer science, while elective credit must be earned in engineering, mathematics and science.

Master's Degrees

NJIT Distance Learning also coordinates distance learning versions of the institute's graduate programs in information systems (MSIS), computer science (MSCS) and engineering management (MSEM).

The MSIS is a 36-credit program that allows participants to specialize in information systems analysis and design, software development and software engineering methodology. Students seeking advanced training in artificial intelligence; graphics and image processing; software engineering; systems analysis, simulation and modeling; or other subdisciplines may wish to enter the 30-credit MSCS program. Individuals with suitable technical qualifications who intend to assume a managerial role in the public or private sector may consider enrolling in the 30-credit MSEM program.

The institute also offers a master of business administration (MBA) in technology management.

Graduate Certificates

NJIT awards 12-credit graduate certificates in one of eight disciplines: computer networking, eCommerce, information systems design and development, Internet applications development, object oriented design, technical communication practice, project management or telecommunications networking. The Graduate Certificate is both a stand-alone credential and a springboard to the corresponding MS degree at NJIT or elsewhere. Graduate Certificate students pay in-state tuition regardless of their state of residence.

New Jersey Institute of Technology

•

Distance Learning Programs

Program Delivery and Student Support

NJIT Distance Learning courses consist of a tele-lecture and electronic discussion between students and mentors. Tele-lectures are produced at NJIT or in the studios of other colleges or universities. A set of tele-lectures is leased and sent to the student's home or office for an entire semester. Students who have opted to view tele-lectures on the Cable Television Network are sent a programming schedule. Electronic discussions occur through NJIT email or a computer conferencing system known as Virtual Classroom®. NJIT Distance Learning recommends that students own a 486 DX100 personal computer with 8 MB of memory, VGA monitor and 14.4 baud modem.

NJIT's distance learning programs also use interactive television, satellite video distribution, streaming video and CD-ROMs.

Institute and Location

The New Jersey Institute of Technology was founded in 1881 as the Newark Technical School. NJIT enrolls more than 8,200 students in bachelor's, master's and doctoral degree programs and 5,000 students in continuing education programs. The university's academic units include two schools devoted to architecture and management, one college to engineering and another to science and liberal arts. NJIT is accredited by the Middle States Association of Colleges and Schools and ranked by the Carnegie Foundation as a Doctoral II University.

NJIT operates on a yearly budget of US$146 million, a figure that includes US$29 million in research funds. The computer science department maintains 14 specialized computing labs. Nearly 1,000 students live in the university's three professionally staffed, air-conditioned residence halls. The Fleisher Fitness Center houses an indoor pool, weight room, racquetball and tennis courts, a soccer field, aerobics and dance studio, martial arts center and three gymnasiums.

NJIT makes its home in Newark, a city of 275,000 that serves as the commercial, banking and insurance center of New Jersey. The beaches of the Atlantic Coast and the ski areas of the Pocono Mountains are several hours away by car.

Contact Information

Distance Learning Programs
Division of Continuing Professional Education
University Heights New Jersey 07102 USA
phone: 1-973-596-3060
fax: 1-973-596-3203
email: zimmerman@njit.edu
internet: http://cpe.njit.edu/dl

Delivery Mode

• Streaming video/audio
• CD-ROMs
• Tele-lectures (videotaped classes)
• Electronic discussions (NJIT email, Virtual Classroom®, chat)

Program Facts

	Program Entry	Program Length	Total Enrollment	# of Int'l Students	Total Program Costs	Application Fee	Prerequisites
BS in Computer Science	Sep, Jan, May	4–7 years	–	–	US$216–434 per credit	US$35	high school diploma; SAT or ACT
Graduate Certificates	Sep, Jan, May	12–18 months	–	–	US$406 per credit	US$50	bachelor's degree
Information Systems (BA, BS)	Sep, Jan, May	4–7 years	–	–	US$216–434 per credit	US$35	high school diploma; SAT or ACT
MBA in Technology Management	Sep, Jan, May	1–2 years	–	–	US$406–558 per credit	US$50	bachelor's degree; GMAT or GRE
MS in Computer Science	Sep, Jan, May	1–2 years	–	–	US$406–558 per credit	US$50	bachelor's degree; GMAT or GRE
MS in Engineering Management	Sep, Jan, May	1–2 years	–	–	US$406–558 per credit	US$50	bachelor's degree; GMAT or GRE
MS in Information Systems	Sep, Jan, May	1–2 years	–	–	US$406–558 per credit	US$50	bachelor's degree; GMAT or GRE

Northwest Missouri State University

•

- In 1987, NWMSU became the first fully electronic campus in the US
- NWMSU business graduates have secured employment with major companies
- Scholarships and other financial aid available for business majors

Programs Offered

Degree Programs:
- Accounting
- Business Management

General Business Curriculum:
- Accounting
- Business Finance Fundamentals
- Business Law
- Economics
- International Business
- Management Information Systems
- Management Process & Behavior
- Marketing Principles
- Organizational Policy & Decision Making
- Production Operations Management

Management Curriculum:
- Economics
- Entrepreneurship
- Human Resources Management
- Managerial Accounting
- Negotiations
- Organizational Theory

University Statistics

Year Founded:	1905
Total Enrollment:	6,042
Undergraduate Enrollment:	5,083
Graduate Enrollment:	729
Distance Education Enrollment:	230

Program Overview

Northwest Missouri State University (NWMSU) is committed to expanding learning options for business students. The Department of Marketing and Management delivers an online version of the university's four-year, 124-credit bachelor of science in business management program. Applicants should have, or be working towards, an associate of applied science (AAS) in business.

Career Opportunities

Business management graduates enter careers in public, financial and health care administration, as well as property, real estate, retail, transportation, production, purchasing, insurance, nonprofit organization and facilities management. Graduates also enter careers in the hospitality industry, food service, personal service, amusement and recreation management. Black and Decker, Farmland, Hallmark, Hershey's, Hormel, Hy-Vee and the Federal Reserve Bank have employed NWMSU business graduates.

Curriculum

The general business curriculum consists of courses in accounting, economics, management process and behavior, marketing principles, business finance fundamentals, business law, production operations management, management information systems, international business, and organizational policy and decision making. Many of these requirements will have been completed during the applicant's AAS degree program.

The management specialization requires students to take additional courses in economics, organizational theory, negotiations, entrepreneurship, human resources management and managerial accounting.

Finally, the program contains a liberal arts component in which participants study American history and government, composition, oral communication, fine arts, humanities, philosophy, lifetime wellness, multiculturalism and science.

During the senior year, six business elective credits and eight additional elective credits must be taken from a pre-approved curriculum.

Advanced Standing

Business students preparing to major in management must achieve advanced standing before registering in advanced coursework.

Advanced standing constitutes formal membership in the department. To attain this status, students must acquire a minimum cumulative 2.0 grade point average in five courses: finite mathematics, general statistics, accounting and the first two levels of economics.

Students who do not achieve advanced standing can register in only two major courses per semester. Those who fail to achieve advanced standing by their senior year cannot register in any major course until advanced standing is attained.

Tuition and Financial Aid

Tuition during the 2000–01 academic year wa US$180 per credit. During their studies, BS in Business Management or Accounting participants may be eligible for institutional and federal financial aid. NWMSU awards the Northwest Grant, while the Department of Marketing and Management awards scholarships to management majors.

The state of Missouri oversees the Charles Gallagher Grant, as well as the Advantage Missouri, Missouri College Guarantee, Missouri Bright Flight and Marguerite Ross Barnett Memorial Scholarship programs.

The federal government administers the Pell Grant, Supplemental Educational Opportunity Grant, Perkins Loan and William D. Ford Direct Subsidized, Unsubsidized or Parent PLUS loans.

Northwest Missouri State University

Program Delivery and Student Support

The BS in Business Management and Accounting degree programs are delivered via Northwest Online. Through Northwest Online, students can also obtain academic advising and career counseling, register for courses, pay bills, purchase textbooks and browse the university library's catalogs.

NWMSU maintains 30 computer labs across the campus, as well as specialized labs for student publications and chemistry, mathematics and graphic design courses. The library's computer lab provides assistance with web page construction, CD-ROM recording, color scanning, photographic editing, and color and B/W transparency printing.

University and Location

Established in 1905, Northwest Missouri State University is a public four-year institution offering bachelor's and master's degree programs as well as one- and two-year certificate programs. More than 6,000 students are enrolled and 235 full-time faculty are employed at NWMSU. The student body represents 42 states and 22 countries. The university is accredited by the North Central Association of Colleges and Schools.

NWMSU has the distinction of being the first academic institution in the country to equip every residence hall room and faculty office with a networked computer station. The main library on campus contains over 600,000 volumes and special collections devoted to the US Civil War and authors such as Willa Cather. The university operates eight residence halls, as well as fitness and recreation centers. Athletic affiliations include the National Collegiate Athletic Association (Division II) and Mid-America Intercollegiate Athletics Association for men and women.

NWMSU's home is Maryville, Missouri, a community of 10,000 centered between Kansas City, Des Moines and Omaha. The city's chief employers are the university, Eveready Battery, Kawasaki Motors, LMP Steel and Wire and Laclede Chain.

Contact Information

Office of Admissions, 800 University Drive
Maryville Missouri 64468-6001 USA
phone: 1-660-562-1562
fax: 1-660-562-1121
email: admissions@mail.nwmissouri.edu
internet: http://www.NorthwestOnline.org

Delivery Mode

• Northwest Online (email, Internet)

Program Facts

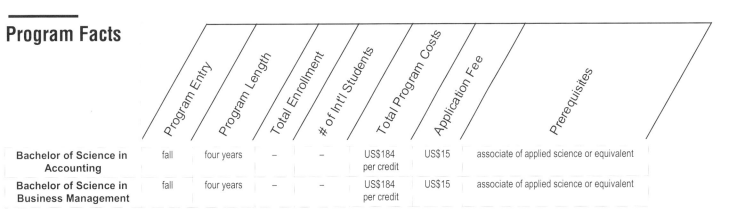

	Program Entry	Program Length	Total Enrollment	# of Int'l Students	Total Program Costs	Application Fee	Prerequisites
Bachelor of Science in Accounting	fall	four years	–	–	US$184 per credit	US$15	associate of applied science or equivalent
Bachelor of Science in Business Management	fall	four years	–	–	US$184 per credit	US$15	associate of applied science or equivalent

Northwestern College

●

Center for Distance Education

Highlights

- Credit obtained through distance courses is equivalent to regular Northwestern credit
- CDE ideally suited for missionaries or military personnel working overseas
- Credit earned in certificate program is transferable to degree programs
- Tuition and application fee for PSEO students are paid by the State of Minnesota for state residents

Programs Offered

Degrees
    Bachelor of Arts in Intercultural Ministries
Degrees Under Development
    Associate of Arts
    Bachelor of Arts in Biblical Studies
Other Programs
    Certificate of Bible
    Postsecondary Enrollment Options

University Statistics

Year Founded:	1902
Total Enrollment:	2,500
Undergraduate Enrollment	1,800
Graduate Enrollment:	n/a
Distance Education Enrollment:	700

Program Overview

Established in 1994, Northwestern College's Center for Distance Education (CDE) offers a Certificate of Bible, Bachelor of Arts in Intercultural Ministries, postsecondary enrollment options and 23 courses in Bible, history, science and general education that can be applied to the previous programs. CDE is accredited by the North Central Association of Colleges and Schools and all credit obtained through distance courses is equivalent to regular Northwestern credit. CDE courses are designed by Northwestern faculty, accessible by Internet anywhere around the world and are ideally suited for missionaries or military personnel working overseas. Registering for CDE courses is straightforward. Applicants must first complete the online registration form at the college website, mail the nonrefundable application fee to CDE, pay a tuition deposit and arrange a payment plan.

Certificate of Bible

The CDE Certificate of Bible program is also known as the 30/30 Plan and prepares students for Christian ministry through the completion of 30 credits in biblical studies in 30 months. All credits earned in the certificate program may be applied to a degree program at Northwestern. The 30/30 Plan curriculum is comprised of five learning modules:Old Testament History & Literature and Bible Study Methods in Christian Education; Christian Discipleship and Isaiah; New Testament History & Literature and Romans & Galatians; Mark and any two of Introduction to Christian Education, Old Testament Archaeology, New Testament Archaeology or Biblical Foundation of Intergroup Relations; and Evangelism & Missions and Christian Theology.

Bachelor of Arts in Intercultural Ministries

The 125-credit bachelor of arts in intercultural ministries (ICM) is a degree completion program that is sponsored by Northwestern College and the Institute of International Studies, a ministry of the US Center for World Mission. ICM expands upon the popular program known as Perspectives on the World Christian Movement, from which more than 20,000 students have graduated. Program objectives include the following: deliver a liberal arts education in a global context; survey Western and non-Western civilizations and folk cultures; develop intercultural communication skills; focus on working in economically developing countries; and overview intercultural ministry methods.

The curriculum focuses on missions, theology, Biblical anthropology, comparative religion, global history, basic science, Greek and Hebrew. General education courses cover English, speech, global perspectives, mathematics, science, social science and computer literacy. Instructional content is arranged in four modules, each worth 12 credits. Graduation requirements, including general education courses, can be fulfilled within 18 to 24 months. General education requirements can be fulfilled through CLEP or life experience. Each student chooses a mentor, or advisor, who will encourage the student throughout the duration of the program.

Postsecondary Enrollment Options

Northwestern College participates in the postsecondary enrollment options (PSEO) program through the CDE. This program enables Minnesota juniors and seniors in public and private high schools or home schools to fulfill high school requirements by completing nonsectarian courses at a participating institution. In addition, children of missionaries who are normally residents of Minnesota are eligible to apply for admission to PSEO. In such cases, a US mailing address is required and students must pay for the shipment of course materials overseas.

Applicants must have a composite ACT score of 18 or higher, a letter of recommendation from a high school official, suitable scores on the state benchmark examination, as well as demonstrate competence in college-level work. PSEO courses can be completed at home or in a school. Credits earned under this program are applicable to degree programs at Northwestern or other institutions. Tuition, books and the application fee are paid by the State of Minnesota for residents of that state.

Northwestern College

●

Center for Distance Education

Program Delivery and Student Support

The Center for Distance Education supplies students with course guides, textbooks, video and audio tapes, and lab kits. The Berntsen Resource Center at Northwestern aids distance students with research and resource acquisition for projects and papers. Staff communicate with students via telephone, facsimile, email or regular mail. Each CDE course has a CourseSite on the Internet used for interaction between students and instructors through discussion forums. Youth Educated at Home conducts classes for some CDE courses, including College Algebra and Mathematics for the Liberal Arts. The CDE website contains helpful links to other sites related to Biblical studies, church history, mission agencies and reference resources.

University and Location

Northwestern Bible and Missionary Training School was founded in 1902 by its first president, Dr. William B. Riley. Northwestern students can choose from one of 20 preprofessional programs or obtain one or more of nearly 50 majors. Beginning in the 2001–2002 academic year, agribusiness and athletic training majors, education endorsement in TESL and a youth ministry minor are available. Northwestern is accredited by the North Central Association of Colleges and Schools, and holds membership in the Council of Christian College and Universities, Evangelical Training Association and Association of Christian Schools International.

Music and performing arts students can join or participate in the A cappella Choir, Drama Ministries Ensemble, Symphonic Band and Women's Choir. The Bultman Center houses a 2,200-seat gymnasium, athletic training facility, wrestling and aerobics room, and human performance laboratory. Residence halls are wired to the campus computer network.

Saint Paul, Minnesota, the home of Northwestern, is located at the juncture of the Minnesota and Mississippi Rivers. In addition to being the state capital, Saint Paul is a major center for insurance, printing and publishing, and computer hardware and software development.

Contact Information

Center for Distance Education
3003 Snelling Avenue North
Saint Paul Minnesota 55113-1598 USA
phone: 1-800-308-5495
fax: 1-651-631-5133
email: distance@nwc.edu
internet: http://www.distance.nwc.edu

Delivery Mode

- Course guides and textbooks
- Videotapes
- Blackboard Internet sites

Program Facts

	Program Entry	Program Length	Total Enrollment	# of Int'l Students	Total Program Costs	Application Fee	Prerequisites
Associate in Arts & Bible	continuous	2 years	n/a	n/a	US$200/credit	–	under development; single courses available
Biblical Studies (ICM) Degree Completion	continuous	2 years	n/a	n/a	US$180/credit	US$50	77 semester credits from elective, or transfer
Certificate in Bible	continuous	30 months	n/a	n/a	US$180/credit	US$25	–

Ohio University

•

Independent and Distance Learning

- Three associate degrees and interdisciplinary bachelor's degree offered
- Four study formats available, including correspondence, web-based, Course Credit by Examination and Independent Learning Projects
- Independent study is open to anyone who can pursue college credit and can benefit from the program

Programs Offered

Associate Degrees:
    Associate of Arts (AA)
    Associate of Individualized Studies (AIS)
    Associate of Science (AS)

Bachelor's Degrees:
    Bachelor of Specialized Studies (BSS)

Individual Courses:
    290 credit courses available

University Statistics

Year Founded:	1804
Total Enrollment:	19,000
Undergraduate Enrollment	16,500
Graduate Enrollment:	2,500
Distance Education Enrollment:	2,500

Program Overview

The Ohio University (Ohio) Independent and Distance Learning Program (IDL) allows students to earn college credit without some of the limitations imposed by the traditional university structure. Independent study is open to anyone capable of pursuing college-level credit who can benefit from the program.

Independent Learning Options

IDL students can select from one of four instructional delivery methods, depending on the course of enrollment.

Correspondence courses divide content into individual lessons to guide student learning. Course material is delivered through a printed study guide, audiocassette, videotape or computer disk, and students submit assignments and interact with instructors via postal mail, fax or email. Correspondence courses normally require supervised examinations or the completion of a course project or paper. More than 250 courses are currently available for correspondence study.

Web courses deliver content via the Internet and students submit assignments and correspond with their instructors by email. Course content is similarly structured to that of correspondence courses; however, students are required have a computer with an Internet connection, be able to use a graphical web browser, and be comfortable communicating via email.

Course Credit By Examination (CCE) is appropriate for students already familiar with a subject or those who can master course content without assistance. CCE students receive a course syllabus and textbook via mail, and prepare independently for a course examination, which must be written within six months of enrollment. The grade achieved on the examination becomes the student's grade in the course.

If a course is not regularly offered through other methods, students may undertake course study through an Independent Learning Project. The proposed course must be offered in the regular Ohio undergraduate curriculum, must not include a lab component and must be approved by the appropriate department. An Ohio faculty member must agree to direct the student's work in the course. The student and the instructor determine the text and other materials to be used and what activities will be required to satisfy course requirements. Students can have up to six months to complete a project; special course examinations may be arranged. A complete list of courses that may apply to the Independent Learning Project option are available in the Ohio undergraduate catalog.

Associate and Bachelor's Degree Programs

Through the External Student Program, Ohio's Division of Lifelong Learning enables students to complete degree coursework for the Associate in Arts, Associate in Science, Associate in Individualized Studies or Bachelor in Specialized Studies degrees.

The Associate in Arts and Associate in Science degrees provide a general liberal arts background emphasizing arts & humanities or social sciences (AA) or science & mathematics (AS). For the AA and AS degrees, students complete 96 quarter-credit hours in requisite arts and humanities, social sciences and natural sciences and/or mathematics courses, and choose their remaining 36 hours from available Ohio courses.

Awarded through University College, the Bachelor of Specialized Studies enables adult students to create a self-designed major. After admission to the program, students choose an area of concentration and develop their degree program with an external advisor. The area of concentration comprises two disciplines and requires a minimum of 45 hours of coursework; it cannot duplicate an existing degree program currently offered on campus. To earn their baccalaureate, students must complete a total of 192 quarter credit hours.

Like the BSS program, the Associate of Individualized Study (AIS) is a self-designed degree program that requires students to submit a proposed course of study and indicate an area of concentration. The AIS degree requires the completion of 30 Ohio credits to satisfy residency requirements.

Admission Requirements

Formal admission to the university is not required for independent study. Students may enroll at any time throughout the year and can commence studies as soon as registration is complete. Adult students are not required to have a high school diploma, and current high school students may be eligible to enroll in lower-division courses with recommendation from their principal or guidance counselor. A noncredit study option is also available.

Prospective IDL students can visit the Independent and Distance Learning office online (http://www.ohio.edu/independent) to review eligibility and enrollment requirements.

Ohio University

●

Independent and Distance Learning

Program Delivery and Student Support

Students enrolled in Independent and Distance Learning can choose a number of study options, from highly structured correspondence and web formats to Course Credit by Examination and Independent Learning Projects. All forms of independent study allow students to learn at the time, place and rate suited to their particular needs.

The Ohio University Libraries assist distance learners with information and research resources required for independent study. The Libraries' web pages serve as a gateway to library collections worldwide and to electronic reference, research and course-related materials. IDL students can access the Libraries' website (http://www.library.ohiou.edu/libinfo/disted.disted.htm) for information and assistance.

University and Location

Athens, Ohio is a small, picturesque city on the banks of the Hocking River and is situated approximately 75 miles southeast of Columbus. The city is surrounded by farms, woodlands and state parks, and is home to the nearly 19,000 students enrolled in studies at Ohio University. An Ordinance of 1787 first provided for the university, which was eventually founded in 1804. The university is accredited by the North Central Association of Colleges and Schools.

Adult and nontraditional learners are part of the diverse student population at Ohio. Many students at the Athens Campus are adult learners who have returned to the classroom to fulfill career goals. The university also connects nearly 2,500 distance learners to various avenues of continued and undergraduate study. Ohio's Independent and Distance Learning Program has served Ohio residents for over 78 years.

Contact Information

Independent and Distance Learning

USA
phone: 1-740-593-2910
fax: 1-740-593-2901
email: independent.study@ohio.edu
internet: www.ohiou.edu/independent

Alternate Internet:
www.ohiou.edu/adultlearning/overview.htm

Delivery Mode

- Printed materials (course guides)
- Audiotape, videotape, CD-ROM, computer disk
- Internet and World Wide Web
- Email, fax, postal mail

Program Facts

	Program Entry	Program Length	Total Enrollment	# of Int'l Students	Total Program Costs	Application Fee	Prerequisites
Associate of Arts	all yr	varies			US$75/yr + course fees		
Associate of Individualized Studies	all yr	varies			US$75/yr + course fees		
Associate of Science	all yr	varies			US$75/yr + course fees		
Bachelor of Specialized Studies	all yr	varies			US$75/yr + course fees		
Course Credit by Examination	all yr	6 mos			US$126–210 per course	n/a	
Courses by correspondence	all yr	1 yr			US$240–400 per course	n/a	
Web-based courses	all yr	1 yr			US$240–400 per course	n/a	

The Pennsylvania State University

•

Distance Education Programs

Programs Offered

Associate Degrees:
  Business Administration
  Dietetic Food Systems Management
  Hotel, Restaurant & Institutional Management
  Human Development & Family Studies
  Letters, Arts & Sciences
Bachelor's Degree Completion:
  Letters, Arts & Sciences
Credit Certificates:
  Postbaccalaureate
  Undergraduate
Dual Degree Program:
  LionHawk
Master's Degree:
  Adult Education

University Statistics

Year Founded:	1855
Total Enrollment:	80,790
Undergraduate Enrollment:	70,796
Graduate Enrollment:	9,994
Distance Education Enrollment:	21,566

Program Overview

Pennsylvania State University is a pioneer in distance learning. PSU's first distance courses in agriculture were offered by correspondence in 1892. More than one hundred years later, PSU still offers distance courses through the World Campus (WC), independent learning (IL) and distributed learning (DL) programs. The Distance Education Report has referred to PSU as a "bellwether institution" in high-technology distance learning and Money.com has ranked World Campus among the country's top 10 virtual campuses.

Penn State Distance Education (PSDE) accepts applications year round. Course length and registration deadlines vary by program, and the campus website contains the most up-to-date program information.

Associate degree program applicants should have a high school diploma, or general education diploma (GED) and acceptable SAT or ACT scores. Other admission options include 18 credits acquired from a regionally accredited institution with a minimum cumulative 2.0 grade point average (GPA), or nine credits acquired from PSU. PSDE also admits high school seniors who expect to receive a 2.0 GPA or higher based on SAT or PSAT results.

The language of instruction of PSDE courses and programs is English. The Test of English as a Foreign Language is therefore required for international degree program applicants, but only recommended for international credit course or certificate program applicants.

Applicants may choose from several credit transfer options. Credit can be applied directly from other regionally accredited institutions, high school advanced placement examinations, college level examinations or military experience. Credit can also be applied through the American Council on Education's College Credit Recommendation Service. Applicants over the age of 60 who are also Pennsylvania residents, PSU alumni or former PSU employees can take credit courses at half tuition.

World Campus Courses and Programs

Initiated in 1998, WC expects to offer between 25 and 30 programs, instruct 300 online credit courses and attain 10,000 enrollments by 2003.

WC enables participants to acquire a master's degree in adult education, in addition to associate degrees in hotel, restaurant, and institutional management and dietetic food systems management (with health care or school food service emphases). PSU grants a postbaccalaureate certificate in logistics and supply chain management.

Independent Learning Courses and Programs

IL enables students to obtain a bachelor's degree in letters, arts and sciences and associate degrees in business administration, human development and family studies, and letters, arts and sciences. The university grants a certificate in one of ten disciplines: adult development and aging services, business management, dietetics and aging, general business, human resources, marketing management, purchasing management, retail management, writing social commentary, and child, youth and family services. Students can apply credit from more than 150 individual courses toward associate or bachelor's degree requirements.

In cooperation with the University of Iowa (UI), PSU has established the LionHawk program, which permits distance learners to earn an associate degree in letters, arts and science from UI and a bachelor of liberal arts studies from PSU. As well, IL offers a variety of noncredit courses and programs.

The Pennsylvania State University

●

Distance Education Programs

Program Delivery and Student Support

WC students should have access to a 100MHz or higher processor. Other hardware features should include 32MB of RAM, 100MB of free disk space, a 14-inch monitor, graphics-capable (inkjet or laser) printer, and 28.8 kbps or higher-speed modem. WC recommends that participants use operating systems such as Windows 95, Windows 98, Windows NT, or Macintosh System 8.1 or higher, in addition to browser software such as Netscape 4.0 or Internet Explorer 4.0 (or higher).

WC students utilize a selection of online services, including bulletin board discussions, chat rooms, reference materials, learning resources, news updates for adult students, study skills, writing workshops and a calendar of WC events. World Campus 101 is a free online course that familiarizes students with online instruction and procedures. WC students can also access the PSU library via an online catalog ("The Cat") and various online research databases.

University and Location

Pennsylvania State University was founded by private charter in 1855, but the Commonwealth of Pennsylvania recognizes PSU as a "state-related" institution. PSU oversees more than 160 baccalaureate and 150 graduate programs and awards nearly 14,000 degrees each year. During the 1998-99 fiscal year, PSU's research expenditures approached US$393 million.

More than 80,000 undergraduate and graduate students attend classes at PSU's 25 campuses. Slightly more than one half of the student body is enrolled at the University Park campus. During the 1999–2000 academic year, 3,000 international students from more than 100 countries studied at PSU. The university has a student to faculty ratio of 19 to 1.

The PSU library collection houses more than 3.7 million volumes and 31,000 serials and periodicals. Staff handle more than five million transactions each month. Various offices provide services related to audiovisual learning aids, computing and microcomputer purchases, health and wellness, student physical disabilities, hospitality, campus policing and travel.

Centre County, the home of PSU's University Park campus, has a population of approximately 133,000 and is situated at the geographic heart of Pennsylvania. The county's four state parks provide areas for hiking, camping, hunting and fishing.

Contact Information

Distance Education Programs
207 Mitchell Building
University Park Pennsylvania 16802-3601 USA
phone: 1-814-865-5403
fax: 1-814-865-3290
email: psuwd@psu.edu
internet: http://www.worldcampus.psu.edu

Delivery Mode

- World Campus (online instruction, email, chat rooms)
- Independent Learning (textbooks; audio & video tapes; audio, video & computer teleconferences)
- Distributed Learning (classroom instruction, interactive videoconferences)

Program Facts

	Program Entry	Program Length	Total Enrollment	# of Int'l Students	Total Program Costs	Application Fee	Prerequisites
Associate Degree (IL)	year round	varies	566	23	US$130–240 per credit	US$50	high school diploma, GED or 18 credits from a regionally accredited institution with a 2.0 GPA
LionHawk Dual Degree Program	year round	varies	–	–	varies	US$30/UI, $50/PSU	contact LionHawk Program at PSU or UI
Master's Degree in Adult Education (WC)	year round	varies	250	–	US$266 per credit	US$50	bachelor's degree from a regionally accredited institution
Postbaccalaureate Certificate (IL)	year round	varies	244	–	US$130–240 per credit	US$50	bachelor's degree from a regionally accredited institution
Undergraduate Certificate (IL) (WC)	year round	varies	232 IL, 2600 WC	14 IL, 24 WC	US$130–240 per credit	US$50 WC	high school diploma, GED or college credit

Purdue University

•

Distributed Learning Services

Program Overview

The Center for Lifelong Learning (CLL) at Purdue University supports the production of complete master's degrees in four areas of engineering (MS/MSE), in business administration (EMBA), in executive education (two degrees) and in technology (MS). A doctoral degree in educational administration can be completed partially by distributed learning. Continuing education credit can also be earned in pharmacy and in audiology & speech science. Individual courses include those in veterinary technology, physics and women's studies.

Purdue has been fully accredited by the North Central Association of Colleges and Schools since 1913. Education for off-campus learners has been offered since 1922 when Purdue first broadcast electrical engineering courses on the university-owned radio stations.

Distance learning courses are offered through the Indiana College Network (ICN) from member institutions of the Indiana Higher Education Telecommunication System/Indiana Partnership for Statewide Education (IHETS/IPSE). Courses are delivered using a variety of media including satellite, Internet, World Wide Web, two-way interactive, videotape, CD-ROM and correspondence.

Application to Purdue must be done through individual departments. Basic requirements for graduate programs include an undergraduate degree with a 3.0 GPA, three letters of recommendation and a statement of purpose. Further requirements for individual programs may exist.

Engineering - MS/MSE

Purdue's Schools of Engineering and Continuing Engineering Education offer a Master's of Science (MS) or Master's of Science in Engineering (MSE) in an interdisciplinary format or with specialization in electrical (MSIE), industrial (MSEE) or mechanical engineering (MSME). Students with degrees in engineering can earn the MSE, and students with undergraduate education in related areas can work toward the MS.

The interdisciplinary program incorporates engineering, mathematics, statistics, psychology, business administration and related subjects in a course of study organized according to students' educational background. Specialty degrees are offered through separate departments. The required 30 semester hours of courses are televised or provided online.

Management - MSM

The Krannert Executive Education Programs (KEEP) began in 1983 with the creation of the Executive Master's Program (EMS). An alternative to traditional MBA programs, the EMS was developed specifically for mid-level managers and managers-to-be who are unable to attend classes on a full-time basis. This cohort program combines on-campus residency (third module residency is at an international location) with distance learning over a 22-month period.

In 1991, the International Master's Management Program (IMM) was introduced. Modeled after the EMS program, this cohort program is also 22 months in length and combines residency and distance learning. IMM residencies alternate between the Purdue main campus in West Lafayette and the partnering institutions: Budapest University of Economic Sciences (BUES) and Tilburg University in the Netherlands.

Food & Agribusiness - MBA

Leaders in food and agricultural businesses around the world can build managerial skills through the Executive MBA offered by Purdue's Krannert Graduate School of Management and the School of Agriculture. This unique program is accredited by the International Association for Management Education.

A residency requirement of nine weeks brings students into repeated contact with each other. Two weeks of the residency are held on the campus of an international partner institution. Weekly coursework totals 18 to 21 hours.

Applicants are required to have previous work experience in the field of agriculture and food.

Technology - MS

The School of Technology offers a weekend program for graduate education that provides individuals working full-time in business and industry with the opportunity to complete the Master of Science degree in Technology.

The program duration is five academic semesters and students move through the program as a cohort. The program combines on-campus residencies (extended weekends, Friday to Sunday afternoons) with distance learning.

Purdue University

●

Distributed Learning Services

Program Delivery and Student Support

Courses are delivered by satellite, interactive television, videotape, Internet, CD-ROM and correspondence. Students require standard reception equipment, including computers with Java-enabled web browsers, Internet connections and modems. For EMBA students, program staff will download required tools onto recommended multimedia Windows laptops during the on-campus orientation week.

The extensive university library system includes special collections in the history of economics, engineering and industrial management, as well as special school and departmental collections. There are over 1,400 electronic data files, and a searchable online catalog of the university's 2,200,000 volumes and microforms.

University and Location

Purdue University enrolls close to 38,000 graduate and undergraduate students in 200 areas of specialization. Twelve academic schools are spread over five campuses throughout Indiana: West Lafayette, Indianapolis, Fort Wayne, Hammond and Westville. There are more than 400 research laboratories on the main West Lafayette campus. The entire university is located on a total of 17,528 acres, which include an airport, research park, golf courses, recreation areas and agricultural lands.

The university was founded in 1869, at which time it began to establish a reputation in agriculture and engineering. The school of aeronautical engineering at Purdue was founded in part by Amelia Earhart. Purdue has graduated more astronauts than any other university.

West Lafayette is a diverse city of 26,500 in north central Indiana, two hours south of Chicago and one hour northwest of Indianapolis. The city, surrounded by major urban centers and city, county and state parks, offers a wealth of cultural and recreational experiences including hiking, swimming, horseback riding, boating and fishing.

Contact Information

Distributed Learning Services
Camilla Lawson, 1586 Stewart Center, Rm 116
West Lafayette Indiana 47907-1586 USA
phone: 1-765-496-7454
fax: 1-765-496-7696
email: cmlawson@purdue.edu
internet: http://www.cll.purdue.edu/dls

Delivery Mode

- Satellite broadcasts
- Interactive television
- Online via Internet/WebCT software
- Correspondence
- Videotape
- CD-ROM

Program Facts

	Program Entry	Program Length	Total Enrollment	# of Int'l Students	Total Program Costs	Application Fee	Prerequisites
EMBA	Aug, Jan	2 years	35	n/a	n/a	US$50	GMAT, work experience, academic record, 3 letters of recommendation
Graduate programs: in-state	Aug, Jan	varies	1,071	63	n/a	US$50	undergraduate degree, 3.0 GPA, statement of intent, 3 letters of recommendation
Graduate programs: out-of-state	Aug, Jan	varies	1,071	63	n/a	US$50	undergraduate degree, 3.0 GPA, statement of intent, 3 letters of recommendation
Management	varies	varies	n/a	n/a	n/a	US$50	n/a
MSE/MS	Aug, Jan	30 semester hours	n/a	n/a	n/a	US$50	undergraduate degree, 3.0 GPA, statement of intent, 3 letters of recommendation
Technology	n/a	5 semesters	n/a	n/a	US$4,000	US$50	undergraduate degree, 3.0 GPA, stmt of purpose, 3 letters of rec, 5 yrs full-time exp

Rensselaer Polytechnic Institute
•
Office of Professional & Distance Education

Programs Offered

Graduate Certificates:
  Bioinformatics
  Computer Graphics, Networks, Science
  Database Systems Design
  Electric Power Engineering
  Graphical User Interfaces
  Human-Computer Interaction
  Management & Technology
  Manufacturing Systems Engineering
  Mechanical Engineering
  Microelectronics Manufacturing Engineering
  Microelectronics Technology & Design
  Quality & Reliability; Service Systems
  Software Engineering

Master's Degrees: (MS, MEng, MBA)
  Business Administration (MBA)
  Computer & Systems Engineering
  Computer Science
  Electric Power Engineering
  Electrical Engineering – Microelectronics
  Engineering Science (two streams)
  Industrial/Mgmt Engineering (two streams)
  Information Technology
  Management
  Mechanical Engineering
  Technical Communications

Institute Statistics

Year Founded:	1824
Total Enrollment:	10,000
Undergraduate Enrollment:	5,000
Graduate Enrollment:	4,000
Distance Education Enrollment:	1,000

Program Overview

Rensselaer Polytechnic Institute offers master's degrees, certificates and courses in 16 areas within science, engineering, computer science and management through its distance learning program, RSVP. Delivered through the Professional and Distance Education (PDE) office, RSVP programs are taken by both individual students and employee groups from participating corporate sponsors.

The Master's of Science (MS) and Master's of Engineering (ME) degrees can take between two to five years to complete and consist of at least 30 credits, where a one-semester course is typically three credits. The Master's of Business Administration (MBA) degree is a 60-credit program. Certificates, generally comprising four course series, can be earned in all RSVP degree areas.

Prospective degree or certificate students must apply to Rensselaer for graduate admission. Prerequisites include a baccalaureate degree and technical experience in engineering, science or other field according to individual program requirements.

Computer Science; Computer Systems & Engineering

The MS in computer science is designed in consultation with industry professionals; students and faculty work on real projects.

Students in the ME in computer and systems engineering concentrate on computer networking or software engineering and take courses in management and manufacturing.

Management & Technology

Rensselaer's Lally School of Management and Technology offers an MBA (60 credits) and an MS (30 credits) in management with several concentrations available. These programs are designed for professionals who have both a technical background and managerial skills and goals.

Students in these programs take a core of management courses, and may also concentrate electives in areas of interest such as service systems or production and operations management.

Industrial & Management Engineering

The Department of Decision Sciences and Engineering Systems (DSES) offers an industrial and management engineering degree, the only such degree in the US, with concentrations in quality engineering and service systems. The Center for Services

Research and Education, one of few centers in the world for research on the service sector, brings together people, systems and technology in the curriculum for this degree.

Engineering Science

The Engineering Science program offers MS and MEng degrees with a concentration in Manufacturing Systems or Microelectronics Manufacturing. The former focuses on advancements in system design, planning and operations, with courses from the fields of management, engineering and science.

Microelectronics Manufacturing is an interdisciplinary program, developed with the Semiconductor Research Center, that adds basic concepts in semiconductor materials, electronics and statistics to a microelectronics manufacturing core.

Information Technology; Technical Communication

The MS in Information Technology is an interdisciplinary program offered by the Faculty of Information Technology, who are also faculty members of Rensselaer's five schools. The program provides an intensive technological core with a specific application discipline, giving working professionals the IT skills needed to harness the power of information in their enterprise.

The MS in Technical Communication, from the Department of Language, Literature and Communication, focuses on the issues inheren in communication through technology.

Electrical/Electric Power/Mechanical Engineering

Students can pursue MS or MEng degrees in Electrical Engineering with a concentration in the design and manufacture of microelectronics (semiconductor devices). This interdisciplinary program draws on the expertise of faculty and researchers in the Electrical, Computer & Systems Engineering Department and the Center for Integrated Electronics and Electronics Manufacturing.

The MS and MEng in Electric Power Engineering provide engineers in the highly competitve power industry with the diverse skills now required by equipment manufacturers, energy management specialists and power brokers.

The MEng in Mechanical Engineering allows professionals to update their skills with concentrations in advanced design or manufacturing techniques.

Rensselaer Polytechnic Institute

●

Office of Professional & Distance Education

Program Delivery and Student Support

Most students complete degrees and certificates while employed full time by the 27 corporations across Canada, Mexico, Europe and the US that have corporate sponsorship agreements with Rensselaer. Individual students take courses via videostreaming or other modes on the WWW.

To register, students must be admitted to Rensselaer. Workplace-based students have on-site coordinators responsible for course administration. Students beginning degree programs must submit a plan of study, and meet regularly with advisors via phone, email or computer forums.

Courses are delivered through satellite, interactive videoconferencing, or videotape mailed at additional cost. Many courses are available via videostreaming (live or on-demand) or using Rensselaer's 80/20 Interactive Distance Delivery Model, which combines live (synchronous) and individual (asynchronous) learning sessions on the Internet.

Institute and Location

Rensselaer, the oldest private engineering school in the US, was founded more than 175 years ago, "for the purpose of ... the application of science ... to the common purposes of life." Established in 1987, the RSVP distance learning program was designed to extend the mission of the institute, by facilitating the transfer of new developments in science, engineering and management to industry.

Distance students benefit from Rensselaer's focus on technology, both in research and education. Twenty-two multidisciplinary research centers, including the Electronics Agile Manufacturing Center and the Scientific Computation Research Center, make their home on campus. Recent rankings by US News & World Report and Success magazines have placed Rensselaer's graduate engineering program 17th nationwide and ranked the Lally School of Management & Technology 7th in the US.

Rensselaer is located in Troy, in central eastern New York, 10 minutes from Albany and 150 miles north of New York City.

Contact Information

Office of Professional & Distance Education
CII - Ste. 4011; 110-8th Street
Troy New York 12180 USA
phone: 1-518-276-8351
fax: 1-518-276-8026
email: rsvp@rpi.edu
internet: http://www.pde.rpi.edu

Delivery Mode

• Satellite
• Interactive videoconferencing
• Videotape
• Live or on-demand on the World Wide Web

Program Facts

	Program Entry	Program Length	Total Enrollment	# of Int'l Students	Total Program Costs	Application Fee	Prerequisites
Certificates	–	1-3 years	50	–	US$8,400-11,200	US$45	undegraduate degree; requirements vary
Courses, 3–4 credits each	–	1 semester	n/a	–	US$700 per credit	US$45	undegraduate degree; requirements vary
MBA	–	2-5 years	–	–	US$42,000	US$45	undegraduate degree; requirements vary
MS and MEng degrees	–	2-5 years	1,000	–	US$21,000-22,400	US$45	undegraduate degree; requirements vary

ei's guide to distance and online learning programs in the usa - 2001 edition

Rogers State University

RSU Online

Highlights

- Nine-year history of online course delivery
- Four complete two-year degrees and four four-year bachelor degrees offered online
- Credit for naval training through US Navy agreement

Programs Offered

Associate Degrees:
   Applied Tech, Business Admin,
   Comp Sci - Bus Option, Liberal Arts
Bachelor's Degrees:
   BA in Liberal Arts, BS in Bus. Info. Tech,
   Bachelor of Technology in Applied Tech
Credit Courses:
   Accounting, Accounting Info Systems,
   Amer Federal Gov't, Art History, Astronomy,
   Bus. Communications, Business Law,
   College Algebra, Composition,
   Computer & Telecomm Applications,
   Computer Architecture, Programming C/C++
   Creative Writing, Drug Abuse,
   Economics, Emerging Technologies,
   Fundamentals of Supervision,
   General Environmental Biology,
   Gov't Regulation of Business,
   Human-Computer Interface, Humanities I&II,
   Industrial Psychology, Intro to Business,
   Intro to Computers, Intro to Safety Mgmt,
   Java Programming, Ldrship/Change Dynam.,
   Mass Comm, Micro-comp Applications,
   Mgmt: Leadership & Dec. Making, Marketing,
   Multimedia Development, Music Apprec.,
   Object-oriented Programming, Principles
   of Accounting I & II, Principles of Mgmt,
   Psychology, Software Engineering,
   Spanish, Statistics, Systems Analysis,
   US History, Website Design & Development

University Statistics

Year Founded:	1909
Total Enrollment:	2,875
Undergraduate Enrollment	–
Graduate Enrollment:	–
Distance Education Enrollment:	1,500

Program Overview

Rogers State University (RSU) has delivered online degrees and courses through RSU Online since 1992. RSU opened the first fully operational university television station in Oklahoma in 1986, with courses broadcast to 3,000 students annually. RSU Online now provides distance learning to over 60 percent of the RSU student body.

Four associate degrees are offered in business administration, liberal arts, computer science, and in applied technology for navy personnel. Complete four-year online degrees are offered in applied technology, business information technology and liberal arts.

Online programs and courses are approved by the Southern Regional Electronic Campus (SREC), a collective of online programs offered throughout the southern US. The SREC reviews programs through the application of common standards, as outlined in its Principles of Good Practice. RSU's degrees are accredited by the North Central Association of Colleges and Schools.

Students applying to RSU Online must provide proof of high school education or GED certificate; to be granted full admission, students must also provide ACT or SAT scores. Students over 21 years of age must provide ACT Compass scores if they do not have other test results. Special student status is available for students who meet minimum admission requirements and who wish to take a maximum of nine credit hours (equivalent to three semester-long courses). International students, including those international students living outside a 60 mile radius of RSU campuses, must submit a TOEFL score greater than 500 and an official high school transcript, and may need to include an ACT score.

Business Administration

The Associate of Arts in Business Administration comprises 60 credit hours. A 38 credit-hour core in general education includes English, math, humanities, science and communication. Twenty-four business program credits in accounting, economics, marketing, management and communications are supported by courses in accounting, statistics, business and administration.

Liberal Arts

The Associate of Arts in Liberal Arts requires the basic 38-credit core of general education courses. Students then must choose a total of 12 electives from four disciplines and 10 other courses as they apply to students interests and needs. Substitution of the communication requirement with creative or technical writing online can be a valuable asset to students interested in writing as a career.

Computer Science

The Associate of Science in Computer Science is a business-oriented program of study. In addition to the core of general education requirements, the program involves the study of microcomputer applications, C and C++ Programming, operating systems and software engineering. Students also take courses in accounting.

Applied Technology for Naval Personnel

RSU Online's new agreement with the US Navy allows naval personnel to receive 30 college credits for naval block training, and with the completion of an extra 30 credit hours of online college courses, to receive an Associate of Applied Science in Technology degree. The application of credit for navy training follows the American Council on Education guidelines. Online technology is accessible to students on ships or Naval bases around the world, though courses follow RSU's tri-semester schedule.

Credit can be received for eight areas of Navy Ratings including advanced electronics and computer fields; aviation electronics technician; fire control technician; nuclear field electrician's mate; nuclear field electronics technician; and nuclear field machinist mate.

Several courses in the areas of computer science, English and political science are designed for students in this program. Student may enroll in any of the 50 classes offered online each semester. Core requirements include English, math, communications, humanities, science, US history and US government, with 15 credit hours of electives.

Rogers State University

•

RSU Online

Program Delivery and Student Support

The RSU Online website is designed as a user-friendly source for all aspects of program delivery. Students can experience an online course by opening the sample course, which explains the interactive components of the online delivery system administered by eCollege.com.

Students can access technical assistance and academic advising online. Textbooks can be ordered online from the campus bookstore. Videos required for some RSU Online courses can also be ordered online for a rental fee from the RMI Media.

Necessary equipment includes java-capable browser (Microsoft Explorer 5.0 or higher for PC or 4.5 for Mac); Windows 98, 2000 or NT for PCs and a 90 MHz Pentium Processor, or the Mac OS 8.1 and a Power PC Processor; 32 MB of RAM or more; 56 kbps modem; sound card; speakers; RealPlayer software; Internet Service Provider; email account.

University and Location

Rogers State University consists of three geographical campuses in addition to the online component, and enrolls 2,875 students. A faculty of 164 delivers RSU's programs, which include 37 associate degrees in arts, science and applied sciences, bachelor's degrees in applied technology, business information technology and liberal arts, and a master's degree in school administration. Cooperative agreements for the administration of upper level programs currently exist between RSU, the University of Oklahoma, the OU Health Sciences Center and Northeastern University. RSU also offers courses by television broadcast from the on-campus studio in Claremore.

The main university campus is located in Claremore, northeastern Oklahoma, where it was established in 1909, two years after the state's formation.

Contact Information

RSU Online
Lane Wood, Coordinator, 1701 W. Will Rogers Blvd.
Claremore Oklahoma 74017 USA
phone: 1-918-343-7751
fax: 1-918-343-7595
email: online@rsu.edu
internet: http://www.rsuonline.edu/

Delivery Mode

• Online
• Videotape
• Television broadcasts

Program Facts

	Program Entry	Program Length	Total Enrollment	# of Int'l Students	Total Program Costs	Application Fee	Prerequisites
Associate degree for navy personnel	Jan, Jun, Aug	30 credit hrs	–	–	US$91 per credit hr	–	Navy Rating training
Associate degrees: in-state	Jan, Jun, Aug	60 credit hrs / 2 years	–	–	US$103.53 per credit hr	–	High school diploma or GED certificate, SAT or ACT scores
Associate degrees: out-of-state	Jan, Jun, Aug	–	–	–	US$196.53 per credit hr	–	High school diploma or GED certificate, SAT or ACT scores
Bachelor's degrees: in-state	Jan, Jun, Aug	120 credit hrs / 4 yrs	–	–	US$103.53 per credit hr	–	High school diploma or GED certificate, SAT or ACT scores
Bachelor's degrees: out-of-state	Jan, Jun, Aug	120 credit hrs / 4 yrs	–	–	US$196.53 per credit hr	–	High school diploma or GED certificate, SAT or ACT scores

The State University of New Jersey – Rutgers

●

Continuous Education and Outreach

- Three graduate certificates and master's program in nursing
- Certificate in horticulture offered
- Interactive delivery includes threaded discussion, chat rooms and email
- Student can apply for various forms of financial aid with their application

Certificate Programs
  Horticulture (CPE)
Graduate Programs
  Certificate in Childhood Literacy (15 cr)
  Certificate in Comm and Literacy (15 cr)
  Certificate in Government Accounting (12 cr)
  Nursing (30 cr)

Year Founded:	1766
Total Enrollment:	49,300
Undergraduate Enrollment	35,000
Graduate Enrollment:	14,300
Distance Education Enrollment:	1,000

Program Overview

Through RutgersOnline, Rutgers University offers Internet courses leading to completion of certificate and graduate programs in several academic areas. The new virtual campus extends the university's services and provides students with the opportunity to telecommute to campus from virtually anywhere. RutgersOnline courses are equivalent to traditional courses offered on campus.

Internet courses are asynchronous in design, allowing students to view lectures and work on assignments at times that are convenient to them. Classes are designed to be interactive and are limited in size to facilitate discussion.

In addition to its online courses, Rutgers also delivers instruction through Interactive Video Classrooms (IVC). IVC connects two or more sites in a live two-way interactive video and audio setting.

Graduate Programs

RutgersOnline primarily offers graduate-level courses. Since 1999, the virtual campus has offered graduate programs in nursing and library studies. Current programs include a master's degree in nursing and graduate certificates in childhood literacy, communication & literacy and government accounting. A certificate program in horticulture is also available.

The development of additional additional certificate programs and courses is underway. Prospective students are encouraged to visit the RutgersOnline course web page (ce1766.rutgers.edu/online) for up-to-date course listings.

Admissions

Distance learning students must apply through the respective school offering the online course. Students wishing to enroll may take advantage of the online registration available on the Rutgers University website (http://www.rutgers.edu). Students have the option to either download an application or request a printed form.

Application requirements vary by graduate program; generally, students should have an undergraduate grade point average (GPA) of B or better and provide the appropriate test scores and letters of recommendation with their application. For some programs, an internship or relevant work experience can strengthen the application.

In many programs, students can enroll on a nondegree basis for up to 12 credits.

Nondegree registration provides graduate credit, which may be applied to a program once a student is accepted. Prospective students should contact the program for course availability before submitting an application for nondegree study.

Financial Aid

Rutgers offers all forms of financial aid to assist students enrolling in undergraduate or graduate distance learning degree programs. Students can apply for academically-based assistance by answering questions on the application form pertaining to financial aid. US citizens or permanent residents can apply for need-based aid in the form of loans, grants and work-study by completing a Free Application for Federal Student Aid (FAFSA) which is available through the Office of Financial Aid or online through the US Department of Education (http://www.fafsa.ed.gov/).

Information on the financial aid application process and eligibility requirements can be accessed through the Office of Financial Aid website (http://studentaid.rutgers.edu).

Tuition

Tuition fees vary depending on the school offering the online course. On average, graduate course tuition for New Jersey residents is approximately US$900 for a three-credit course. Non-resident tuition is approximately US$1300 per course. At the time of enrollment, all students must pay the mandatory US$75 application fee and are subject to other student fees.

The State University of New Jersey – Rutgers

•

Continuous Education and Outreach

Program Delivery and Student Support

In order to participate successfully in an online course, students must have reliable Internet access including an email account, graphical browser and access to the World Wide Web. Online courses feature interactive delivery including threaded discussion, chat rooms and email. The RutgersOnline website offers a complete list of technical requirements (http://rutgersonline.net).

All interactive video classrooms provide full two-way real-time audio and video, so students and faculty can interact as if they were face-to-face. Classrooms are equipped with multiple cameras that record both instructors and students.

University and Location

Founded in 1766, Rutgers is one of the oldest institutions of higher learning in the US. Comprised of 29 undergraduate colleges, graduate schools and professional schools, Rutgers is the flagship institution of New Jersey's public higher education system, and offers more than 100 graduate programs as well as opportunities for interdisciplinary study, joint-degree programs and nondegree study. Rutgers is also a member of the Association of American Universities, which comprises the 62 leading research universities in North America.

Contact Information

Continuous Education and Outreach
83 Somerset St, Queens Bldg, College Ave Campus
New Brunswick New Jersey 08901 USA
phone: 1-732-932-5935
fax: 1-732-932-9225
email: caprio@andromeda.rutgers.edu
internet: http://www.rutgers.edu

Delivery Mode

The majority of Rutgers distance learning courses are fully asynchronous and Internet-based. The horticulture program is delivered through an integrated CD/Internet model.

Program Facts

	Program Entry	Program Length	Total Enrollment	# of Int'l Students	Total Program Costs	Application Fee	Prerequisites
Graduate Certificate in Childhood Literacy	Sep or Jan	1–2 years	25	--	US$13,500	US$75	bachelor of arts or science
Graduate Certificate in Comm. and Literacy	Sep or Jan	1–2 years	25	–	US$13,500	US$75	bachelor of arts or science
Graduate Certificate in Government Accounting	Sep or Jan	1–2 years	30	–	US$15,000	US$75	bachelor of arts or science
Graduate Program in Nursing (MS)	Sep or Jan	Generally 3 years	40	–	US$27,000	US$75	bachelor of arts or science in nursing
Horticulture Certificate	Monthly	1 year	New	–	US$3,000	US$75	high school diploma

ei's guide to distance and online learning programs in the usa - 2001 edition

Saint Mary-of-the-Woods College

•

Women's External Degree Program

Programs Offered

Associate Degree Majors:
  Accounting, Early Childhood Education, General Business, Gerontology, Humanities, Paralegal Studies

Baccalaureate Degree Majors:
  Accounting, Accounting Info Systems, Applied Science: Occup. Therapy Apps., Business Administration, Comp Info Systems, Digital Media Comm, Education (three specializations), English, Gerontology, History/Political Science/Pre-law Track, Human Resource Mgmt, Human Services, Humanities, Journalism, Marketing, Mathematics, Not-for-Profit (several areas), Paralegal Studies, Professional Writing, Psychology, Social Science/History, Theology

Certificate Programs:
  Gerontology, Paralegal Studies, Theology

Master's Degree Programs:
  Art Therapy, Earth Literacy, Music Therapy, Pastoral Theology

Post-baccalaureate:
  Legal Nurse Certificate, Teacher Licensure

College Statistics

Year Founded:	1840
Total Enrollment:	1,439
Undergraduate Enrollment	1,354
Graduate Enrollment:	85
Distance Education Enrollment:	1,046

Program Overview

Through the Women's External Degree (WED) Program, Saint Mary-of-the-Woods College offers students the opportunity to earn their college degree through distance learning. The undergraduate program is intended to be flexible, affording women the opportunity to control when and where they study in a wide range of academic disciplines. Academic guidance and support, both on- and off-campus, are important components of the program. Four MA programs are also offered, and are open to both women and men.

Bachelor's, Associate & Certificate Programs

WED Program students are recommended to take two courses in their first semester, to adjust to the schedule, pacing and requirements of distance study. Once comfortable, students can then choose to take as little as one or as many as five courses per semester, or vary their semesters depending on additional commitments. Semesters are typically 20 to 22 weeks long.

Program participants can undertake baccalaureate study in the following fields: Accounting, Accounting Information Systems, Applied Science: Occupational Therapy Applications, Business Administration, Computer Information Systems, Digital Media Communication, Education (Early Childhood, Elementary or Secondary: English, Math and Social Studies), English, Gerontology, History/Political Science/Pre-law Track, Human Resource Management, Human Services, Humanities, Journalism, Marketing, Mathematics, Not-for-Profit (in several areas), Paralegal Studies, Professional Writing, Psychology, Social Science/History and Theology. The degree requires the completion of 125 semester hours of study, of which 30 hours must be earned through the college. Students in Accounting Information Systems must complete 150 hours to meet CPA standards.

Associate degree programs are offered in Accounting, Early Childhood Education, General Business, Gerontology, Humanities and Paralegal Studies and comprise 65 semester hours. Certificate programs are also offered to WED students in Gerontology, Paralegal Studies and Theology.

A post-baccalaureate certificate program is offered in Legal Nursing for students with a bachelor's degree in nursing. Teacher licensure is also available for those students who have a bachelor's degree and who wish to become licensed teachers. Education majors must live within 200 miles of campus for supervision of field experiences.

MA Programs

SMWC also offers distance education graduate programs in Art Therapy, Earth Literacy, Music Therapy and Pastoral Theology. These programs begin most coursework with three to five days on campus; summer weeklong intensives are also required for some programs.

MA in Art Therapy students complete 45 curriculum hours, and integrate theories of art therapy through practical fieldwork and internships. The program is based on the educational guidelines of the American Art Therapy Association.

The MA in Earth Literacy is an interdisciplinary major designed for individuals who wish to work toward planetary sustainability. The 36-hour program emphasizes internships and practica experiences. A graduate certificate is also available.

The MA in Music Therapy is a 39 credit hour program. Qualified music therapists will gain advanced understanding of the therapeutic uses of music; counseling and psychotherapy are emphasized.

The MA in Pastoral Theology prepares women and men for service in pastoral ministry and is also appropriate for those who wish to develop a theological foundation for the Christian Life. The 36-credit-hour program requires the completion of a Spiritual and Professional Component. A graduate certificate is also available.

Admission Requirements & Procedures

Applicants to undergraduate WED programs should have a high school diploma or GED certificate and demonstrate potential for success in a distance learning program. Applicants who have been out of high school for less than five years should submit SAT I scores along with their application.

Master of Arts and graduate certificate applicants should have a bachelor's degree from an accredited institution and submit the following materials with their application: official transcripts of all collegiate work, a completed application form, two letters of recommendation, and a non-refundable application fee. Individual programs may have additional requirements, and can be consulted through the SMWC website (www.smwc.edu).

Saint Mary-of-the-Woods College

•

Women's External Degree Program

Program Delivery and Student Support

New SMWC students travel to campus for two-and-a-half days to consult with academic advisors, plan current and future courses of study and meet with fellow students and instructors. During the balance of the semester, work is undertaken at a distance with regularly-submitted assignments, and students interact with their professors via telephone, mail and email. Each semester, students return to campus for one day to review and plan their continued course of study.

WED staff are dedicated to providing assistance to distance learning students in the form of advocacy, registration assistance and information, referral to additional campus services and distribution of library materials and quarterly newsletters. The Career Development Center (CDC) can help students focus interests, assess skills and explore the academic options that will best support their job search.

College and Location

SMWC was founded in 1840, and is the oldest Catholic liberal arts college for women in the US. The college is accredited by the North Central Association of Colleges and Schools. Over 100 full-time and adjunct SMWC faculty serve as WED instructors and academic advisors, and sixty percent of full-time faculty have doctoral or terminal degrees in their fields.

Located five miles northwest of Terre Haute, Indiana, SMWC's 67-acre wooded campus features a fitness trail, gymnasium, indoor swimming pool, lake and stables. Saint Mary-of-the-Woods is situated approximately 75 miles from Indianapolis and 175 miles from Chicago, Illinois. Terre Haute's Hulman Field airport is served by commuter flights (via Chicago), and Indianapolis International Airport is served by most major airlines.

Contact Information

Women's External Degree Program
Guerin Hall
St. Mary-of-the-Woods Indiana 47876 USA
phone: 1-812-535-5263
fax: 1-812-535-4900
email: wedadm@smwc.edu
internet: http://www.smwc.edu

Delivery Mode

• Faculty members & students communicate by telephone, voice mail, email and postal service. Textbooks, course manuals and workbooks are used. Some courses require Internet connections, videotapes, audiotapes or optional computer programs.

Program Facts

	Program Entry	Program Length	Total Enrollment	# of Int'l Students	Total Program Costs	Application Fee	Prerequisites
Associate (General Business)	Sep, Nov, Feb, Apr	65 credit hours	22	not avail	US$294/cr hr	US$30	–
Baccalaureate (all programs)	Sep, Nov, Feb, Apr	125 credit hours	921	not avail	US$294/cr hr	US$30	–
Post-baccalaureate (Legal Nurse)	Oct, Nov, Mar, May	31 credit hours	89	not avail	US$294/cr hr	US$30	–
Post-baccalaureate (Teaching Licensure)	Sep, Nov, Feb, Apr	–	1	not avail	US$294/cr hr	US$30	–

Salve Regina University

●

Graduate Extension Study

Program Overview

Graduate Extension Study (GES) at Salve Regina University (SRU) provides a forum for distance learners to obtain a master's degree in one of four 36-credit (12-course) programs or one of two certificates.

At present, the GES curriculum consists of 39 three-credit online courses. Tuition per credit hour is US$350, while prerequisites are US$500 per course. Each course must be completed within six months of registration. Master's degree candidates taking seven or more GES courses must comply with SRU residency policy by registering in at least one on-campus course or attending the Graduate Extension Study Institute. The institute is a four-day conference in June that permits students to interact with faculty.

In addition to the application form, students must submit a US$50 nonrefundable application fee, official transcripts and two letters of recommendation from previous instructors. They should also submit the results of one of five standardized tests: Miller's Analogies Test (MAT), Graduate Record Examination (GRE), Graduate Management Aptitude Test (GMAT), Law School Admissions Test (LSAT) or Medical College Admissions Test (MCAT). International applicants must include the results of the TOEFL or IELTS and a transcript evaluation.

Graduate requirements are lowered for applicants with military credentials or insurance certification. Students in the military can transfer up to 18 credits, while students with insurance certification can transfer up to 12 credits.

Master of Arts Programs

SRU awards a master of arts (MA) in human development, and in international relations with a concentration in regional studies. The regional studies concentration is only available through GES.

The human development program entails four core courses and eight electives. Three of the four core courses are devoted to developmental psychology from infancy to adulthood, while the other examines personality psychology. Electives include such courses as ethical perspectives on global issues, great writers, systems consultation or concept approaches through mind/emotions.

The international relations master's program entails coursework in international relations foundations, international law, contemporary international issues, global business and ethical perspectives on global issues. Program participants who wish to specialize in regional studies elect courses that focus on Russia and Eastern Europe; Africa; China, Japan and the Pacific Rim; Central Asia and India; the United States and North America; Central and South America; and the Middle East.

Master of Business Administration

The university offers a master of business administration (MBA) program. Prerequisites include SRU courses PRE561, PRE 518 and PRE510 or six credits each in accounting, economics, and quantitative methods and/or calculus.

Program participants must take nine business administration courses and three electives from the same curriculum. Core courses include organizational theory and behavior, law and business organizations, human resources management, operations research, economic principles, marketing management, managerial ethics, financial management, and strategic management & business policy. A research seminar is required.

Master of Science in Management

SRU awards a master of science (MS) in management with one of three concentrations: management, insurance or correctional administration. Students in the MS program must take a research seminar and seven core courses: organization theory and behavior, law and business organizations, human resources management, economic principles, marketing management, managerial ethics, and strategic management and business policy.

Students concentrating in management elect four courses from among operations research, financial accounting, global business labor relations, financial management, systems analysis and design, business data communications and knowledge-based systems. In place of the research seminar, those concentrating in insurance take an additional management course. Students concentrating in correctional administration undertake courses in incarceration literature, correctional administration, personality psychology and systems consultation instead of marketing management coursework.

Certificate Programs

The university confers a certificate through one of two programs: a 15-credit graduate certificate in management or a 12-credit certificate in management with a concentration in correctional administration.

Salve Regina University

Graduate Extension Study

Program Delivery and Student Support

GES students interact with instructors by correspondence, telephone and email. Those taking online courses must have access to a personal computer, modem and Internet service. Students are obligated to use SRU web resources in a manner consistent with the university mission. The university library's website contains a catalog, periodical lists, course reserves, as well as electronic databases, journals and newspapers.

Instructors at SRU are well-trained to guide students to successful completion of their course of study.

University and Location

The Roman Catholic order Sisters of Mercy of Providence founded Salve Regina College by state-granted charter. The college opened its doors to students in 1947 and adopted its present name, Salve Regina University (SRU), in 1991. SRU is accredited by the New England Association of Schools and Colleges and is a member of the National Catholic Educational Association.

The student body consists of 1,700 undergraduate students and 415 graduate students; alumni total over 12,000. The student to faculty ratio is 13 to 1. Students benefit from the following student centers and services: academic and career development centers; counseling, health and student activities offices; student government association; and academic clubs. The spiritual mission of the university is reflected in ministries such as retreats for staff, faculty and students, spirituality workshops, and mass and other sacramental rituals. SRU's 60-acre shoreline campus features several Gilded Age summer estates including Ochre Court, which was built in 1892.

SRU is located in Newport, Rhode Island, a community of 28,227. The city is a mecca for sports enthusiasts who enjoy sailing, scuba diving, spearfishing and surfing. The country's oldest tavern (1673) and the internationally renowned Newport Jazz Festival make Newport their home.

Contact Information

Graduate Extension Study
100 Ochre Point Avenue
Newport Rhode Island 02840-4192 USA
phone: 1-800-637-0002
fax: 1-401-849-0702
email: sruexten@salve.edu
internet: http://www.salve.edu.geshome.html

Delivery Mode

- Correspondence
- Internet (email, online instruction)
- Telephone

Program Facts

	Program Entry	Program Length	Total Enrollment	# of Int'l Students	Total Program Costs	Application Fee	Prerequisites
Certificate in Correctional Administration	year round	6 months per course	–	–	US$350 per credit	US$50	some undergraduate study
Graduate Certificate in Management	year round	6 months per course	–	–	US$350 per credit	US$50	bachelor's degree
Master of Arts in Human Development	year round	5-year maximum	–	–	US$350 per credit	US$50	bachelor's degree, standardized test
Master of Arts in International Relations	year round	5-year maximum	–	–	US$350 per credit	US$50	bachelor's degree, standardized test
Master of Business Administration	year round	5-year maximum	–	–	US$350 per credit	US$50	bachelor's degree, standardized test, SRU courses PRE561, PRE 518 and PRE510
Master of Science in Management	year round	5-year maximum	–	–	US$350 per credit	US$50	bachelor's degree, standardized test

Sinclair Community College

Distance Learning

- Associate in Arts and Associate in Science in Business Administration programs
- Degrees can be earned completely at a distance, through distance learning and independent study methods
- Students can transfer to four-year business administration and distance liberal arts programs

Programs Offered

Certificate:
　　Software Applications for the Professional
Degrees:
　　Associate in Arts
　　Associate in Science in Business Admin.

College Statistics

Year Founded:	1887
Total Enrollment:	20,086
Undergraduate Enrollment	20,086
Graduate Enrollment:	n/a
Distance Education Enrollment:	4,287

Program Overview

Sinclair Community College (Sinclair) offers two complete degree programs, a short-term certificate and over 150 courses through its Distance Learning Program (DLP). In addition, Sinclar offers more than 80 associate degrees that range from 91 to 110 quarter-credit hours in length, of which 30 credits must be taken at Sinclair. Students can transfer into programs from regionally accredited institutions, provided they meet basic grade-point average (GPA) requirements.

Sinclair offers students distance learning opportunities through a number of individualized technologies. Students get course lectures and instructional materials by videocassette, audiocassette, CD-ROM and/or in print. Through the Sinclair Electronic College, students can take a collection of courses via the Internet, accessing assignments and information, interacting with instructors and fellow students, and linking to online resources. A few distance courses involve alternative testing (e.g. case studies, online tests) but testing for most courses is done via a proctor near the student's location.

Associate in Arts

The Associate in Arts is a 94 quarter-credit-hour program, combining twenty-three distance learning courses with seven courses offered through independent study or on-campus courses. Students undertake study in English, speech, computers, mathematics, natural & physical sciences, social & behavioral science and arts & humanities, as well as interdisciplinary multicultural studies. Additional elective hours can be chosen from a variety of available courses. In partnership with Governors State University (GSU), Sinclair offers Associate in Arts graduates the ability to transfer to GSU to complete a Bachelor of Arts through distance education.

Associate in Science, Business Administration

DLP offers the Associate in Science in Business Administration, which combines study in accounting, English composition, mathematics, business software, economics, natural science and humanities. The program requires the completion of 98 quarter credit-hours or 30 courses, 23 of which may be taken through distance learning methods. Remaining courses are offered through independent study or on-campus courses. For those students who wish to transfer to a four-year institution to continue their business studies, a University

Parallel program option is available.

Certificate Program

Sinclair also offers a certificate program in Software Applications for the Professional that can be completed through a combination of distance learning methods. Certificate students must complete a total of 21 credit hours of coursework.

Admission Requirements

Sinclair welcomes all students to enroll in distance education courses and programs. Students who are degree-seeking or who are taking English or mathematics courses must take a Sinclair placement test, which determines their initial level of course placement. A one-time $10 application fee is required of all students.

Tuition fees are determined on a per-credit basis, depending on the student's geographical area of residence: Montgomery County (Ohio) residents pay US$29.45 per credit hour, other Ohio residents pay US$48.45 per credit hour and out-of-state residents pay US$81.45 per credit hour. Sinclair distance education students can submit applications for admission and register for courses online through the Sinclair Distance Learning Web site (http://www.sinclair.edu/distance). Admission is offered on a rolling basis, and Associate and certificate programs begin in September, January, March and mid-June.

International applicants must have a high school diploma, a certificate of completion and be eligible for admittance to a university in their home country. Students should have completed mathematics study at the secondary level. International applicants are advised to begin their application process at least four months in advance of their intended date of enrollment. Students applying from outside the US should submit their application materials at least two months prior to the start of the quarter in which they wish to enroll.

Financial aid is available to Sinclair students in a number of forms, including federal and state grants, low-interest loans and student employment. Information on financial aid opportunities can be obtained from the main Sinclair web site (http://www. sinclair.edu).

Sinclair Community College

Distance Learning

Program Delivery and Student Support

For web-based courses, Sinclair DLP students should have access to a 486 computer (or higher) or Macintosh equivalent with the following components: 8 MB RAM (or higher); 8 MB free hard disk space; a 28.8 kbps modem (or higher); Windows 3.1 or higher; telephone line; an Internet account with access to the World Wide Web; and an Internet browser that is version 4.0 or higher.

Internet access to the college library, International Student Services, online tutoring, academic advising, disability services and career planning is available to Sinclair DLP students through the Sinclair Distance Learning web site (http://www. sinclair.edu/distance).

Contact Information

Distance Learning
444 West Third Street
Dayton Ohio 45402 USA
phone: 1-937-512-2694
fax: 1-937-512-2891
email: lpahud@sinclair.edu
internet: http://www.sinclair.edu/distance

College and Location

Sinclair College originates under the auspices of the YMCA, which began offering courses to local residents in 1887. By 1929, the college offered curriculum in several disciplines including liberal arts, office training, law and technical study. The YMCA College was renamed Sinclair College in 1948, after David A. Sinclair, founder of the YMCA educational program. In 1968, twenty acres of downtown property were acquired for development of a new campus, which was subsidized by municipal levy; a new Sinclair campus opened its doors to students in September 1972. Sinclair College was re-accredited by the North Central Association of Colleges and Schools in 1997, and has enjoyed Montgomery County citizen support for nearly forty years.

Sinclair's main campus is adjacent to Interstate 75 on the western edge of downtown Dayton. The now 50-acre campus blends modern architecture and greenspace, and is interconnected through a series of underground corridors and third-floor walkways. Dayton features numerous museums and art venues, including the United States Air Force Museum & IMAX Theater, the Dayton Art Institute and the Dayton Visual Arts Center, and is home to growing high technology, service and distribution sectors.

Delivery Mode

- Internet (World Wide Web)
- CD-ROM
- Videotape
- Audiotape
- Print Materials

Program Facts

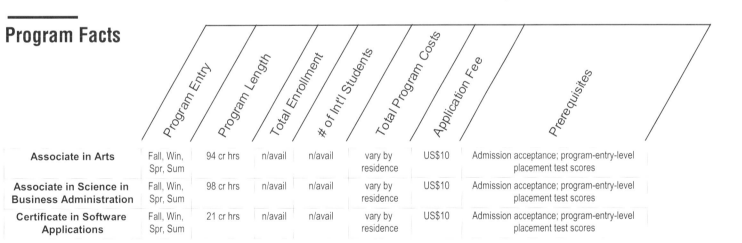

	Program Entry	Program Length	Total Enrollment	# of Int'l Students	Total Program Costs	Application Fee	Prerequisites
Associate in Arts	Fall, Win, Spr, Sum	94 cr hrs	n/avail	n/avail	vary by residence	US$10	Admission acceptance; program-entry-level placement test scores
Associate in Science in Business Administration	Fall, Win, Spr, Sum	98 cr hrs	n/avail	n/avail	vary by residence	US$10	Admission acceptance; program-entry-level placement test scores
Certificate in Software Applications	Fall, Win, Spr, Sum	21 cr hrs	n/avail	n/avail	vary by residence	US$10	Admission acceptance; program-entry-level placement test scores

Southern New Hampshire University

●

Distance Education Program

Programs Offered

Master's Degrees:

    Accounting

    Business Administration

    Business Education

    Community Economic Development

    Computer Information Systems

    International Business

Undergraduate Degrees:

    Accounting

    Business Administration

    Business Studies (17 concentrations)

    Computer Information Systems

    Economics & Finance

    International Business

    Liberal Arts

    Management

    Management Advisory Services

    Marketing & Retailing

    Psychology

    Teacher Education

Undergraduate/Graduate Certificates:

    Various Fields

College Statistics

Year Founded:	1932
Total Enrollment:	8,900
Undergraduate Enrollment	7,200
Graduate Enrollment:	1,700
Distance Education Enrollment:	7,000

Program Overview

Southern New Hampshire University (formerly New Hampshire College) is a business and liberal arts college that resides on a 350 acre campus in Manchester NH. Initiated in 1996, the university's Distance Education (DE) program presently enrolls 7,000 students each year from 47 states and 24 countries.

Students enrolled in DE may earn a certificate or an associate's, bachelor's or MBA degree online. The program is designed to support those who travel frequently, have difficult schedules, work long hours or rotating shifts, have physical limitations that preclude class attendance, or who want to start, continue or finish their education and have issues that prevent them from attending site-based and scheduled classes.

The undergraduate DE program delivers over 100 business and liberal arts courses online every eight weeks, leading to 26 undergraduate certificates and degrees. All necessary classes are offered and there are no proctored examinations at the undergraduate level. There are six undergraduate terms per year, and each term is eight weeks in length. All online courses are worth 3 semester hours.

The MBA offers several electives choices including marketing, accounting, business education, computer information systems and international business. The program undergoes regular updates, and prospective students are encouraged to contact the Academic Advisor for the latest program information. MBA students may be required to pass one proctored examination upon completion of all coursework. Graduate terms are twelve weeks in length, and there are four terms per year. All MBA students interact asynchronously with faculty and peers in a collaborative workspace (at any time, 24 hours a day, 7 days a week).

While MBA courses may have chat requirements, undergraduate courses are 100 percent asynchronous (no graded or required chat sessions). Courses are delivered through the Web using Blackboard Course Info(TM) educational delivery software. All DE classes are kept relatively small to allow maximum interaction among students and faculty.

Prospective students can apply to SNHU and register for DE courses online, or in person at any one of nine continuing education centers in New England and Puerto Rico. In addition to a completed application, applicants must submit official high school transcripts, and college transcripts if credit is to be evaluated and transferred.

Students can transfer up to 90 under-graduate hours into a bachelor's degree program; for matriculation, at least 30 semester hours must be completed through SNHU. Typically, no more than six hours may be transferred into the MBA program. Credit earning options include College-Level Examination Program (CLEP) and portfolio assessments, and students are advised to consult the Academic Advisor for more information.

Distance Education students can apply for merit-based scholarships administered by SNHU or need-based government assistance. The DE program at SNHU qualifies for and accepts GI-Bill, military tuition assistance, federal work-study, Perkins Loan, Supplemental Educational Opportunity Grant, Stafford Student Loan, Pell Grant and all forms of corporate reimbursement.

Undergraduate Programs

SNHU currently offers business and liberal arts programs through distance education. A hospitality program is anticipated in the near future. Business and certificates are awarded with concentrations in accounting, business administration, computer information systems, economics & finance, international business, management advisory services, marketing, retailing, sport management, technical management and business studies in eleven concentrations.

Liberal arts certificates and degrees are awarded in communication, English language and literature, humanities, psychology, social science and teacher education in three concentrations.

Hospitality confers undergraduate certificates and degrees in hotel management, restaurant management, and travel & tourism.

School of Management

The School of Management (SoM) offers Master of Business Administration (MBA) and Master of Science (MS) degrees in accounting, business education, community economic development, computer information systems, finance and international business.

Students may obtain graduate certificates in independent programs, or in conjunction with the MBA. Certificate options include accounting, artificial intelligence & expert systems, computer information systems, database management & design, finance, health administration, human resources management, international business, marketing, operations management, school business administration, taxation, networking & telecommunications, and training & development.

Southern New Hampshire University

•

Distance Education Program

Program Delivery and Student Support

The DE program relies on Blackboard(R) software to deliver its online educational programs. All online services are password protected and classes are asynchronous, which means students can participate in their classes at their own convenience. However, courses are not self-paced, correspondence or independent study in nature. Students must meet instructor requirements for interaction and will have turn-in dates for papers, projects, quizzes or examinations. Requirements are outlined in each class syllabus.

DE students must have access to a Pentium-class PC with Windows 95 or higher, or a Mac with System 7.5 or higher, with the following specifications: 32MB RAM, 30MB of free hard drive space or alternate storage (e.g. Zip drive), and Internet access. The DE technical support staff recommend MS Office 97 or higher (PC) or MS Office 98 (Mac), and a fast modem.

College and Location

Southern New Hampshire University is a private, coeducational institution established in 1932 and awards certificates, associate's, bachelor's, master's and doctoral degrees. SNHU operates continuing education centers in Manchester, Dover, Laconia, Nashua, and Portsmouth, New Hampshire, as well as Puerto Rico.

All SNHU programs are fully accredited. Accrediting agencies include the New England Association of Schools and Colleges (NEASC), New Hampshire Postsecondary Education Commission, New Hampshire State Department of Education for Teacher Certification and the Association of Collegiate Business Schools and Programs (ACBSP).

Through a special arrangement with the Polytechnic of North London, SNHU students may study in England. SNHU's membership in the New Hampshire College & University Council enables SNHU students to take courses at eleven other four-year institutions in the consortium.

Contact Information

Distance Education Program
2500 North River Road
Manchester New Hampshire 03106-1045 USA
phone: 1-603-645-9766
fax: 1-603-645-9706
email: depinfo@minerva.nhc.edu
internet: http://de.nhc.edu/

Delivery Mode

- Blackboard software (threaded discussions, student drop-box, on-line testing)
- Email is typically reserved for private correspondence and is discouraged for classroom interaction

Program Facts

	Program Entry	Program Length	Total Enrollment	# of Int'l Students	Total Program Costs	Application Fee	Prerequisites
Associate of Arts	six times per year	2 years	–	–	US$645/ 3 sem hr class	n/a	high school diploma or GED
Associate of Science	six times per year	2 years	–	–	US$645/ 3 sem hr class	n/a	high school diploma or GED
Bachelor of Arts	six times per year	4 years	–	–	US$645/ 3 sem hr class	n/a	high school diploma or GED
Bachelor of Science	six times per year	4 years	–	–	US$645/ 3 sem hr class	n/a	high school diploma or GED
Graduate Certificate	four times per year	18 months	–	–	US$1320/ 3 sem hr class	n/a	four-year degree
Master of Business Administration	four times per year	12–18 months	–	–	US$1320/ 3 sem hr class	n/a	four-year degree
Master of Science	four times per year	12–18 months	–	–	US$1320/ 3 sem hr class	n/a	four-year degree
Undergraduate Certificate	six times per year	–	–	–	US$645/ 3 sem hr class	n/a	high school diploma or GED

ei's guide to distance and online learning programs in the usa - 2001 edition

Southern Oregon University

•

Extended Campus Programs

Highlights

- Licensed Oregon teachers living in southwest Oregon can earn their MEd and Continuing Teaching License through synchronous learning
- Students can work toward their criminology degree via upper level distance courses
- Courses involve online interaction with students and faculty, and assignments are received via a number of distance methods

Programs Offered

Graduate Credit Courses:
  Education Courses
Undergraduate Credit Courses:
  Upper Division Criminology Classes

Program Overview

Students enrolled in the Distance Learning Program at Southern Oregon University (Southern) can undertake the Master of Education and Continuing Teaching License (MEd/CTL) through distance education, or take upper division criminology classes toward their bachelor's degree in criminology. Criminology courses are offered via the World Wide Web, and many of the required courses for the MEd/CTL program are available via distance learning methods.

Master of Education/Continuing Teaching License

The MEd/CTL program is designed for licensed teachers residing in the southwestern Oregon region who wish to earn their Master of Education and/or Oregon Continuing Teaching License, and for whom distance learning is the appropriate method of instruction. Approximately half of course credit hours can be earned during the academic year through Southern's Distance Learning Program (DLP), and are offered via 2-way television and the Internet. The remaining 12–23 credits of the program can be completed on campus during the summer. The program requires the completion of 45–48 credit hours of instruction.

In undertaking the MEd/CTL program, candidates build core competency in research, assessment, pedagogy, diversity, foundations and leadership. Courses address issues such as classroom instruction and management, curriculum design and educational change, leadership, evaluating and assessing second language learners, working with exceptional and at-risk children, and classroom creativity. Seminar and project work, including the development of work samples and a professional portfolio, are also part of the program.

Most classroom teachers complete the program in two to three years, but students can take up to seven years, or as little as 18 months, to complete degree requirements. The program follows the term schedule, and students must meet course requirements within specific start and end dates.

Prospective applicants can visit the program online at www.sou.edu/education.

Upper Level Criminology

Through DLP, students can fulfill upper division requirements for the social science degree in criminology through web-based instruction. The degree is appropriate for those who wish to enter the criminal justice field and for practicing professionals who have difficulty continuing their education due to work shifts or geographic location.

Courses offered asynchronously through Southern's criminology department include the following: Parole and Probation, Corrections, Juvenile Delinquency, The Law of Crimes, Community Policing, Crime Control Theory, Criminal Justice Administration and Current Topics. The practicum for the department's degree program is also available through asynchronous delivery. An orientation for remote students enrolling in criminology courses is available on videotape.

Admission Requirements

To be admitted to the MEd/CTL program, program applicants must have the following qualifications: a baccalaureate degree from an accredited college or university; a cumulative GPA of at least 3.0 in the last 90 quarter hours (60 semester hours) of undergraduate work; basic literacy skills in reading, writing and mathematics as indicated through a passing grade on one of several competency or standardized tests (CBEST, PPST, CBT or NTE) or through documentation of five years of successful full-time employment in a licensed public school position; and eligibility for an Oregon Basic or Initial Teaching License. In addition, applicants must submit minimum test scores for one of the following tests: Praxis II MSAT Content Knowledge and Content Area Exercises (310, with no score less than 147 on any section); Graduate Record Exam (GRE) (1200 combined, minimum score of 400 verbal); or the former NTE Core Battery Tests of Communication Skills and General Knowledge (667 and 666, respectively).

Applicants should submit a completed Application for Graduate Admission form to Southern's Office of Admissions, along with the application fee, transcripts of undergraduate and previous graduate work, a completed Character Question form (as supplied with admission materials), and two supervisor recommendations.

To enroll and register in criminology courses, Distance Learning students who were not students in the prior academic term should contact Extended Campus Programs at the main Southern campus (telephone: 1-541-552-6332; email: huftill@sou.edu).

University Statistics

Year Founded:	1925
Total Enrollment:	5,772
Undergraduate Enrollment:	5,096
Graduate Enrollment:	676
Distance Education Enrollment:	150/term

Southern Oregon University

●

Extended Campus Programs

Program Delivery and Student Support

For web-based course components, students should have access to a computer linked to the Internet and running Internet Explorer or Netscape browser software versions 4.0 or higher, and have an email account. Course instructors are available for questions and feedback from distance students via phone and e-mail. Most MEd/CT classes use electronic discussion boards to connect students to each other and to the instructor. All MEd courses involve some meeting time, which is included in the course schedule, and course assignments are accepted via email, fax or mail.

Students enrolling in the MEd/CT program can register directly via telephone (1-800-552-5388), and all distance students can order textbooks by telephone or via the Southern bookstore web site (www.sou.edu/bookstore).

University and Location

In 2001, Southern Oregon University will celebrate its 75th anniversary. Originally founded as a private institution in 1869, the school was established as the Southern Oregon State Normal School in 1925, and in 1940 was renamed a college of education. In 1956, the institution became Southern Oregon College and in 1957 was again renamed as Southern Oregon State College. In 1997, the name was changed a final time to Southern Oregon University, reflecting its present role as a regional institution serving the state and the southern region of Oregon.

The main Southern campus is located on 175 acres in Ashland, and comprises four schools: Business; Arts and Letters; Social Science, Education, Health and Physical Education; and Science. Southern offers 36 degree programs, including eight master's degrees. Eighty percent of its student population originate in the state of Oregon; however, Southern currently welcomes 148 international students. Ashland is home to the Oregon Shakespeare Festival, the largest regional Shakespeare Festival in the world, and is located near the Pacific Crest Trail, a hiking and equestrian trail that spans 2,650 miles from Canada to Mexico.

Contact Information

Extended Campus Programs
1250 Siskiyou Boulevard
Ashland Oregon 97504 USA
phone: 1-541-552-6332 or 1-800-552-5388
fax: 1-541-552-6047
email: huftill@sou.edu
internet: http://www.sou.edu/ecp/distlearn

Delivery Mode

• Web (Criminology)
• Two-way video to downlink sites in neighboring counties (Education)

Program Facts

	Program Entry	Program Length	Total Enrollment	# of Int'l Students	Total Program Costs	Application Fee	Prerequisites
Continuing Teaching License	ongoing	varies	30	n/a	US$190/credit	US$50	Teaching license
Master of Education	ongoing	varies	50–80	n/a	US$190/credit	US$50	Teaching license

Southwest Texas State University

•

Office of Correspondence & Extension Studies

Programs Offered

Graduate Credit Courses:
  Geography
  Math

Non-credit Certification Courses:
  Master Reading Teacher (MRT) Program
  Medicaid Fraud Prevention
  TILE Assessment (Comm-Based Altern)
  TILE Assessment Work (Nursing Facilities)

Undergraduate Credit Courses:
  Art & Design
  Biology
  Criminal Justice
  Dance
  English
  Geography
  Health Management Information
  History
  Long-term Healthcare Administration
  Math
  Music
  Philosophy
  Political Science
  Psychology
  Sociology
  Spanish
  Theater Arts

University Statistics

Year Founded:	1899
Total Enrollment:	24,825
Undergraduate Enrollment	19,447
Graduate Enrollment:	2,378
Distance Education Enrollment:	2,429

Program Overview

Since 1954, SWT has offered correspondence courses to students. For those interested in educational advancement, the Office of Correspondence & Extension Studies currently offers more than 50 accredited graduate and undergraduate university courses, delivered online and through audio or video cassettes. Both in-state and out-of-state correspondence students can take courses developed and taught by professors for a cost that is consistently among the lowest in the nation.

Application Procedures

Students can enroll in a correspondence course at SWT at any time, but should call to make sure a course is available. Applications can be obtained from Correspondence Studies or downloaded from the website (www.ideal.swt.edu/correspondence). Students can enroll via mail, online application, telephone, fax or in person. All courses fees must be paid in full at enrollment.

Formal acceptance to SWT is not required to take a correspondence course and course enrollment does not constitute admission to the university. Courses are open to all students as long as departmental and course prerequisites are met and TASP (Texas Academic Skills Program) guidelines are complete. Out-of-state students and those from private institutions must verify their status by submitting a copy of their latest semester transcript or grade report, or a letter of good standing from their university registrar's office.

Students enroll in courses for a 12-month period, which begins the day a student's payment is received by the Office of Correspondence Studies. Students who do not complete a course within 12 months can apply to have enrollment extended for a period of six months. After the initial 12-month period, lessons and exams will not be processed if the student has not paid an extension fee. No enrollment can last more than 18 months.

Correspondence study students can transfer to a different course within six months of their original enrollment date. Transfer fees apply and only one transfer is allowed per course. Students cannot transfer from on-campus or extension courses to correspondence courses.

Undergraduate Courses

Undergraduate courses are offered in Art & Design, Art Theory & Practice, Biology, Career & Tech Education, Criminal Justice, Dance, English, Geography, Health Information Management, History, Long-Term

Health Care Administration, Math, Music, Philosophy, Political Science, Psychology, Sociology, Spanish, and Theater Arts. All undergraduate courses include several written assignments, and at least one examination. The undergraduate tuition rate is US$63 per credit hour.

Graduate Courses

SWT offers graduate courses in geography and math. Though available to all students, geography courses are designed for students interested in receiving a Master of Applied Geography through the SWT Department of Geography as part of the "Step Up to Geography" program. Students interested in pursuing this degree should contact the SWT Graduate School (http://www.gradschool.swt.edu/) or the SWT Department of Geography (http://www.geo.swt.edu/). Graduate tuition is US$95 per credit hour.

Non-Credit/Certification Courses

Created in 1999, the Master Reading Teacher (MRT) Program prepares students to teach reading and serve as a reading mentor for other teachers. The program consists of six online modules, one for each MRT standard.

The Identifying & Preventing Medicaid Fraud, Waste and Abuse course provides training for healthcare workers. It includes real life examples, self-help exercises and an exam to ensure healthcare workers comprehend the material and can apply it on the job. This course is only available online.

TILE (Texas Index of Level of Effort) Assessment Workbooks are available in Nursing Facilities and Community-Based Alternative. SWT offers print-based and online versions of these courses.

Southwest Texas State University

●

Office of Correspondence & Extension Studies

Program Delivery and Student Support

Students begin their course as soon as they have received their study guide and textbook(s), which contain all the instructions and lessons needed to complete each course. A list of the required textbooks and materials can be found in every study guide. Textbooks are available through the SWT bookstore.

    Once a student completes the first lesson, written assignments are sent to the Office of Correspondence & Extension Studies, where it is then posted and sent to the instructor for grading. Lessons and examinations are mailed to professors daily. On average, it takes approximately four weeks for graded assignments and exams to be returned to students, including mail time. Every assignment and exam report will be returned with a grade and the instructor's comments.

University and Location

Authorized by the Texas Legislature in 1899, Southwest Texas State Normal School opened its doors in 1903. Over the years the Legislature broadened the institution's scope and changed its name in succession to Normal College, Teachers College, College, and in 1969, University. Each name reflects the university's growth from a small teacher preparation institution to a multipurpose university.

    Located in San Marcos, the gateway to the Texas Hill Country, SWT offers undergraduate and graduate instruction to citizens across Texas as well as those from other states and countries. Undergraduate degree programs are offered through colleges of Applied Arts, Business, Education, Fine Arts & Communication, Health Professions, Liberal Arts and Science. In addition, over 80 degree programs are offered through the Graduate College. Today, SWT is the seventh largest public university in the state of Texas and enrolls close to 25,000 students.

Contact Information

Office of Correspondence & Extension Studies
Debi Perkins, 601 University Drive
San Marcos Texas 78666 USA
phone: 1-512-245-2322
fax: 1-512-245-8934
email: DP01@swt.edu
internet: http://www.ideal.swt.edu/correspondence

Delivery Mode

- Audio cassettes
- Video cassettes
- Study guides
- Textbooks
- Internet sites

Program Facts

	Program Entry	Program Length	Total Enrollment	# of Int'l Students	Total Program Costs	Application Fee	Prerequisites
Graduate Credit Courses	year round	varies	n/a	n/a	US$95/credit hour	US$25	bachelor's degree
Non-credit Certification Course	year round	varies	n/a	n/a	varies	–	varies
Undergraduate Credit Courses	year round	varies	n/a	n/a	US$63/credit hour	US$25	high school diploma, GED or good standing at other accredited institutions

Southwestern Adventist University

•

Adult Degree Program

- ADP courses are identical to campus-based courses in credit awarded
- Many opportunities for credit transfer through tests and portfolio assessments
- ADP students pay 20 percent less tuition than full-time SWAU students
- Six months permitted to finish a course, with possible extensions

Programs Offered

Associate Degree:
  Science
Bachelor's Degrees:
  Arts
  Business Administration
  Science
Majors:
  Business Administration
  Communication
  Criminal Justice
  Education
  English
  Mathematics
  Office Systems Administration
  Office Technology
  Psychology
  Religion
  Social Science
  Theology

University Statistics

Year Founded:	1893
Total Enrollment:	1,150
Undergraduate Enrollment	870
Graduate Enrollment:	n/a
Distance Education Enrollment:	280

Program Overview

The Adult Degree Program (ADP) at Southwestern Adventist University (SWAU) enables distance learners over the age of 22 to earn undergraduate degrees in a variety of disciplines. Specific degrees include an Associate of Science, Bachelor of Arts, Bachelor of Science and Bachelor of Business Administration.

The ADP is appropriate for young adults who wish to complete their degrees, homemakers who cannot engage in full-time studies, employees who cannot attend day classes, students who are physically challenged, senior citizens and students seeking self-improvement.

Majors and Minors

The ADP facilitates study in the following major areas: business administration with a concentration in accounting, management or computer information systems; communication with a concentration in broadcasting, journalism or corporate communication; criminal justice; education with teacher certification and a concentration in elementary or secondary education; English; mathematics; office systems administration; office technology; psychology; religion; social science with a concentration in history, international affairs or social science; and theology. Most minors that are available through campus-based study are also available through the ADP. Students may customize majors, but some degree programs, such as lab science, nursing or social work, are not delivered at a distance.

Accounting or management program graduates enter careers in nonprofit, commercial and governmental accounting or management. Computer information systems graduates design, develop and implement computer information systems in business settings. Communication graduates enter careers in media law and the radio, television, advertising, public relations, photographic and recording industries.

In addition to completing SWAU degree requirements, ADP students seeking K-12 teacher certification in Texas must sit for comprehensive state examinations. Prospective teachers must be US citizens or intend to become naturalized citizens.

Admission and Registration

University admission is necessary for entrance into the ADP. Applicants must submit a copy of their high school or general education diploma or official transcripts of previous postsecondary education, and must have acceptable SAT/ACT scores or college English and Math courses. International applicants should attain a score of 550 on the paper-based TOEFL.

Students must register in a minimum of 12 credits per year. University residency policy obligates students to compile at least 32 credits on campus or through the ADP. Baccalaureate programs require the fulfillment of 128 credits. The general education requirements for all bachelor's degrees entail 54 to 66 credits of English, health science and physical education, mathematics and science, religion, and social science and humanities.

Program participants must be prepared to devote at least 15 to 20 hours per week to their studies. Six months are permitted to finish a course and extensions cost US$25 per course. Throughout their studies, students must maintain a minimum 2.0 GPA (2.5 GPA in Education) to avoid dismissal.

Tuition for ADP courses is the same as that charged for campus-based courses: US$400 per credit hour. Fees are charged for the admission seminar and each SWAU course for which the ADP committee determines the student should receive experiential credit. Following the seminar, tuition refunds are made on a decreasing percentage basis until the end of the fifth month, after which no refunds are made.

Portfolio Assessment

Upon acceptance and submission of a nonrefundable deposit, students must attend one of three one-week admission seminars held in March, June or October. The seminar counts for three credits and gives students the tools to assemble a portfolio with which to request experiential credit. As well, the seminar enables distance learners to meet their instructors and other students.

Students have three months to complete the autobiographical section of the portfolio and another three months to compile the experiential credit requests. Experiential credit options include previous academic work, corporate- or military-sponsored educational programs and proficiency tests administered by SWAU or the College Level Examination Program.

Southwestern Adventist University

•

Adult Degree Program

Program Delivery and Student Support

ADP students engage in independent study and communicate with instructors via mail, email, telephone or facsimile. Some courses are delivered by videotape or at a college near the student's hometown. The office of information services staffs a computing help desk.

Program participants can borrow materials from the university's Chan Shun Centennial Library and other libraries with which SWAU has established loan agreements. The loan period for distance learners is six weeks. Textbooks can be purchased from the university bookstore.

Contact Information

Adult Degree Program
PO Box 58
Keene Texas 76059-0058 USA
phone: 1-817-645-3921 or 1-800-433-2240
fax: 1-817-556-4742
email: mizherj@swau.edu
internet: http://www.swau.edu

University and Location

Southwestern Adventist University is a private, coeducational, four-year liberal arts institution that is accredited by the Southern Association of Colleges and Schools, Association of Texas Colleges and Universities and National Adventist Board of Regents. SWAU confers associate degrees in five majors, bachelor's degrees in 28 majors and a master of education in elementary education. The university also oversees 19 nondegree preprofessional programs.

The university's new library, opened during SWAU's centennial celebration in 1993, is 36,000 square feet. The MicroGarden, which is operated by the office of information services, is a 25-station computer lab containing Pentium MMX hardware. Sports enthusiasts can join six varsity teams and three club teams. Aspiring writers and editors can work for the student newspaper, The Southwesterner.

SWAU was founded as Keene Industrial Academy by pioneers who settled in Keene, Texas. Keene is located 45 miles southwest of Dallas and is home to 4,450. Brandon Manufacturing and Southwestern Colorgraphics are the city's two largest employers. Local attractions include Tomsen Observatory, Hopps Museum, Calicott Park and Cleburne State Park.

Delivery Mode

• Independent study (mail, email, telephone, facsimile, videotapes)

Program Facts

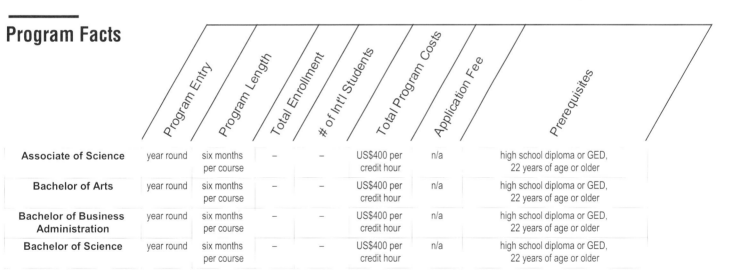

	Program Entry	Program Length	Total Enrollment	# of Int'l Students	Total Program Costs	Application Fee	Prerequisites
Associate of Science	year round	six months per course	–	–	US$400 per credit hour	n/a	high school diploma or GED, 22 years of age or older
Bachelor of Arts	year round	six months per course	–	–	US$400 per credit hour	n/a	high school diploma or GED, 22 years of age or older
Bachelor of Business Administration	year round	six months per course	–	–	US$400 per credit hour	n/a	high school diploma or GED, 22 years of age or older
Bachelor of Science	year round	six months per course	–	–	US$400 per credit hour	n/a	high school diploma or GED, 22 years of age or older

Syracuse University

•

Independent Study Degree Programs

- Founded in 1966, ISDP is one of the oldest independent study programs in the US
- Baccalaureate program accepts a maximum of 90 transfer credits
- Matriculated and nonmatriculated students can take online courses
- Residencies enrich distance studies through face-to-face interaction with instructors

Programs Offered

Master's Degrees:
- Advertising Design
- Business Administration
- Communications Management
- Engineering Management
- Illustration
- Information Resource Management
- Library Science
- Nursing
- Social Science
- Telecommunication & Network Management

Undergraduate Degrees:
- Associate of Arts in Liberal Studies
- Bachelor of Arts in Liberal Studies

University Statistics

Year Founded:	1870
Total Enrollment:	18,293
Undergraduate Enrollment	12,130
Graduate Enrollment:	6,163
Distance Education Enrollment:	1,000

Program Overview

Founded in 1966, Independent Study Degree Programs (ISDP) at Syracuse University (SU) constitutes one of the three oldest independent study degree programs in the US. Each program consists of brief on-campus residencies and self-directed study at home.

The university confers two undergraduate degrees through ISDP: an associate of arts in liberal studies (AALS) or bachelor of arts in liberal studies (BALS). The selection of graduate degree programs is more extensive: a master of arts in advertising design (MAAD) or illustration (MAI); master of business administration (MBA); master of library science (MLS); master of social science (MSSc); or master of science in information resource management (MSIRM), telecommunications and network management (MSTNM), communications management (MSCM), engineering management (MSEM) and nursing (MSN).

Admission Requirements

Undergraduate degree applicants should hold a high school diploma or equivalent. Points of entry for admission are January, May or August. Master's degree applicants should hold a bachelor's degree with a cumulative grade point average (GPA) of preferably 3.0 or better. All applicants must submit three letters of recommendation and a personal essay. Other admission requirements and points of entry for admission vary from program to program.

The 30-credit master of arts program is designed for students with professional advertising design or illustration experience. A portfolio and interview are necessary. The only point of entry is August.

Business professionals are encouraged to enter the 54-credit MBA program. Candidates must submit GMAT scores and a resume. Points of entry are January, May or August.

Government officials, corporate executives, librarians, college instructors and secondary school teachers have enrolled in the 30-credit MSSc program. The curriculum integrates the study of international relations and societal foundations. Admission is available year round.

The 36-credit MLS program is the first such program in the US delivered in a limited residency distance learning format. Fulfillment of degree requirements leads to librarian certification for New York state. Candidates must attain a GRE (general) score of 1000. The only point of entry is July.

Registered nurses are encouraged to enter the 45-credit MSN program. Participants must acquire CPR certification and malpractice insurance coverage within the first two years of the program. The only point of entry is June.

The 36-credit MSCM program is designed for applicants with five years of professional communications management experience. Candidates must submit GRE (general) scores and a recommendation from their current employer. A portfolio is required and an interview encouraged. The only point of entry is August. The MSEM program integrates engineering studies and technology management studies, and comprises 36 credits. August is the only point of entry.

The 42-credit MSTNM program is tailored for students with three years of professional telecommunication and network management experience or sufficient related coursework. Candidates must attain a GRE (general) score of 1000. The only point of entry is July. The MSIRM program also requires that applicants attain a GRE (general) score of 1000. The program comprises 42 credits and July is the only point of entry.

Residencies

ISDP residencies permit students to meet their instructors and fellow students. Depending on the program, residencies consist of classes, assignments, readings, research or studio projects.

Participants in the AALS, BALS, MBA, MSCM and MSEM degree programs meet for one-week residencies in August, January and May. Those in the MSIRM, MSTNM and MLS degree programs meet in the summer for one to four weeks, in the fall for three or four days and again for three or four days in the spring. Those in the MAAD and MAI degree programs meet for two weeks in August and another two weeks during the academic year. Participants in the MSSc degree program attend a two-week residency every summer, while those in the MSN program begin residencies in June of each odd year.

Tuition and Financial Aid

Tuition per credit for undergraduate courses is US$390, while tuition per credit for graduate courses is US$647. Twenty-five percent of the tuition for an ISDP degree program must be paid at registration. Refund policies vary from program to program. ISDP students may be eligible for financial aid from federal grant and loan programs as well as New York State's TAP program, as long as they are New York State residents.

Syracuse University

●

Independent Study Degree Programs

Program Delivery and Student Support

ISDP utilizes asynchronous email and Internet communications, correspondence, telephone, facsimile and limited residencies. Online services maintained by the university facilitate registration and textbook purchases, and provide access to the following resources: undergraduate and graduate catalogs; course syllabi and class schedules; information about financial aid, graduate funding and grades; and library resources.

The university's center for career services and career resources library assist students in their job searches. In addition, the management, citizenship and public affairs, nursing, information studies and public communications colleges publish information on job vacancies for their graduates.

Contact Information

Independent Study Degree Programs
700 University Avenue
Syracuse New York 13244-2530 USA
phone: 1-315-443-3480 or 1-800-442-0501
fax: 1-315-443-4174
email: suisdp@uc.syr.edu
internet: http://www.yesu.syr.edu/DistanceEd

University and Location

Syracuse University was founded in 1870 and today awards degrees through 15 schools and colleges devoted to architecture, arts and sciences, education, engineering and computer science, human development, graduate studies, information studies, law, management, citizenship and public affairs, public communications, nursing, social work, visual and performing arts, and continuing education. SU is chartered by the New York State Board of Regents, accredited by the Middle States Association of Colleges and Schools and holds membership in the Association of American Universities.

All states in the union and more than 90 countries are represented in the student body, which totals 18,293. SU employs 805 full-time faculty, 86 percent of whom have a PhD or professional degree. The university libraries hold 2.7 million volumes, 3.7 million microforms, 16,000 periodicals and serials, and 1,700 tapes, computer-readable disks and CD-ROMs. Students have access to 14 public and over 20 departmental computer labs, all of which are networked.

SU is located in Syracuse, New York, a community of 150,563 (1999 estimate) in the geographic heart of the state. Every major urban center in the northeast US is within a 350-mile radius of Syracuse.

Delivery Mode

- Asynchronous communication (email, Internet)
- Correspondence
- Facsimile
- Online instruction
- Residencies
- Telephone

Program Facts

	Program Entry	Program Length	Total Enrollment	# of Int'l Students	Total Program Costs	Application Fee	Prerequisites
Associate of Arts **Bachelor of Arts**	Jan, May, Aug	2–3 years 4–6 years	– 150	–	US$371 per credit	US$40	high school diploma or equivalent, TOEFL 550 (pbt)
Master of Arts in Ad Design or Illustration	Aug	2 years	–	–	US$613 per credit	US$40	bachelor's degree, portfolio, interview, TOEFL 550 (pbt)
Master of Business Administration	Jan, May, Aug	2–3 years	–	–	US$613 per credit	US$40	bachelor's degree, GMAT, resume, TOEFL 580 (pbt)
Master of Library Science	Jul	2–3 years	–	–	US$613 per credit	US$40	bachelor's degree with 3.0 GPA, GRE 1000 (general), TOEFL 550 (pbt)
Master of Science (Eng Mgmt, Comm Mgmt)	Aug	2–3 years	–	–	US$613 per credit	US$40	varies between the two specializations
Master of Science (Info Resources Mgmt)	Jul	2–3 years	–	–	US$613 per credit	US$40	bachelor's degree with 3.0 GPA, GRE 1,000
Master of Science (Nurs, Telecom/Ntwk Mgmt)	Jun, Jul	varies	–	–	US$613 per credit	US$40	varies between the two specializations
Master of Social Science	year round	2–3 years	–	–	US$613 per credit	US$40	bachelor's degree, TOEFL 600 (pbt)

Teikyo Post University

●

TPU Online

- Certificate and degree programs available completely online
- Associate degrees in Early Childhood Education and Management
- Bachelor degrees in five fields
- Certificates include International Business Administration and Legal Assistant
- Accredited by the New England Association of Schools and Colleges

Programs Offered

Associate Degrees:
- Early Childhood Education
- Management

Bachelor Degrees:
- Criminal Justice
- Integrated Business
- International Business Administration
- Management
- Management Information Systems

Certificates:
- Early Childhood Education
- International Business Administration
- Legal Assistance

University Statistics

Year Founded:	1890
Total Enrollment:	1,500
Undergraduate Enrollment	1,500
Graduate Enrollment:	n/a
Distance Education Enrollment:	200

Program Overview

Established in 1890, Teikyo Post (TPU) is a small business and liberal arts university located in Waterbury, Connecticut. TPU offers certificates, associate (AS) and bachelor of science (BS) degrees through online study.

Early Childhood Education

TPU Online offers certificate and AS programs in Early Childhood Education (ECE). Students can also fulfill course credit toward the Child Development Associate (CDA) credential.

The AS comprises 61 credit hours and covers key areas including Foundations of Early Childhood Education, Teaching the Exceptional Child and Child Development. Three practicums form part of the curriculum. A direct Career Track and a Transfer Track for teacher certification are also offered.

The ECE certificate provides professional training leading to the educational requirements of the CDA credential. Students complete 21 credits for the certificate or undertake two psychology courses and two early childhood education courses to fulfill the CDA education requirement. Additional requirements apply; students should visit the CDA Council online for further details (http://www.cdacouncil.org).

Management

The Management program offers both AS and BS options, and prepares students to become organizational leaders with understanding of sound management principles and practices. Management students can elect to minor in Management Information Systems.

BS students complete business, major, general education and elective courses, for a total of 120 credits. AS degree students complete 15 credits of General Education courses, 18 credits of major courses and a three-credit elective. A minor is also available.

Criminal Justice, Legal Assistant

The BS in Criminal Justice develops understanding of the criminal and juvenile justice systems. The core curriculum comprises 54 credits plus 66 credits of General Education and elective courses. For students studying outside Connecticut or the US, transfer credits are accepted from previous accredited college experience or professional development training programs.

The Legal Assistant certificate readies students to enter or advance in the profession.

A total of 10 courses (30 credits) is required.

Integrated Business, International Business

The BS in Integrated Business (INB) assists students in developing the skills required to manage people, resources and information in an integrated business environment. INB students can select from the following concentrations: Early Care & Education, International Business, Law Office Management, Management, Marketing or Management Information Systems (MIS). The degree comprises 120 credits including 36 hours of business core courses, 39 credits of Integrated Business requirements and 15 credits in the area of concentration.

The certificate and BS programs in International Business provide students with the background and skills needed for a global business environment. The certificate program requires the completion of five online courses for a total of 15 credits. The BS degree in International Business Administration (IBA) assists students in preparing to conduct business effectively in other cultural settings. Courses cover areas such as International Business Law, International Management, International Marketing and International Logistics, Sourcing & Production. The degree comprises 120 credits.

Management Information Systems (MIS)

The BS program in MIS combines business coursework with advanced training in applying computer technology to management. The BS program comprises 120 credits including 45 credits of business core and major courses. Students have the option to undertake an MIS seminar or an internship.

The Computer Information Skills certificate program emphasizes the use of word processing, spreadsheet and database software to solve problems. Upon completion of this program, students will have applicable knowledge in MS Windows, Word, Excel, and PowerPoint. The certificate requires a total of 15 credits (five courses).

Course Registration

TPU students must have a working knowledge of the Internet and email/attachments before registering for an online course. TPU programs do not require the fulfillment of prerequisites prior to enrollment. Course schedules and registration forms are available online (http://www.teikyopost.edu/registrar/).

Teikyo Post University

●

TPU Online

Program Delivery and Student Support

TPU Online courses are structured to allow students to complete course work any time during the week. Successful students are highly motivated and able to work independently to complete their assignments according to the online course schedule. Exams and other evaluation mechanisms are completed online.

Most online courses use asynchronous threaded discussion, which is available at any time (24/7). Some courses offer real time chat room discussions. Online courses normally follow the same accelerated eight-week or weekend timeframe, calendar dates, and policies as other Accelerated Degree Program courses.

TPU Online students must have access to a computer with Windows 95 or 98, Microsoft Office, up-to-date virus scan software, an established Internet connection and an email account.

University and Location

In May of 1990, Post College became affiliated with the worldwide Teikyo University Group. The name change to Teikyo Post University signalled the regional college's partnership with one of the world's largest international education consortia.

Teikyo Post enrolls 1,500 full- and part-time students from more than 35 countries and maintains a 15 to one student-to-faculty ratio. More than 200 students are currently enrolled in online degree and certificate programs. Online instructors undergo individualized training in teaching strategies to develop effective, personalized instruction that encourages student participation. Instructors are full-time faculty at Teikyo Post University or adjunct faculty with a minimum master's degree and current experience in their discipline.

Teikyo Post is fully accredited by the New England Association of Schools and Colleges.

Delivery Mode

- Degree programs are delivered asynchronously via the Internet
- Online programs meet the same course requirements and quality standards as on-campus programs; TPU Online students communicate with instructors and students through email and class discussion forums

Program Facts

	Program Entry	Program Length	Total Enrollment	# of Int'l Students	Total Program Costs	Application Fee	Prerequisites
Associate of Science in Management	year round	varies	n/a	n/a	US$975 per course	US$40	None
Associate of Science or Certificate in ECE	year round	varies	n/a	n/a	US$975 per course	US$40	None
Bachelor of Science in Criminal Justice	year round	varies	n/a	n/a	US$975 per course	US$40	None
Bachelor of Science in Integrated Business	year round	varies	n/a	n/a	US$975 per course	US$40	None
Bachelor of Science in Management Information	year round	varies	n/a	n/a	US$975 per course	US$40	None
Bachelor of Science or Cert. in Int'l Bus Admin	year round	varies	n/a	n/a	US$975 per course	US$40	None
Bachelor or Associate of Science in Management	year round	varies	n/a	n/a	US$975 per course	US$40	None
Legal Assistant Certificate	year round	varies	n/a	n/a	US$975 per course	US$40	None

Thomas Edison State College

Programs Offered

*All offered year round including
  certificate programs

Associate in Applied Science:
  Radiologic Technology

Associate in Science:
  Applied Science & Technology
  Management
  Natural Science & Mathematics
  Public & Social Services

Bachelor of Science:
  Applied Science & Technology
  Business Administration
  Health Sciences
  Human Services
  Nursing

BSN students must either live or work
  in New Jersey

Graduate Degrees:
  Master of Arts in Professional Studies
  Master of Science in Management

Other Programs:
  Certificate

Other Undergraduate Degrees:
  Associate in Applied Science
  Associate in Arts
  Bachelor of Arts

College Statistics

Year Founded:	1972
Total Enrollment:	8,137
Undergraduate Enrollment	–
Graduate Enrollment:	–
Distance Education Enrollment:	8,137

Program Overview

Thomas Edison State College (TESC) offers 15 degrees in 100 major areas of study. Students can pursue certificates, or undergraduate or graduate degrees. TESC's commitment to adult education has achieved national recognition; graduates are regularly admitted to other prestigious universities around the country. TESC employs 550 consulting faculty who teach at accredited colleges and universities across the US.

Applications for admission are accepted throughout the year. Credit transfer options include the Thomas Edison State College Examination Program (TECEP), American College Testing Proficiency Examination, Advanced Placement, College Level Examination or New York University Foreign Language Proficiency Examinations. Other options include professional license, registry or certificate assessment, portfolio assessment, or previous academic experience. With the exception of the nursing program, in which students must reside or work in New Jersey, residency is unnecessary for undergraduate or graduate degree programs.

Tuition is payable under two options. The comprehensive fee is paid annually and includes enrollment, transfer credit evaluation, technology services and course fees. New Jersey residents pay US$2,500, while out-of-state residents pay US$3,600. The per service fee is paid as students use each service. Accordingly, the annual enrollment and technology fee is US$685 for New Jersey residents, US$1,175 for out-of-state residents and US$1,580 for international students.

In addition to regular distance degree programs, the college coordinates two other adult education programs. Corporate-higher education organizes degree completion programs in the workplace. Military degree completion permits armed forces personnel to fulfill degree requirements on base.

Associate Degrees

The college awards an associate in arts; an associate in applied science; and associate in applied science in radiologic technology; or an associate in science in management, applied science and technology, natural science and mathematics, or public and social services.

Bachelor's Degrees

Upon completion of 120 credits of coursework, TESC awards a bachelor of arts (BA) in many major areas of study including chemistry, economics, music, journalism and history, or a bachelor of science (BS) with a concentration in applied science and technology, business administration, health sciences, human services or nursing. In cooperation with the University of Medicine and Dentistry of New Jersey, the college also awards a BS in health sciences. The degree pathways program allows community college students to transfer a maximum of 80 credits to a baccalaureate program.

Master's Degrees

TESC has developed two master's degrees that can be earned by taking courses online, to accommodate the needs of adults pursuing master's-level education. Both programs require students to participate with their colleagues in classroom discussions. Individuals may also work in a small group with other students. Students can arrange an individualized study schedule to suit their particular circumstances.

The Master of Science in Management (MSM) degree attracts managers from many fields. Entrepreneurs enroll, as do managers from companies such as American Cyanamid, AT&T, Bristol Myers Squibb, Dime Savings, First Union, Head Start, Lucent, MicroWarehouse, Prudential, Verizon, as well as from all branches of the US military. MSM students may select from tracks in Leadership, Project Management or Management of Substance Abuse Programs. During weekend residencies, students participate in two courses in professional leadership development.

The Master of Arts in Professional Studies (MAPS) provides working professionals with the opportunity to study the liberal arts from an applied perspective. The program benefits from a diverse student body, including participants who work as museum curators, college business managers, computer networking specialists, nuclear engineers and teachers.

No more than six credits for either program can be transferred from graduate study completed at other institutions. A thesis/applied project is necessary.

Certificates

The college offers a 30-credit certificate program in 12 disciplines: finance, labor studies, human resources management, marketing, operations management, public administration, accounting, administrative office management, computer-aided design, computer science, computer information systems and electronics. The college has also developed an online e-Commerce certificate.

Thomas Edison State College

Program Delivery and Student Support

Students take courses through one of three delivery modes: guided, or mentored, study at home or in the workplace; contract learning, in which instructors and students interact on a one-to-one basis; or through online courses which employ the Internet and email. The college is currently integrating interactive television classes into its distance learning programs. Cable access and satellite downlinks will form an important component of such classes.

Distance learners at TESC can access the services of the advisement center by telephone, fax and email. They also have borrowing privileges at the New Jersey State Library, which is administered by the college.

College and Location

Thomas Edison State College opened its doors to students in 1972 and since then has conferred associate, bachelor's and master's degrees to more than 17,200 people. TESC currently enrolls 8,137 adult learners, the average age of which is 38, from all 50 states and 79 countries. The New York Times has characterized the college as "one of the brighter stars of higher learning," while Forbes has placed it among the country's top 20 colleges and universities in the use of technology.

TESC is a component of the New Jersey System of Higher Education, which includes Rutgers University, The State University and the New Jersey Institute of Technology. The college is accredited by the Middle States Association of Colleges and Schools. It operates in conjunction with the John S. Watson Institute for Public Policy and National Institute on the Assessment of Experiential Learning.

TESC is located in Trenton, the capital of New Jersey since 1790 and briefly capital of the US in 1784 and 1799. Trenton is the preeminent commercial, manufacturing and transportation hub of the state. George Washington devised his march to Princeton in the city's Douglas House.

Contact Information

Office of Admissions, 101 West State Street
Trenton New Jersey 08608-1176 USA
phone: 1-609-984-1150 or 1-888-442-8372
fax: 1-609-984-8447
email: info@tesc.edu
internet: http://www.tesc.edu

Delivery Mode

- Contract learning (one-to-one learning sessions between student and instructor)
- Guided study (mentored instruction at home or in the workplace)
- Online courses

Program Facts

	Program Entry	Program Length	Total Enrollment	# of Int'l Students	Total Program Costs	Application Fee	Prerequisites
Associate in Applied Science	year round	–	3	–	comprehensive or per service	US$75	–
Associate in Applied Science (Radiol. Tech)	year round	–	13	–	comprehensive or per service	US$75	–
Associate in Arts; Associate in Science	year round; year round	–; –	377; 1104	–; –	comprehensive or per service	US$75	–
Bachelor of Arts; Bachelor of Science	year round; year round	–; –	2922; 5053	–; –	comprehensive or per service	US$75	–
Certificate	year round	–	–	–			–
Master of Arts in Professional Studies	year round	–	new program	–	US$298 per credit	US$75	bachelor's degree, relevant work experience, top writing, presentation and computer skills
Master of Science in Management	year round	–	162	–	US$298 per credit	US$75	bachelor's degree, relevant work experience, top writing, presentation and computer skills

University of Bridgeport

Online Programs

Highlights

- MS in Human Nutrition can be undertaken online or through on-campus weekend instruction
- 18–24 month program combines nutrition science, clinical nutrition, nutrition education & counseling, public health issues and nutritional epidemiology
- Science and non-science backgrounds welcome

Programs Offered

Master's Degree:
   Master of Science in Human Nutrition

Program Overview

The University of Bridgeport (UB) offers a Masters of Science (MS) in Human Nutrition through on-campus weekend instruction, or through online asynchronous & text-based instruction. The online program, delivered by the Nutrition Institute and UB Online, combines independent study with intense faculty-student interaction: lessons and activities are completed offline, and students receive individual guidance from instructors and participate in classroom discussions over the Web.

The MS program is designed for students with undergraduate degrees who wish to pursue a graduate degree preparing them for general work in the field of human nutrition. The degree is not designed for those who wish to receive training or clinical experience in dietetics, and is not intended to prepare students for the registered dietician's examination.

MS in Human Nutrition

The MS in Human Nutrition program provides students with a core of basic and advanced courses in nutrition science, clinical nutrition, nutrition education and counseling, issues in public health nutrition and nutritional epidemiology. Courses are offered three semesters per year, and students enroll in the program beginning in September or January.

To complete the program, students must undertake a minimum of 31 semester credit hours and maintain a grade point average (GPA) of 3.0 or above. Twenty-eight credit hours of core courses are required and students select three credit hours from elective courses such as Botanical Medicine, Nutrition & Exercise or a Nutrition Seminar for those entering without a basic nutrition course.

The program curriculum focuses on the intervening role of human nutrition in the disease process. Students undertake coursework in Biochemistry of Nutrition, Vitamins and Minerals, Clinical Biochemistry, Nutritional Therapeutics, Developmental Nutrition and Biostatistics, as well as Assessment of Nutritional Status. At the completion of studies, on-campus students undertake a three-credit thesis in nutrition research. Online students travel to the Bridgeport campus to write a one-day comprehensive examination.

On average, students take between 18 and 24 months to complete the program. Courses are 16 to 20 weeks in duration; although online students can structure their progress, courses require the completion of regularly scheduled assignments and exams.

The Human Nutrition program is licensed and accredited by the Connecticut Board of Governors for Higher Education and the Commission on Institutions of Higher Education, New England Association of Schools and Colleges.

Admission Requirements

Applicants to the MS in Human Nutrition program should have a baccaulaureate degree from an accredited college or university, and demonstrate a 3.0 grade point average (out of 4.0) in undergraduate coursework. Students from both science and non-science backgrounds are considered; however, prospective students should have completed coursework in anatomy and physiology, organic chemistry or introductory biochemistry, and basic nutrition during their previous studies. An elective nutrition seminar is offered as part of the program, for those students who do not have basic coursework in nutrition.

Applications for admission should include a completed application form, US $40 application fee, undergraduate and graduate records, two letters of recommendation and a personal statement. International applicants must demonstrate proficiency in English, either by submitting a paper-based TOEFL test score of 550, providing proof of a C grade or better in one semester of English at an accredited US college or university, or achieving an acceptable score on the English Language Proficiency Test, administered by UB's English Language Institute. Total program tuition for in-state, out-of-state and international students in US$12,000.

University Statistics

Year Founded:	1927
Total Enrollment:	n/a
Undergraduate Enrollment	n/a
Graduate Enrollment:	n/a
Distance Education Enrollment:	170

University of Bridgeport

Online Programs

Program Delivery and Student Support

Students undertaking UB Online courses should have a basic level of computer literacy, and understand how to complete functions such as the following: creating, naming, finding, moving and navigating between files and folders; switching between open applications; cutting and pasting; using Save and Save As commands; printing; backing up saved work; and working in a "desktop" environment. Simple word processing, graphics, email and web-browsing skills are also required.

Students should have access to a fairly new Macintosh or PC with the following specifications: 100mb of free hard drive space; 16 megabytes of RAM (minimum); floppy disk or backup drive; good color monitor (minimum 640x480 pixels and 16 bit color); Internet access (33.6 kbps or 56 kbps); Internet Explorer or Netscape versions 4.0 or higher; email software (e.g. Eudora Pro); Microsoft Office. Students should have an Internet account and email address.

University and Location

Founded in 1927 as the Junior College of Connecticut, The University of Bridgeport is a private, non-sectarian, comprehensive university and is fully accredited by the New England Association of Schools and Colleges. The university benefits from ongoing financial support from the Professors World Peace Academy (PWPA), a non-profit international organization of academicians dedicated to world peace through education.

UB maintain's a student-faculty ratio of 11 to one, offering more than 30 undergraduate and 14 graduate degree programs. International students are welcome, and the student population represents over 60 countries, as well as 30 domestic states. UB faculty number 200 full- and part-time members, including Fulbright Scholars, National Science Fellows and National Endowment for Humanities Fellows, among numerous fellows and scholars.

The University of Bridgeport's Seaside Park campus comprises 86 acres, bordered by the city of Bridgeport to the north and Long Island Sound to the south. Located fifty-five miles from New York City, the campus schedules a regular variety of entertainment events, including art exhibits, theatre productions, dance ensembles, lectures and concerts.

Contact Information

Online Programs
303 University Avenue
Bridgeport Connecticut 06601 USA
phone: 1-203-576-4851 or 1-800-470-7307 (Toll
fax: 1-203-576-4852
email: ubonline@bridgeport.edu
internet: http://www.bridgeport.edu/disted/

Delivery Mode

• Internet (asynchronous instruction)
• On-campus weekend program also offered

Program Facts

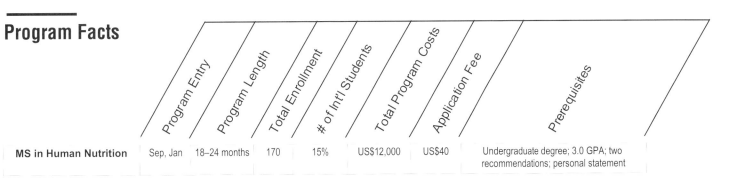

	Program Entry	Program Length	Total Enrollment	# of Int'l Students	Total Program Costs	Application Fee	Prerequisites
MS in Human Nutrition	Sep, Jan	18–24 months	170	15%	US$12,000	US$40	Undergraduate degree; 3.0 GPA; two recommendations; personal statement

University of California Extension

•

Center for Media and Independent Learning

Highlights

- Over 200 individual college- and professional-level courses
- Five certificate programs and two professional course sequences
- Choice of online and independent learning methods
- Faculty include UC, UC Extension and 'visiting' instructors from US universities and colleges

Programs Offered

Certificate Programs:
  Business Administration
  Computer Information Systems
  E-Commerce
  Marketing
  Project Management
Professional Sequences:
  Integrated Marketing Communications
  Telecommunications Fundamentals
Professional-level Courses:
  Behavioral & Health Sciences, Business,
  Computer Science, Education,
  Healthcare, Marketing,
  Publishing & Editing,
  Technical Communication
Undergraduate Credit Courses:
  Biological & Physical Sciences,
  Computer Science, Film, Health,
  Mathematics, History,
  Society & Culture, Personal Development,
  Writing

University Statistics

Year Founded:	1868
Total Enrollment:	31,277
Undergraduate Enrollment	22,678
Graduate Enrollment:	8,599
Distance Education Enrollment:	5,000

Program Overview

The Center for Media and Independent Learning (CMIL), is administered through the University of California (UC) Berkeley campus. As part of UC Extension, CMIL offers certificate programs, professional sequences and individual courses in a range of study areas to distance learning students. CMIL students can undertake studies without the need for classroom attendance, and programs and courses are open to students anywhere in the world. UC Extension is the University of California's continuing education division.

Through CMIL, students can take both online and independent learning courses. In online courses, participants access course syllabi and lecture notes over the Internet, visit electronic libraries and other sites to aid with studies, and communicate with instructors and fellow students through message boards and chat rooms. Students in independent learning courses work with print-based course materials, sending and receiving assignments by email or regular mail. Independent learning courses also involve one-on-one interaction between students and instructors.

Certificate Programs

CMIL offers a number of certificate programs including E-Commerce, Marketing, Business Administration, Project Management and Computer Information Systems. The E-Commerce certificate program focuses on developing students' understanding of the business and technical issues that drive e-commerce. Students enrolled in the Marketing Certificate undertake seven courses; the program emphasizes professional practices and direct applications of marketing concepts. The Certificate in Business Administration is a seven-course program designed to provide comprehensive coverage of the fundamentals of business management. The Certificate in Project Management allows students to develop tools for project management from concept through completion, and consists of five required courses and an elective. The Certificate in Computer Information Systems: Analysis and Design, enables students to define, manage and execute a systems approach to business.

Professional Sequences

CMIL offers professional sequences in Integrated Marketing Communications and Telecommunications Fundamentals.

The Integrated Marketing Communications sequence prepares students to produce cost effective integrated marketing programs through coursework in advertising, direct marketing, sales promotion and public relations. The program covers contemporary marketing principles and involves the identification and analysis successful marketing campaigns and strategies. The program is suitable for professionals who wish to develop integrated marketing strategies, and small business and marketing department representatives who wish to broaden their level of experience. Students complete four courses over a maximum of three years, and must maintain an overall GPA of 3.0.

Telecommunications Fundamentals provides an introduction to the basics of telecommunications, including key concepts, principles and terminology of data communications, computer networks and digital communications. Courses are designed for a range of technical professionals working in telecommunications or related fields, as well as those in entry level positions in the industry. The program requires the completion of three two-unit courses over a maximum of two years, and students must maintain an overall GPA of 3.0.

Individual Courses

CMIL offers over 200 college and professional-level courses, in addition to 21 core curriculum high school courses. Undergraduate credit courses can be undertaken in Biological & Physical Sciences, Computer Science, Film, Health, Mathematics, History, Professional Development, Society & Culture and Writing. Students can also take coursework to build professional skills in the areas of Behavioral & Health Sciences, Business, Computer Science, Education, Healthcare, Marketing, Publishing & Editing and Technical Communication. College-level courses earned through distance learning may be accepted for transfer to the University of California or to other accredited institutions.

Admission Procedures

Enrollment in lower-division courses is open to students who have satisfied specific prerequisites outlined in course descriptions. Enrollment in upper-division courses requires two years of college-level work or the equivalent. Most courses are offering on a rolling basis, and students may apply at any time. However, some courses have specific start and end dates. Students may apply to CMIL by mail, fax, telephone, email or in person. An orientation is not required.

University of California Extension

Center for Media and Independent Learning

Program Delivery and Student Support

UC Extension Online is a collaboration between CMIL and UC Berkeley Extension, combining Berkeley Extension's program offerings with CMIL's experience in developing distance learning courses and supporting students at a distance. In 1998, UC Extension Online received a Significant Achievement Award from the University Continuing Education Association for its high-quality curriculum and innovative approach to providing students and instructor services online. CMIL courses typically feature message boards, email, online resources, chat rooms and course materials that are posted online. CMIL maintains a tech-help line for students who experience technical problems with online courses, and students can order course textbooks through an online bookstore (http://www.specialty-books.com/uc-books).

University and Location

The Center for Media and Independent Learning is the distance learning division of UC Extension, the continuing education arm of the University of California. Established over 80 years ago to expand the resources of the university, CMIL offers online and independent learning courses to more than 5,000 students each year. Approximately 170 instructors participate in CMIL, and nearly half have doctoral degrees in their fields. Instructors include UC faculty members, UC Extension instructors and faculty members from other colleges and universities. The University of California System comprises a total of ten campuses, including UC Berkeley and UC Los Angeles (UCLA). CMIL is administered through the UC Berkeley campus.

Contact Information

Center for Media and Independent Learning
2000 Center Street, Suite 400
Berkeley CA 94704 USA
phone: 1-510-642-4124
fax: 1-510-643-9271
email: askcmil@uclink.berkeley.edu
internet: http://learn.berkeley.edu

Delivery Mode

- Online via Internet (including streaming audio & video)
- Correspondence
- Online Message Boards
- Online Chat Rooms
- Textbooks with Web or CD Components
- Email, Fax

Program Facts

	Program Entry	Program Length	Total Enrollment	# of Int'l Students	Total Program Costs	Application Fee	Prerequisites
Certificate in Business Administration	varies	7 courses	n/a	n/a	US$4,225	US$60	business background
Certificate in Computer Information Systems	varies	6 courses	n/a	n/a	US$3,400	US$60	business background; two years of experience in information systems
Certificate in E-Commerce Bus & Tech	varies	8 courses	n/a	n/a	US$4000–5,000	US$60	Web basics, networking concepts, programming concepts
Certificate in Marketing	varies	7 courses	n/a	n/a	US$4,225	US$60	none
Certificate in Project Management	varies	6 courses	n/a	n/a	US$3,000–4,000	US$60	none
Prof Seq in Integrated Marketing Comms	varies	4 courses	n/a	n/a	US$2,000	US$40	none
Prof Seq in Telecomm Fundamentals	varies	3 courses	n/a	n/a	US$1,500	US$40	none

University of Colorado at Colorado Springs

●

Graduate School of Business Administration

Program Overview

The Graduate School of Business Administration at the University of Colorado at Colorado Springs (UCCS) delivers a Distance Master of Business Administration program via the Internet. The UCCS Distance MBA (DMBA) program has been highlighted in Forbes Magazine as among the top 20 Cyber-University programs in the US. The program is fully accredited by AACSB: The International Association for Management Education.

Master of Business Administration

The DMBA program is comprised of 21 hours of core courses, 15 hours of electives and up to four preparatory courses. Core and elective courses address current issues in general management, information systems and international business.

The core curriculum of the DMBA includes the following courses: Contemporary Issues in Acccounting, Corporate Financial Management, Information Systems, Leading & Managing in Changing Times, Marketing Management, Operations: Competing through Capabilities and Strategic Management (capstone course).

Distance MBA students may choose to complete an Area of Emphasis in Finance or Information Systems (IS) by completing nine hours of coursework in the Finance or IS areas and six hours of 600-level MBA courses. Finance courses include Investment Management and Analysis, International Financial Management, and Managerial Economics and the Business Cycle. Information Systems courses cover topics in Visual Basic, database design, networking and systems analysis & design.

DMBA students must fulfill preparatory requirements before enrolling in specific core courses. Preparatory courses include the following: Business Communication; Business, Government & Society; Macroeconomics; and Statistics. This coursework may be waived at the discretion of the Graduate School, based on equivalent coursework already completed. Students can also take waiver exams to satisfy some of these requirements.

Semester Schedule and Faculty

The academic year begins in the summer term and ends with the following spring term. Students usually take between two and five years to complete the program, averaging up to two courses per semester.

Most core and preparatory courses are offered at least two terms per year. Course offerings are subject to the faculty availability. If student enrollments exceed class limits, the school will make every effort to offer the class in the following semester. A complete course schedule is available online (http://web.uccs.edu/business/dmbasched.htm) and lists when core, elective and preparatory courses are scheduled to be offered.

Faculty in the DMBA program maintain academic and professional emphases in areas such as technology management, global competitiveness and strategic planning. Many come from leading US institutions such as the Universities of Arizona, Colorado, Minnesota. Texas and Washington. All DMBA faculty have PhDs and many maintain active positions in industry, academic publishing and research.

Admission Requirements and Tuition

UCCS Distance MBA (DMBA) students exhibit high academic and professional experience. In 1999, newly admitted students had average GMAT scores of 590 and an average of approximately nine years of post-baccalaureate professional work experience.

Prospective DMBA students must have the equivalent of a four-year bachelor's degree from a regionally accredited institution. Complete application forms are available online (http://web.uccs.edu/business/dmbasvcap.htm). Applicants should submit the following materials: Part I and II of the application for admission; the US$75 application fee; two official copies of transcripts from all higher learning institutions attended; official GMAT scores; current resume; three letters of recommendation (optional). International students should submit TOEFL scores if their education was completed in a language other than English; grade transcripts from foreign institutions must be translated if not in English.

Applicants should submit all of their materials by the following deadlines: June 1 (fall admission), November 1 (spring admission) or April 1 (summer admission). The Graduate School will contact each applicant in writing about the admission decision once all credentials have been reviewed.

Total estimated cost for tuition and course materials is US$17,400, plus the basic cost of maintaining an Internet Service Provider. Students may pay up to US$23,000 for the program depending on the number of additional preparatory courses required. Tuition per three-credit-hour course is US$1200.

University of Colorado at Colorado Springs

Graduate School of Business Administration

Program Delivery and Student Support

MBA program students interact with classmates and PhD faculty in cyber classrooms, with software provided and maintained by JonesKnowledge.com. Prospective students should have access to a Pentium or better computer with 28.8 kbps modem (minimum), sound card, speakers and Web access (Netscape 7.0 or higher). For courses with video components, access to a television and VCR is also required.

Disabled students who need special accommodations can contact MBA program advising staff by telephone (1-800-990-8227, ext. 3408) or by email (busadvsr@mail.uccs.edu).

Contact Information

Graduate School of Business Administration
1420 Austin Bluffs Parkway
Colorado Springs CO 80918 USA
phone: 1-719-262-3408
fax: 1-719-262-3100
email: busadvsr@mail.uccs.edu
internet: http://web.uccs.edu/business

University and Location

The UCCS campus is nestled on a bluff overlooking Colorado Springs, in view of Pikes Peak, one of the most prominent of the Rocky Mountains. Twelve new buildings, including an advanced computer classroom building have been constructed in the past few years. Every classroom has a computer and electronic display screen to facilitate classes, and is not dissimilar to the current technology that helps deliver materials and information for the DMBA program. Faculty involved in the DMBA program hold doctoral degrees and are actively involved in research, industry consulting and academic publishing.

The UCCS DMBA program, while administered around the world, holds the same accreditation as the on-campus MBA program and DMBA students earn the same degree as campus MBA students. The DMBA is accredited by AACSB: The International Association for Management Education, which is the highest accreditation available for a university-level business program.

Delivery Mode

- Internet - virtual classroom
- Videotapes
- Textbooks
- Supplemental readings

Program Facts

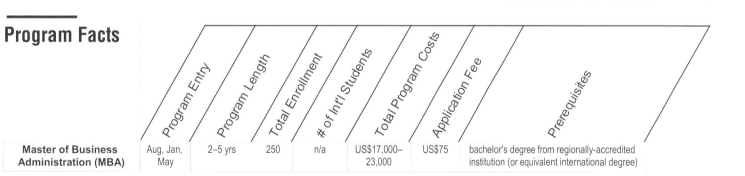

	Program Entry	Program Length	Total Enrollment	# of Int'l Students	Total Program Costs	Application Fee	Prerequisites
Master of Business Administration (MBA)	Aug, Jan, May	2–5 yrs	250	n/a	US$17,000–23,000	US$75	bachelor's degree from regionally-accredited institution (or equivalent international degree)

University of Colorado at Denver
•
CU Online

Program Overview

The University of Colorado at Denver has been offering online courses since the fall of 1996, and continues to develop courses and degree programs online. CU Online is the virtual campus of the University of Colorado system, with eleven collegiate and professional development programs offering more than 200 courses via the Internet.

CU Online offers core curriculum and elective courses in a variety of disciplines, representing the same courses taught throughout the University of Colorado system.

CU Online courses are not self-paced. However, students enjoy greater scheduling flexibility than in a traditional classroom. By logging in to class students can view lectures, review assignments and participate in class discussions. CU Online courses are appropriate for students who, because of time and/or distance limitations, may not be able to take traditional on-campus courses.

Programs of Study

Today, CU's catalog of online courses includes over 200 core curriculum, elective and professional development courses in a wide range of disciplines as well as five complete online degree/certificates.

CU Online offers courses in liberal arts and sciences, arts and media, business, education, engineering, public affairs and architecture and planning. All courses may be applied to a degree program at the University of Colorado at Denver or may be transferred to a student's home institution, upon approval.

Complete online degree programs are offered, including a bachelor of arts in sociology and master's degrees in business administration , engineering in engineering management, engineering in geographic information systems and public administration.

Admission

Students living in Colorado must be accepted to the University either as degree-seeking or non degree-seeking students. Students living outside the state do not need to be admitted to take CU Online courses; however, if students wish to complete their degree through CU Online, formal admission must be made.

Admission requirements vary by college and school. For freshmen, CU Online bases admission on several factors, the most important being grade point average, high school rank, and ACT or SAT scores.
To find specific information about applying, students may visit CU Online (www.cudenver.

edu/cuonline/ei), or contact the specific school or college for graduate study requirements.

To register for an online class, students will need the course call number (available on the website). Once registered for an online course, it usually takes 24 to 36 hours to have access to the course.

Credit Options

Students may take credit and noncredit courses through CU Online. Credit granted from CU Online is identical to that earned on the CU-Denver campus. Because CU-Denver is a fully accredited institution, credit is easily transferable to other universities.

Faculty

Online courses follow the same faculty governance policies as the established on-campus courses. All CU Online faculty members are approved by the department and often instruct the on-campus courses. Many of the instructors are experts who work in the field in which they teach and bring knowledge and resources from their industry.

Tuition and Fees

Online tuition rates are based on the course level and apply to all online courses whether or not on-campus courses are taken. A US$100 online course fee, US$50 lab fee and select student fees may apply in addition to tuition fees.

Tuition rates vary, with most undergraduate courses costing approximately US$126–183 per credit hour, and most graduate courses costing between US$190–$250 per credit hour. CU Denver offers four payment plans, including deferred payments and financial aid.

To be eligible for financial aid, students must be enrolled as degree-seeking students at the University of Colorado at Denver. For more information, students can visit the CU Denver Financial Aid web site (http://finaid.cudenver.edu/).

University of Colorado at Denver

CU Online

Program Delivery and Student Support

CU Online course instructors make use of current technology such as streaming audio, video, and multimedia slide shows to present course content. Most courses also make use of technologies that allow students to interact with their instructors and peers, such as online bulletin boards, live discussions in online classrooms, email and collaborative workspaces.

 CU Online offers a range of online student services. Students can search catalogs, register for courses, order textbooks and other course materials, get academic advice and apply for financial aid through CU Online websites.

University and Location

The University of Colorado at Denver is one of four institutions in the University of Colorado system and the only public university in the Denver metropolitan area. It is an urban, nonresidential campus located in downtown Denver. The University of Colorado at Denver was founded in 1965 and is accredited by the North Central Association of Colleges and Schools.

Contact Information

CU Online
Patty Godbey, Campus Box 198, PO Box 173364
Denver Colorado 80217-3364 USA
phone: 1-303-556-6505
fax: 1-303-556-6530
email: inquiry@cuonline.edu
internet: http://www.cudenver.edu/cuonline/ei

Delivery Mode

- Streaming audio and video
- Multimedia slide shows
- Threaded discussions on bulletin boards
- Live discussions in online classrooms
- Collaborative workspaces

Program Facts

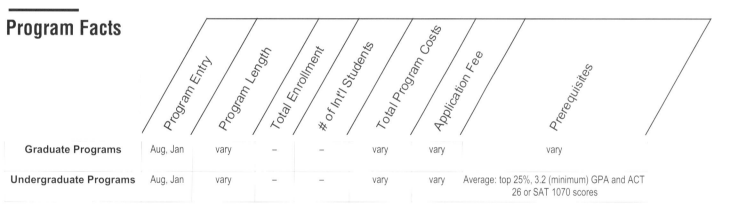

	Program Entry	Program Length	Total Enrollment	# of Int'l Students	Total Program Costs	Application Fee	Prerequisites
Graduate Programs	Aug, Jan	vary	–	–	vary	vary	vary
Undergraduate Programs	Aug, Jan	vary	–	–	vary	vary	Average: top 25%, 3.2 (minimum) GPA and ACT 26 or SAT 1070 scores

University of Delaware

•

College of Health and Nursing Sciences (CHNS)

- Program admission unnecessary prior to course enrollment
- Any site at which a student is employed can participate in the program
- Three one-weekend on-campus courses
- Degree requirements can be fulfilled within 15 months but must be completed within five years after enrollment in first nursing course

Programs Offered

BRN Curriculum:
  BRN Role Practicum
  Community Health Nursing
  Current Perspectives in Nursing
  Health Care Delivery Topics
  Introduction to Nursing Research
  Leadership Organizational Behavior
  Learning Lab: Health Assessment
  Nursing Informatics
  Nursing Research Applications
  Pathophysiology
  Psychopathology
  Transition to Baccalaureate Nursing Education
  Wellness & Health Assessment

University Statistics

Year Founded:	1743
Total Enrollment:	21,206
Undergraduate Enrollment	16,162
Graduate Enrollment:	3,108
Distance Education Enrollment:	1,936

Program Overview

The University of Delaware (UD) awards a Bachelor of Science in Nursing (BSN) degree to students who complete the Baccalaureate for the Registered Nurse Major. The program is offered in a distance learning format and is available through part- or full-time study to meet the needs of busy practitioners. The program is designed for registered nurses (RNs) with an associate degree or diploma in nursing. The program is fully accredited by the National League for Nursing Accrediting Commission and holds preliminary approval from the Commission on Collegiate Nursing Education.

UD's commitment to distance learning technologies has been recognized by the United States Distance Learning Association and Yahoo! Internet Life magazine.

Curriculum

The program is a 125-credit program culminating in a bachelor of science in nursing. A total of 29 credits must be acquired in upper-division nursing courses. Another 66 credits must be acquired from various mandatory and elective courses in the arts and sciences. University policy requires that students obtain their first 90 credits or last 30 credits from UD.

The upper-division nursing curriculum consists of ten videotaped or web courses and three campus-based courses. The ten distance courses address pathophysiology, psychopathology, current perspectives in nursing, nursing informatics, wellness and health assessment, introductory nursing research, health care delivery topics, community health nursing, and leadership and organizational behavior. The three campus-based courses are held on weekends each January and June. These address health assessment, nursing education transition topics and nursing research applications.

Many students complete the program within 15 months; students must complete the program within five years of their initial enrollment in a nursing course. All mandatory nursing courses and many support courses are available year round. The CHNS offers distance courses during the fall and spring semesters and two special sessions in the summer and winter. The college recommends that students consult their advisor prior to enrolling in the special sessions.

A role practicum concludes the program by providing participants with 84 hours of preceptored clinical experience at a health care facility in the student's state of residence. The practicum emphasizes the importance of wellness, short-term hospital care and explores the social, political and economic forces that influence the formation and debate of health care issues.

Admission Procedures

Candidates must submit a distance learning application for admission, US$50 nonrefundable application fee and official transcripts. Upon admission, UD Online sends enrollment information to students and participating worksites. At this time, the college assigns to each student an advisor who formulates a personalized program schedule. Formal university admission is unnecessary for enrollment in distance courses. However, only matriculated students can enroll in nursing courses.

The college awards a maximum of 30 credits to students who have completed an NLN-accredited associate degree in nursing or passed the NLN Nursing Acceleration Challenge Exam (ACE) II. Transfer students must have a cumulative 2.5 grade point average in all prior college studies.

Institutions or corporations that wish to participate in the program as UD Online official worksites must submit an agreement form. The institutional or corporate participant appoints a coordinator to distribute course materials and administer examinations to students. The CHNS has established educational partnerships with 142 health care facilities, businesses and colleges in 15 states and one other country.

RNs can also enroll as individual students. Under this option, they must travel to UD's Newark campus to sit for nursing exams.

Tuition

Tuition is US$217 per credit for distance courses. Tuition for the three weekend courses is assessed on the basis of the student's place of residency. Delaware residents pay US$188 per credit, while nonresidents pay US$553 per credit.

Financial aid is available in the form of employer-sponsored tuition reimbursements or loans for part-time matriculated students. The university disburses more than US$53 million in aid each year to eligible citizens and permanent residents of the US.

University of Delaware

College of Health and Nursing Sciences (CHNS)

Program Delivery and Student Support

Online courses are delivered via three formats: web-based, CD-ROM and videotape. Internet students must have access to Windows or a Macintosh computer. A more powerful computer and higher speed Internet connection may be required for optimum course access.

The university bookstore receives textbook orders online or by telephone or facsimile. Distance learners use electronic services provided by the university library, writing center, career services center, academic advisement office, and financial aid and student loan office. Participants can log on to the listserv and interact with peers.

Contact Information

College of Health and Nursing Sciences (CHNS)
Division of Special Programs
Newark Delaware 19716 USA
phone: 1-800-UOD-NURS
fax: 1-302-831-4550
email: dsp-email@udel.edu
internet: http://www.udel.edu/DSP

University and Location

Founded as a private academy in 1743 and supported by the state since 1833, the University of Delaware currently enrolls 16,162 undergraduate and 3,108 graduate students. UD awards degrees through seven colleges devoted to agriculture and natural resources, arts and science, business and economics, engineering, health and nursing sciences, human services, education and public policy, and marine studies.

Approximately 7,000 students live on campus. The university library houses more than 2.4 million books and serials, three million microforms, 390,000 government documents, 6,000 video cassettes and films, and 120,000 maps. Students with computing needs can use 11 general access sites and 13 departmental sites.

UD makes its home in Newark, a city of 25,098 (1990) in the northern part of the state. The I-95 corridor is a short drive from the campus. On September 3, 1777, soldiers first raised Betsy Ross's flag during the Battle of Cooch's Bridge, near Newark.

Delivery Mode

- Videotaped courses
- Web-enhanced courses (videotaped lectures, web-based syllabi & assignments, online interaction)
- Web-based courses (web-based syllabi & assignments, online interaction)

Program Facts

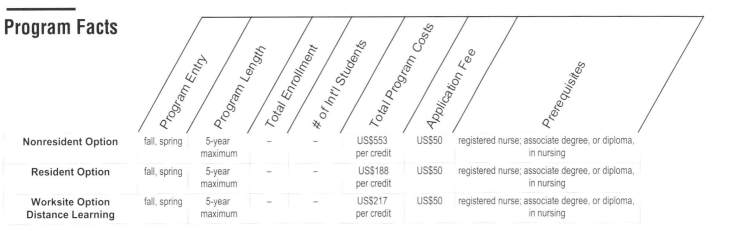

	Program Entry	Program Length	Total Enrollment	# of Int'l Students	Total Program Costs	Application Fee	Prerequisites
Nonresident Option	fall, spring	5-year maximum	–	–	US$553 per credit	US$50	registered nurse; associate degree, or diploma, in nursing
Resident Option	fall, spring	5-year maximum	–	–	US$188 per credit	US$50	registered nurse; associate degree, or diploma, in nursing
Worksite Option Distance Learning	fall, spring	5-year maximum	–	–	US$217 per credit	US$50	registered nurse; associate degree, or diploma, in nursing

University of Georgia

•

University System of Georgia Independent Study

Program Overview

University System of Georgia Independent Study (USGIS) delivers an array of credit courses to adult distance learners who are restricted from attending campus-based classes at participating institutions. University System of Georgia (USG) institutions include the University of Georgia (UGA), Georgia College and State University, Armstrong Atlantic State University, Georgia Southern University, North Georgia College and State University, and Valdosta State University.

Curriculum

The USGIS curriculum offers 121 courses in a variety of disciplines and subdisciplines. The business and communication curricula consist of courses in accounting, economics, journalism and mass communication, management, marketing and speech communication.

The liberal arts curriculum offers courses in anthropology, arts, classical culture, English, educational psychology and measurement, education, French, German, history, Latin, philosophy, political science, religion, sociology, Spanish and women's studies.

The scientific, medical and health curricula consist of courses in agricultural and applied economics, biology, child and family development, counseling and human development services, crop and soil sciences, ecology, foods and nutrition, forest resources, geography, geology, health promotion and behavior, horticulture, mathematics, psychology, recreation and leisure studies, and veterinary medicine.

At present, eight courses are available entirely online. Related subjects include English, history, horticulture, Latin, political science, psychology, recreation and leisure studies, and religion.

Admission and Registration

Admission is open to any person over Georgia's legal school age limit. Subject to the approval of an academic dean, this includes students who have been dismissed from USG programs. Incarcerated students can also apply for USGIS courses.

Admission to USGIS does not constitute admission to any other institution. Submission of transcripts, admission tests or enrollment in a college or university are not required. High school and home school students, however, must enroll in a college or university prior to applying for USGIS.

Course registration is assigned to specific academic terms for purposes of financial aid disbursement and enrollment certification. Students can register in multiple courses during the same term, as well as in courses that they have not finished or passed in previous terms. Courses are normally completed within one year of enrollment. Upon payment of a fee, one three-month extension per course is permissible.

With the exception of UGA students, who may be eligible for resident credit, USGIS offers nonresident credit only. UGA students who wish to apply USGIS resident credit to a baccalaureate program must have a 2.0 grade point average in at least 15 hours of coursework at the time of registration in USGIS. Those who are under academic discipline may not earn resident credit for USGIS courses. Students enrolled in a degree program at another college or university should confirm beforehand that any credit earned through USGIS is transferable to their home institution.

To sit for final examinations, students must complete all mandatory coursework and be enrolled in the course for at least eight weeks. A pass on the final examination is necessary to pass a USGIS course, irrespective of grades achieved on individual lessons. Midterm and final examinations are administered by educators at official test sites throughout the US. Students who cannot travel to regular sites, such as military personnel stationed overseas, should submit a proposal for alternative sites to USGIS.

Tuition and Financial Aid

Tuition is US$104 per semester hour for resident in-state students (at UGA) and non-resident (distance learning) students. Resident out-of-state students at UGA pay $417 per semester hour. Students desiring to audit a course pay the same tuition as resident credit students. All tuition fees or other charges are subject to change at the end of each semester.

Students receiving financial aid or scholarships are not exempt from the tuition payment policy unless they secure a two-week financial aid deferment from UGA. Incarcerated students working toward a general education diploma cannot redeem their US$500 HOPE vouchers until parole. Tuition refunds are remitted to the agency or institution overseeing the financial aid. USGIS does not offer financial aid or scholarships.

University of Georgia

University System of Georgia Independent Study

Program Delivery and Student Support

USGIS employs traditional and electronic distance learning modes. Traditional distance courses use textbooks and other instructional materials, audio- and videotapes and print-based course guides. Electronic distance courses also use textbooks, but the delivery format is enhanced with WebCT, email, and diskette-based course guides. Some course assignments may be submitted via mail or email. All distance learners sit for midterm and final examinations at one of the 33 certified examination sites; UGA will work with non-Georgia residents to locate testing sites near them.

Textbooks and required materials are available through MBSDirect. Students can order online at http://direct.mbsbook.com/uga.htm or by calling 1-800-325-3252.

Contact Information

University System of Georgia Independent Study
1197 South Lumpkin Street, Suite 193
Athens Georgia 30602-3603 USA
phone: 1-706-542-3243 or 1-800-877-3243
fax: 1-706-542-6635
email: usgis@arches.uga.edu
internet: http://www.gactr.uga.edu/usgis/

University and Location

Incorporated in 1785, the University of Georgia is the oldest state-chartered institution in the US. The university awards undergraduate and graduate degrees through 13 schools and colleges devoted to agricultural and environmental sciences, arts and sciences, business, education, environmental design, family and consumer sciences, forest resources, graduate studies, journalism and mass communication, law, pharmacy, social work and veterinary medicine. UGA is accredited by the Southern Association of Colleges and Schools.

Approximately 6,000 students live on the Athens campus. The university library houses 3.3 million volumes and one of the country's largest map collections. Computing and networking services maintains microcomputer clusters, campus email, WebCT instructional resources and a digital media studio. The Ramsey Student Center for Physical Activities offers 430,000 square feet of recreational facilities, while the Rec Sports Complex contains tennis courts, playing fields, fitness trails, running paths, picnic areas, beaches and a lake.

Athens is located in the northeast county of Clarke, which has a population of 86,522 (1990). The people of Athens and Clarke County hosted events for the 1996 Olympic Games.

Delivery Mode

- Audio & videotapes
- Textbooks and instructional materials
- Print & electronic course guides
- Local examination sites
- Flexible country-wide examination sites
- Web courses (online instruction, email, chat rooms)

Program Facts

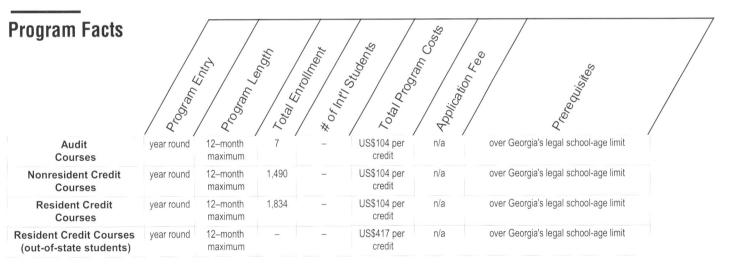

	Program Entry	Program Length	Total Enrollment	# of Int'l Students	Total Program Costs	Application Fee	Prerequisites
Audit Courses	year round	12–month maximum	7	–	US$104 per credit	n/a	over Georgia's legal school-age limit
Nonresident Credit Courses	year round	12–month maximum	1,490	–	US$104 per credit	n/a	over Georgia's legal school-age limit
Resident Credit Courses	year round	12–month maximum	1,834	–	US$104 per credit	n/a	over Georgia's legal school-age limit
Resident Credit Courses (out-of-state students)	year round	12–month maximum	–	–	US$417 per credit	n/a	over Georgia's legal school-age limit

University of Illinois at Urbana-Champaign

•

Office of Continuing Education

- Off-campus students can obtain master's degrees through academic outreach
- Students complete courses within nine months, under guided individual study
- Academic Outreach Library and online resource portal offer support services
- Full refunds for credit courses possible during first quarter of classes

Programs Offered

Master's Degrees:
- Business Administration
- Computer Science
- Crop Sciences
- Curriculum & Education Reform
- Curriculum & Instruction
- Educational Organization
- Educational Psychology
- Electrical & Computer Engineering
- Food Science & Human Nutrition
- General Engineering
- Human Resource Development
- Human Resource Education
- Library & Information Science
- Mechanical Engineering
- Natural Resources
- Rehabilitation or Social Work
- Theoretical & Applied Mechanics

Other Programs:
- Guided Independent Study

University Statistics

Year Founded:	1867
Total Enrollment:	36,303
Undergraduate Enrollment	27,452
Graduate Enrollment:	8,851
Distance Education Enrollment:	–

Program Overview

The University of Illinois at Urbana-Champaign (UIUC) provides distance learning degree programs and credit and noncredit courses through two divisions of the Office of Continuing Education: Academic Outreach (AO) and Guided Individual Study (GIS). Professionals seeking specialization in the fields of education, science and engineering can obtain master's degrees on a part-time basis by enrolling in AO courses. GIS is appropriate for adult students with family- and work-related obligations or UIUC students who face scheduling problems connected to on-campus courses.

Academic Outreach

In cooperation with the college of education, AO offers courses that lead to an MEd in curriculum and instruction; curriculum, technology and education reform; educational psychology; educational organization and leadership; human resource education; and global human resource development. AO also offers an advanced certificate in education. All MEd programs are designed to meet the professional goals of teachers, counselors and administrators or those students desiring certification in these occupations.

In collaboration with the college of engineering, AO delivers courses that lead to a master of computer science and a master of science (MS) in electrical & computer engineering, general engineering, mechanical engineering or theoretical & applied mechanics. In cooperation with the college of liberal arts and sciences, AO offers a certificate of completion (online) in French translation.

In cooperation with the college of commerce and business, AO offers the Executive Master of Business Administration (MBA) Program to corporate managers who wish to hone their competitive edge. Full-time status in the university is unnecessary and classes meet only one day per week. Supplemental material is presented in seminars and workshops coordinated by the Executive MBA Alumni Group.

Additionally, AO delivers courses that culminate in an MS in library and information science, in rehabilitation with a concentration in counseling, in food science and human nutrition, in crop sciences or natural resources, or in environmental sciences.

In total, the UIUC administers more than 130 undergraduate courses and over 100 graduate courses through AO. Content is identical to that of traditional on-campus credit courses. Since AO courses are tied to a semester schedule, students must meet assignment deadlines.

Like on-campus degree programs, enrollment in AO is contingent on admission to the UIUC's graduate college or appropriate academic departments. When reviewing applications, the university gives priority to students who are enrolled in degree programs over those who are not. Some courses are limited to master's degree students.

Full refunds for credit courses are possible during the first quarter of classes.

Students enrolled in off-campus degree programs can apply for federal financial aid by completing and submitting to the appropriate government agency the Free Application for Federal Student Aid. Military scholarship winners do not have to pay the fees that normally accompany AO courses.

Guided Individual Study

GIS offers more than 125 credit courses in 29 fields and a dozen noncredit courses in seven fields. Close to 50 of these courses are available through the Internet.

Enrollment is open to students completing undergraduate or graduate degree programs at UIUC (on or off campus) or at other colleges and universities. Enrollment is also open to senior high school students (with the approval of the school's principal or student's guidance counselor), international students and independent students seeking technical, vocational or professional self-improvement.

Students can enroll in GIS courses year round and under most circumstances courses can be completed within nine months. Those enrolled in credit courses must take at least one examination, on or off campus, under an authorized proctor.

Since completion rates for GIS courses are lower than those for traditional, on-campus courses, the university recommends that students do not undertake more than two GIS courses concurrently. Upon submission of a written request and additional US$20 fee, students can obtain a three-month extension to complete course requirements.

Enrollment in GIS courses does not constitute admission to the UIUC. No graduate credit is available through GIS, although graduate students can obtain undergraduate credit to fulfill the requirements for graduate degree programs. Baccalaureate students who secure the approval of the appropriate dean may apply a maximum of 60 semester hours earned from GIS courses toward degree requirements.

University of Illinois at Urbana-Champaign

●

Office of Continuing Education

Program Delivery and Student Support

The Office of Continuing Education at UIUC delivers credit courses through a variety of electronic media, including online instruction, CD-ROM, compressed video, videotapes and video teleconferencing; traditional distance learning formats, such as correspondence; and regional on-site instruction. Students should own or have access to a personal computer with Internet access, preferably facilitated by Internet Explorer 5.0, or Netscape.

Electronic support services for UIUC's distance learning students are delivered through an online resource portal and the Academic Outreach Library (AOL). Upon request, the AOL will send journal articles and books to students, conduct database searches, provide research and reference assistance, hold individual library orientation sessions, reserve materials at instructional sites and secure items through interlibrary loans.

University and Location

The University of Illinois at Urbana-Champaign was chartered in 1867 as the Illinois Industrial University. UIUC delivers more than 250 undergraduate and graduate programs through 16 colleges, institutes and schools. The 1999 US News and World Report placed UIUC within the top 10 public universities in the country.

The university has a current undergraduate enrollment of 27,452, of which 89 percent includes students from Illinois. Five hundred and ninety international students are enrolled in undergraduate degree programs. The graduate college enrolls 8,851 students and professionals. Alumni include 10 Nobel laureates and 17 Pulitzer Prize winners.

The UIUC library contains more than 17 million items, housing the largest public university library collection in the world. More than 80 centers, labs and institutes conduct research on campus. Students, faculty and staff have access to 30,000 computer network connections.

The university owns 22 undergraduate residence halls, two graduate residence halls and 975 apartments for students with families. Campus recreation facilities offer playing fields and gyms; an ice arena; courts for basketball, racquetball, squash, tennis and volleyball; swimming pools; indoor running tracks; and weight rooms.

Contact Information

Office of Continuing Education
Suite 1405, 302 East John Street
Champaign Illinois 61820 USA
phone: 1-217-333-3060 or 1-800-252-1360
fax: 1-217-244-8481
email: inforequest@talon.outreach.uiuc.edu
internet: http://www.outreach.uiuc.edu

Guided Individual Study
Suite 1406, 302 East John Street
Champaign Illinois 61820 USA
          1-217-333-1321
          1-217-333-8524
          GISinfo@c3po.conted.uiuc.edu
          http://www.outreach.uiuc.edu/gis

Delivery Mode

- CD-ROM
- Compressed video
- Correspondence
- Online instruction
- Regional on-site instruction
- Videotapes
- Video teleconferencing

Program Facts

	Program Entry	Program Length	Total Enrollment	# of Int'l Students	Total Program Costs	Application Fee	Prerequisites
Academic Outreach Undergraduate Courses	Aug, Jan	varies	–	–			high school diploma
Advanced Certificate in Education	–	–	–	–			contact UIUC college of education; phone: 1-217-333-0964
Guided Independent Study	year round	varies	–	–			
Master of Computer Science	Aug, Jan	varies	–	–			bachelor's degree and work experience
Master of Education	Aug, Jan	varies	–	–			bachelor's degree and work experience
Master of Science	Aug, Jan	varies	–	–			bachelor's degree and work experience
Master of Social Work	Aug, Jan	varies	–	–			bachelor's degree and work experience

University of Maine

•

Continuing and Distance Education

- Four-year interdisciplinary degree tailored to student goals
- Web-based certificate in Electric Power Systems
- Courses can be taken for university or continuing education credit

Programs Offered

Certificates:
  Classical Studies
  Electric Power Systems
  Maine Studies
Degrees:
  Bachelor of University Studies
Graduate Certificates:
  Child and Family Services
Graduate Courses:
  Education Database Systems
  Electrical Engineering
  Higher Education
  Information Technology & Public Policy
  Liberal Arts
  Long Term Care
  Social Work
Undergraduate Courses:
  Biology, Child Development,
  Civil Engineering,
  Education, English,
  History, Human Sexuality,
  Interdisciplinary Studies, Internet Marketing,
  Latin Studies, Modern Languages,
  Nursing, Nutrition,
  Peace Studies, Political Science,
  Property Surveying, Psychology,
  Women's Studies,
  Writing - Business & Technical

University Statistics

Year Founded:	1865
Total Enrollment:	10,782
Undergraduate Enrollment	7,500
Graduate Enrollment:	2,200
Distance Education Registrations:	3,980

Program Overview

The Division of Lifelong Learning's Distance Education Program at the University of Maine (UM) offers a four-year undergraduate interdisciplinary degree and courses in a variety of academic disciplines, leading to certficates in electric power systems, Maine studies, classical studies or child and family services.

Distance education courses, which generally follow the academic term system timeline, can be taken for university credit or continuing education credit transferable to degree programs. The continuing education division and distance education program in the Division of Lifelong Learning are closely linked. The UM has been offering distance education for ten years, and the number of courses online has more than doubled since the 1998-99 academic year. Courses are also delivered through interactive television and compressed video.

Students pay in-state fees for online courses. Application may be possible through the Continuing & Distance Education division or through UM admission procedures. Applicants to graduate courses should contact the Graduate School. Students can gain more information on Division of Lifelong Learning (DLL) offerings by visiting the DLL web site (http://dll.umaine.edu).

Bachelor of University Studies

The four-year Bachelor of University Studies (BUS), first launched in 1975, is designed as a part-time, adaptable, interdisciplinary degree. Courses of study are tailored to the needs of students, and are completed entirely by distance education or combined with off-site continuing education courses.

Interested students must first consult with an academic advisor, who will review the prerequisite 18 postsecondary credit hours, high school transcripts, and students' academic goals. Application can then be made to UM.

Students who enroll in the Bachelor of University Studies (BUS) program do not commit to a major as in traditional undergraduate programs. In this degree, tailored courses of study cover a variety of academic interests, as well as general education requirements of writing, ethics, human values and social contacts, mathematics and science. The unique course combinations and interdisciplinary relationships lead to a major project at the end of the final year. More information is available through the BUS web

site (http://dll.umaine.edu/bus).

Electric Power Systems

Students interested in electrical engineering can earn an Electric Power System Certificate that combines junior and senior level material. Twelve one-month modules are undertaken entirely through web-based courses.

If participants wish to apply credits toward the electrical and computer engineering degree at UM, they can choose to take exams rather than receive a pass or fail grade for each module. More information is available through the program web site (http://www.ume.maine.edu/ced/powersys).

Child & Family Services

The Certificate in Child and Family Services is built upon the bachelor's degree in social work to give graduates the expertise to work with children and their families. The certificate cannot be completely earned by distance learning; courses are offered at off-site locations in Maine.

The program requires 15 credit hours or five courses, some of which form the foundation for UM's Master of Social Work degree. Graduate credits earned for the certificate can be applied to this degree if students are accepted into the UM School of Social Work for graduate study.

Classical Studies

The Certificate in Classical Studies: From the Bronze Age to the Fall of the Roman Empire is an 18-credit hour, or six course, program. It allows individuals to explore the classical roots of western civilization, from the Latin language to women in the ancient world, in a series of interdisciplinary courses.

Courses are delivered through a combination of distance learning and continuing education modes.

Maine Studies

Students can take undergraduate distance education courses that form part of the interdisciplinary Certificate in Maine Studies. The program is valuable for students in education or students who hope to work for the state of Maine. Courses are multidisciplinary, exploring all aspects of Maine's history, economy, culture, politics, geology, and sociology. Student's can gain more information on the program by visiting the program web site (http://www.ume.maine.edu/ced/mainestudy).

University of Maine

•

Continuing and Distance Education

Program Delivery and Student Support

For students taking distance education courses offered synchronously or asynchronously on the Web, or by interactive television or compressed video, basic technology requirements include a VCR, television with cable channels, and a computer with an Internet connection capable of playing QuickTime Media at a speed of 56 kbps. Courses online are delivered through WebCt and FirstClass over the university's UNET information technology system. The UNET help desk assists in all aspects of distance course technology; the Distance Ed Helpline can be reached by email or through a toll-free number.

The University of Maine's Fogler Library features an online catalogue, and maintains 950,000 volumes, 6,700 periodical subscriptions, as well as microforms, government publications, and electronic databases, including UM theses and dissertations online.

University and Location

The University of Maine (http://www.umaine.edu) is the state of Maine's land-grant institution, founded in 1865. The campus located next to the town of Orono is the largest in the University of Maine system. It is nine miles from the state's third largest city, Bangor. UM delivers 55 master's degree, 23 doctorates and bachelor's degrees in close to 90 areas through five colleges. Approximately 500 students from other states and 70 countries form part of the university's enrollment of 10,000.

The Orono area is part of classic rural New England. It is known for its autumnal beauty and pristine forests, mountain ranges and coastal scenery, and is a favourite holiday destination for city dwellers along the New England coast. Located between two rivers, the area offers extensive outdoor recreation including whitewater rafting, hunting and fishing, throughout four distinct seasons. The town of Orono is rich in cultural activities such as musical performances, theatre productions, and art galleries and museums.

Contact Information

Continuing and Distance Education
Jim Toner, Director, 122 Chadbourne Hall
Orono Maine 04469-5713 USA
phone: 1-207-581-3142; 1-877-947-4357 (Toll Free)
fax: 1-207-581-3141
email: CEDSS@umit.maine.edu
internet: http://dll.umaine.edu/ced/

Delivery Mode

• Online via Internet
• Interactive television
• Compressed video
• QuickTime Media streaming technology

Program Facts

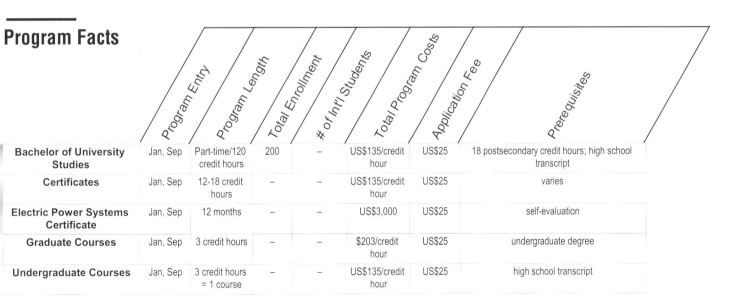

	Program Entry	Program Length	Total Enrollment	# of Int'l Students	Total Program Costs	Application Fee	Prerequisites
Bachelor of University Studies	Jan, Sep	Part-time/120 credit hours	200	–	US$135/credit hour	US$25	18 postsecondary credit hours; high school transcript
Certificates	Jan, Sep	12-18 credit hours	–	–	US$135/credit hour	US$25	varies
Electric Power Systems Certificate	Jan, Sep	12 months	–	–	US$3,000	US$25	self-evaluation
Graduate Courses	Jan, Sep	3 credit hours	–	–	$203/credit hour	US$25	undergraduate degree
Undergraduate Courses	Jan, Sep	3 credit hours = 1 course	–	–	US$135/credit hour	US$25	high school transcript

University of Massachusetts Lowell

•

Online Degree and Certificate Programs

Highlights

- A large selection of credit courses offered entirely online
- Online courses are held over a period of 14 weeks and are available during the spring, summer and fall semesters
- In-state and out-of-state distance learners pay the same tuition

Programs Offered

Certificate Programs:
- Data Telecommunications
- Information Technology Fundamentals
- Intranet Development
- Multimedia Applications
- Plastics Technology
- UNIX

Degree Programs:
- AS in Information Systems
- Bachelor of Liberal Arts
- BS in Information Systems

University Statistics

Year Founded:	1895
Total Enrollment:	12,187
Undergraduate Enrollment	9,503
Graduate Enrollment:	2,684
Distance Education Enrollment:	4,800

Program Overview

The University of Massachusetts Lowell (UML) offers a variety of certificates and degrees entirely online through its Division of Continuing Studies and Corporate Education (CSCE). UML's continuing studies division is one of the largest public continuing education units in New England and the most comprehensive in terms of curriculum in the UMass system.

UML offers over 80 credit courses per semester in writing, communication, social sciences, multimedia, mathematics, management, computer programming and website development. CSCE operates on an open-enrollment, rolling-admissions basis. Registration occurs by mail, telephone, fax or in person.

Students transferring from other accredited institutions into CSCE certificate or degree programs must have a minimum cumulative grade point average (GPA) of 1.7. UML maintains special transfer arrangements with Massachusetts community colleges through the Commonwealth Transfer Compact. Students applying under the compact must have an associate degree consisting of at least 60 credits and a minimum cumulative 2.0 GPA. At least 35 credits should have been earned in the general education curriculum.

Online students pay the same tuition rate of US$615 per course regardless of their state of residence.

Financial aid is available on a limited basis to students admitted to a degree program. Financial aid options include the Hoff Scholarships, Pell Grant, Supplemental Education Opportunity Grant, Federal Direct Loans, Perkins Loan, Mass Plan Family Education Loan and College Work-Study Program.

Online Degree Programs

Students can obtain all credit requirements for an associate of science or bachelor of science in information systems via CyberEd courses. In both programs, first-year students normally take one or two courses during their first semester and then three courses during subsequent semesters. Although students may register for individual courses, admission to CSCE is necessary for degree programs.

The associate of science in information systems (ASIS) is a 60-credit program that students pursue on a part-time basis for four years. The first year of study normally entails courses in college writing, introductory information systems, personal computers and Microsoft Office. The second year includes courses in business writing, C programming and introductory management and organizational behavior. Students take computer or information systems electives during the last three years and general education courses during the last two years.

Applicants to the ASIS program should hold a high school diploma or graduate equivalency diploma (GED). UML residency policy requires online ASIS students to complete at least 24 credits through CSCE's CyberEd program.

The bachelor of science in information systems (BSIS) is a 120-credit program that students pursue on a part-time basis for seven years. In addition to the ASIS degree requirements, BSIS students must complete a variety of courses in liberal arts and the general education curriculum, as well as required and elective courses in computer or information systems. UML residency policy requires online BSIS students to complete at least 30 credits through CSCE's CyberEd program.

Students can now earn a bachelor's degree in liberal arts entirely online from UML. Details are available on the CyberEd website (http://cybered.uml.edu).

Online Certificate Programs

Students can also obtain all credit requirements for a certificate in information technology fundamentals, Intranet development, multimedia applications or UNIX. The first program is designed for students who wish to cultivate a broad understanding of this field before moving into one or more areas of specialization. The Intranet development program equips graduates to develop and maintain corporate intranets. The multimedia applications program provides students with the knowledge and skill sets required to produce compelling interactive multimedia presentations. The UNIX program is tailored for professionals in the computer industry who want to upgrade their operating system and programming skills.

Two other online certificate programs are available to CyberEd students. In collaboration with NYPRO Inc., UML grants a plastics technology certificate and in collaboration with Nortel Networks, grants a data telecommunications certificate.

Applicants should hold a high school diploma or graduate equivalency diploma (GED).

University of Massachusetts Lowell

•

Online Degree and Certificate Programs

Program Delivery and Student Support

UML online students must secure an Internet service to access online coursework and to enable file transfer, as well as obtain a personal email account. Hardware should consist of a Pentium PC, or Macintosh, with 16 MB RAM and a 28.8 baud modem. Software should include a browser such as Netscape Navigator 4.05, Microsoft Internet Explorer 4.0, AOL 4.0 or more advanced versions.

CyberEd participants use password-secure websites, bulletin boards, chat rooms and other collaborative electronic environments. Textbooks and other materials are obtainable from the university bookstore online.

University and Location

The University of Massachusetts Lowell originated in a merger of Lowell State College and Lowell Technological Institute, which were founded in the 1890s. UML was integrated into the state university system in 1991. The university confers six associate degrees, 38 baccalaureate degrees, 30 master's degrees and 12 doctorates. UML's traditional academic programs enroll approximately 12,000 students and employ over 400 faculty members.

UML's facilities are scattered across three campuses in Lowell and Chelmsford. The north campus houses engineering, management and sciences, the south campus, health professions and arts, and the west campus, education. Library holdings include 400,000 volumes, 625,000 microforms, 3,500 videotapes and 3,700 periodicals. UML owns eight undergraduate residence halls, as well as apartments for graduate students, married students and those with children.

Incorporated as a city in 1826, Lowell, Massachusetts has a population of 103,000. The city is known historically for its preeminent role in the New England textile industry. Today, companies such as Wang Laboratories, Coca-Cola, NYNEX, Raytheon and Textron employ local residents.

Contact Information

Online Degree and Certificate Programs
One University Avenue
Lowell Massachusetts 01854-2881 USA
phone: 1-800-480-3190
fax: 1-978-934-4064
email: Continuing_Education@uml.edu
internet: http://cybered.uml.edu

Delivery Mode

• Online courses (Internet, email, chat rooms)
• UML Instructional Network (satellite uplinks, line-of-sight microwave, dedicated fiber-optic analog video, compressed video, consumer cable connections)

Program Facts

	Program Entry	Program Length	Total Enrollment	# of Int'l Students	Total Program Costs	Application Fee	Prerequisites
Associate of Science in Information Systems	three times yearly	4 years	–	–	US$615 per course	–	high school diploma or GED
Bachelor of Science in Information Systems	three times yearly	7 years	–	–	US$615 per course	–	ASIS degree requirements or 60 college credits
Data Telecommunications Certificate	three times yearly	1–2 years	–	–	US$615 per course	–	high school diploma or GED
Information Technology Fundamentals Certificate	three times yearly	1–2 years	–	–	US$615 per course	–	high school diploma or GED
Intranet Development Certificate	three times yearly	1–2 years	–	–	US$615 per course	–	high school diploma or GED
Multimedia Applications Certificate	three times yearly	1–2 years	–	–	US$615 per course	–	high school diploma or GED
Plastics Technology Certificate	three times yearly	1–2 years	–	–	US$615 per course	–	high school diploma or GED
UNIX Certificate	three times yearly	1–2 years	–	–	US$615 per course	–	high school diploma or GED

University of Nevada, Reno

•

Independent Learning Program

Highlights

- 150 academic credit courses in 29 subject areas available through independent study
- On-campus component not required
- Continuous enrollment throughout the year
- Up to one year to complete a course
- High School credit and continuing education (non-credit) options available

Programs Offered

Bachelor's Degree:
  General Studies (requires one semester or one summer attendance)

University Statistics

Year Founded:	1864
Undergraduate Enrollment	–
Graduate Enrollment:	–
Extension School Enrollment:	2,500

Program Overview

Through the Independent Learning Program (Independent Learning), the University of Nevada, Reno (UNR) offers undergraduate, high school and continuing education courses through correspondence and online study. More than 150 academic credit courses are offered at the baccalaureate level in twenty-nine subject areas. Correspondence courses are also offered in conjunction with the University of Nevada, Las Vegas.

Independent Learning students can enroll at any point during the year, either online or through traditional telephone, fax or in-person registration. On campus attendance is not a required component of ILP studies. However, all courses require the completion of proctored examinations, which can be administered in the student's home community by an approved proctor. Arrangements can be made for students outside the US, provided an approved proctor is arranged to facilitate the exam process. All credit courses and instructors are approved by the appropriate UNR department.

Study for University Credit

Independent Learning students can undertake study for university credit in the following areas: Accounting, Anthropology, Basque Studies, Criminal Justice, Curriculum and Instruction, Economics, Education, English, Environment, Foreign Languages (French, German, Italian, Spanish), Gaming Management, Geography, Health Ecology, History, Human Development & Family Studies, Journalism, Managerial Sciences, Mathematics, Music, Nutrition, Political Science, Psychology, Sociology, Western Traditions and Women's Studies. The William F. Harrah College of Hotel Administration at UNLV also offers correspondence courses in the following areas: hotel management, food & beverage, and travel & convention administration. A limited number of correspondence credits from these areas may be transferred to the Hotel Administration baccalaureate program at UNLV.

Independent Learning students can earn a maximum of 60 credits toward a baccalaureate degree at UNR through accepted correspondence study. Students who wish to transfer credit from completed correspondence courses to another institution are required to make specific arrangements with the intended university or college. The University of Nevada System Transfer Guide (www.unr.edu/stsv/trcenter) offers information on course transfer to other postsecondary institutions in Nevada.

For students who wish to pursue teacher certification in Nevada, the State Department of Education can provide information on the application of correspondence study to secure or renew the certificate.

Non-credit and Continuing Education

UNR offers Business CC (Business Writing) correspondence study for continuing education units (CEUs). The CEU is a nationally certified designation for participation in non-credit continuing education activities. One CEU is equivalent to ten hours of independent study instruction.

Political Science CA (Citizenship for New Americans) is a non-credit course offered for non-citizens who cannot attend regular classes. Textbooks are provided by the Immigration and Naturalization service through library loan

High School Credit

Students can earn high school credit through the High School Correspondence Program (HSCP). HSCP students communicate with instructors via mail, and have up to one year to complete correspondence courses. Courses are offered in the following areas: Algebra, American Government, American History, Applied Mathematics, Biology, Calculus, Computer Literacy, English, Geometry, Sociology and World History. Credit is granted by the high school whose requirements students plan to fulfill; students should consult with the school prior to undertaking correspondence study, to ensure that all requirements will be met by the proposed coursework.

Admission Procedures

University admission is not required to enroll in correspondence study. However, prospective students must meet any course prerequisites and provide appropriate verfication if required. High school students who wish to enroll in colleges courses may do so subject to approval.

A correspondence study enrollment form is available online (www.dce.unr.edu/istudy). Along with completed enrollment forms, students should submit payment for total course costs in US dollars, including course fees, stationery, handling and syllabus charges, textbooks and any deposits. Independent Learning students can also register by phone, fax or online with credit card payment. Students who live outside the US must pay an additional US$40–50 per course to receive and return course materials.

University of Nevada, Reno

Independent Learning Program

Program Delivery and Student Support

Independent Learning students can take up to one year to complete a course; instruction is delivered through course syllabi, textbooks, video and audio cassettes as well as reference and additional instructional materials. Course syllabi guide students on how to proceed through their studies, and outline assignment information. Instructors provide feedback and answer student questions prior to returning graded work.

Thirty courses are now delivered through the World Wide Web, and most courses accept email submissions for assignments and inquiries. Students enrolled in online (web) correspondence study courses should have access to a computer with a printer and Internet connection, and arrange an email account to correspond with instructors. Computers are not required for regular correspondence study.

University and Location

Established in 1864, The University of Nevada, Reno is oldest university in the University and Community College System of Nevada, and provides university credit through independent study to the state of Nevada. The university enrolls over 2,500 students in independent study, and has an annual total student population of over 15,000 students engaged in undergraduate and graduate studies. UNR is accredited by the Northwest Association of Schools and Colleges Commission on Colleges.

UNR is located on 255 acres near the Sierra Nevada Range. The surrounding Reno-Sparks metropolitan area is known for its bustling commercial center and entertainment venues, as well as a range of cultural and sporting attractions including The Nevada Museum of Art, the UNR Wolf Pack athletic teams and activities at nearby Lake Tahoe resort.

Contact Information

Independent Learning Program
Attn: Ms. Carley Ries, Asst. Director, Mailstop 050
Reno Nevada 89557 USA
phone: 1-775-784-4652
fax: 1-775-784-1280
email: istudy@nevada.unr.edu
internet: www.dce.unr.edu

Delivery Mode

- Audio tapes
- Videotapes
- Course manuals
- CD-ROMs
- Internet
- Textbooks

Program Facts

	Program Entry	Program Length	Total Enrollment	# of Int'l Students	Total Program Costs	Application Fee	Prerequisites
Baccalaureate Courses	continuous	n/a	2,000	–	varies	n/a	Applicable prerequisites for individual courses; high school students can enroll with approval
High School Credit courses	continuous	n/a	500	–	varies	n/a	Applicable prerequisites for individual courses
Non-credit courses	continuous	n/a	10	–	varies	n/a	n/a

University of North Texas

•

Highlights

- MS degree in six disciplines offered through distance or distance/on-campus components
- BS program in Applied Behavior Analysis
- Teacher School Library certification and Gifted & Talented Education endorsement
- Certificate programs in Volunteer Management and Applied Gerontology

Programs Offered

Bachelor's Degrees:
  Behavior Analysis
Certificates:
  Applied Gerontology
  Volunteer Management
Certifications:
  Gifted and Talented Endorsement
  School Library Endorsement
Master's Degrees:
  Applied Gerontology
  Computer Education & Cognitive Systems
  Hospitality Management
  Information Science
  Library Science
  Merchandising

University Statistics

Year Founded:	1890
Total Enrollment:	27,054
Undergraduate Enrollment	21,059
Graduate Enrollment:	5,995
Distance Education Enrollment:	varies

Program Overview

The University of North Texas (UNT) offers master of science (MS) and bachelor of science (BS) degrees, certificates and teacher endorsements through distance and online learning.

UNT students can complete the two-year MS degree in library science, information science, hospitality management, merchandising, computer education & cognitive systems, or applied gerontology. A graduate Specialist Certificate in Applied Gerontology is also offered. The BS program in Behavior Analysis prepares students for occupations involving behavior analysis and problem-solving in educational, business and institutional settings, and can be completed in four years.

One-year teaching endorsement specializations are offered in School Library or Gifted & Talented Education. The certificate program in volunteer management is designed for professionals and students who wish to enhance their career prospects through specialized training in volunteer management, leadership, community asset mapping, program planning and evaluation.

Master of Science

The Master of Science in Library or Information Science comprises 36 graduate credit hours; a grade point average (GPA) of 3.0 or better and a final comprehensive examination are required. UNT offers the MS both online and via videoconference. The online option includes an eight-day institute on campus in Denton (June 2–10, 2001) or at the University of Minnesota (September 7–10, 2001 and January 10–14, 2002) with the remaining coursework provided online. Videoconference programs are offered to various sites in Texas and also through the UNT Videoconference Network.

The MS programs in Merchandising and Hospitality Management require the completion of 24 credits (eight courses) through web instruction, and a remaining 12 credit hours taken in residence or through transfer credit. A six-hour thesis option is available for students who take less than 50 percent of coursework via the web.

UNT offers the MS in Computer Education & Cognitive Systems, with specialization in either Instructional Systems Technology or Teaching & Learning with Technology. Both specializations require of a minimum of 36 semester hours, and include core courses in Instructional Systems Design, Human Computer Interaction, Analysis of Research in Educational Technology and Readings in Computer Education and Cognitive Systems.

The MS in Applied Gerontology is a 45-hour graduate degree program that combines distance learning instruction with an internship. The program offers specialization in Administration of Long-term Care & Retirement Facilities, Administration of Aging Organizations or Applied Gerontology, and includes 12 semester hours of core courses in aging, plus track-related coursework.

Bachelor of Science

The BS in Applied Behavior Analysis requires a total of 124 semester credit hours, of which 34 hours must be taken in Applied Behavior Analysis. Additional university core requirements and a selected minor or electives complete the program. The combined distance/on-campus curriculum is designed to develop student skills in the areas of measuring, analyzing and changing behavior, and can serve as the basis for career applications or graduate study.

Certificate-level Study

School Library Certification comprises 18 credit hours and endorses certified teachers for elementary or secondary school librarianship. Courses are offered through online instruction or on-campus components at partner universities. Teacher endorsement in Gifted & Talented (GT) Education is available through an online four-course program. The Certificate in Volunteer Management can be taken online at the undergraduate or graduate level; the program involves 12 course hours of study and 48 hours of service with a community agency. An 18-hour graduate Specialist Certificate in Applied Gerontology is also offered.

Admission Requirements

MS applicants should have a bachelor's degree, a grade point average (GPA) of 3.0 in the last 60 hours of coursework (or 2.8 overall) and provide standardized test scores (e.g. GRE, GMAT, MCAT, etc.) as required by each department. International students must demonstrate proficiency in spoken & written English, which may include a TOEFL test score. BS applicants should have a high school diploma and submit SAT/ACT scores.

UNT application deadlines are June 15 (BS, fall), July 15 (MS, fall), November 20 (MS, spring) and December 1 (BS, spring). Summer admission is also available. All applicants should consult UNT online (www.unt.edu) for full application procedures.

University of North Texas

•

Program Delivery and Student Support

UNT students should have access to an IBM/Intel Pentium-90 PC or Apple Macintosh Power-PC or better, with 32 megabytes of RAM (minimum), two gigabyte hard drive, monitor, sound card and speakers, and Internet access. Online course components require PCs to be running Windows 95 or Windows NT 4.0, or Macintoshs to be running System 7.5 or better. Some degree programs have specific software requirements and should be consulted for specifications.

All students enrolled at UNT are eligible for a free email account through the EagleMail email service. Students can register for courses online through WebReg, and can undertake research or receive assistance through online or telephone contact with Financial Aid, the Registrar's Office, Student Accounting, UNT Libraries, and a variety of online campus resources.

University and Location

Originally established as the Texas Normal College and Teacher Training Institute in 1890, the University of North Texas has awarded over 164,900 degrees at the bachelor, master and doctoral levels. UNT was officially designated a university system in 1999, and the newly-built UNT System Center in Dallas now offers junior-, senior- and graduate-level study to students in Dallas and Ellis counties. The UNT system includes UNT in Denton, the UNT Health Science Center at Fort Worth and the UNT System Center at Dallas.

UNT has been listed as one of America's 100 Most Wired Colleges. The UNT Videoconference Network maintains a variety of on- and off-campus classrooms in the Dallas-Forth Worth Metroplex area, equipped with modern techhnological resources for interactive video teaching and learning. The university's library system, named a major research library by the US Department of Education, provides online access to over 2 million catalogued holdings. The main UNT campus occupies 498 acres in Denton, Texas, part of the Dallas-Forth Worth Metroplex area. Denton affords easy access to many attractions, including the Dallas Museums of Art and Natural History, and the Kimbell Art Museum.

Contact Information

PO Box 311277
Denton Texas 76203 USA
phone: 1-800-868-8211
fax: 1-940-369-7619
email: cdl@unt.edu
internet: http://courses.unt.edu

Delivery Mode

- Internet
- Two-way video
- CD-Rom
- Course Manuals
- Teleconferencing
- Email

Program Facts

	Program Entry	Program Length	Total Enrollment	# of Int'l Students	Total Program Costs	Application Fee	Prerequisites
BS - Behavior Analysis	Aug, Jan, Jun	4 years	68	14	$30,000	$25	High school diploma; SAT/ACT scores
Certificate - Volunteer Mgmt	Aug, Jan, Jun	4 courses	92	n/avail	n/avail	$25; $50 (int'l)	Admission to UNT
MS - Applied Gerontology	Aug, Jan, Jun	2 years	44	6	$12,000	$25; $50 (int'l)	Undergraduate degree
MS - Comp Ed & Cognitive Systems	Aug, Jan, Jun	2 years	105	29	$12,000	$25; $50 (int'l)	Standardized test scores (GRE, GMAT, MCAT, etc)
MS - Hospitality Management	Aug, Jan, Jun	2 years	8	3	$12,000	$25; $50 (int'l)	Standardized test scores (GRE, GMAT, MCAT, etc.)
MS - Library or Info Science	Aug, Jan, Jun	2 years	335	46	$12,000	$25; $50 (int'l)	Standardized test scores (GRE, GMAT, MCAT, etc.)
MS - Merchandising	Aug, Jan, Jun	2 years	11	7	$12,000	$25; $50 (int'l)	Standardized test scores (GRE, GMAT, MCAT, etc.)
Teaching Endorsement: School Library /Gifted	Aug, Jan, Jun	1 year	175 / 112	n/avail	$2,000	$25; $50 (int'l)	Teaching certification

University of Tennessee

•

Distance Education and Independent Study

- MS and MBA degrees available
- Applied Statistical Strategies graduate certificate program
- Professional certificate study for Internet Technology careers

Programs Offered

Graduate Certificates:
  Applied Statistical Strategies
Graduate Degrees:
  Business Administration (PEMBA)
  Industrial Engineering (MS)
  Information Sciences (MS)
  Nuclear Engineering (MS)
Professional Certificates (Internet Technology):
  Administrative Technology Assistant
  E-Commerce Analyst
  Help Desk Specialist
  Instructional Technology Developer
  Internet Professional
  Network Systems Engineer
  Technical Sales Professional
  Web Database Developer
  Webmaster Developer

University Statistics

Year Founded:	1794
Total Enrollment:	26,064
Undergraduate Enrollment:	20,334
Graduate Enrollment:	5,730
Distance Education Enrollment:	2,600

Program Overview

Through the Department of Distance Education and Independent Study, the University of Tennessee (UT) offers a variety of flexibly delivered programs for distance learners. Real-time Internet-based courses are being introduced at the upper-undergraduate and graduate levels, allowing both "click-to-learn" self study and voice/data interactive learning. Interactive (two-way) video and videotapes are used to deliver graduate degrees.

Graduate Degree Programs

The university offers a number of master's level programs of study.

The MS in Industrial Engineering/ Engineering Management is available to students via videotape. Prospective students must have a bachelor's degree in engineering or a related scientific or technical field.

The MS in Information Sciences is accredited by the American Library Association. This program is available to students via the Internet and requires 42 semester hours of graduate courses. The core curriculum consists of five courses. The focus of this program is on electronic as well as traditional print media.

The MS in Nuclear Engineering is available to students via the Internet, and requires 24 semester hours of graduate courses. The program is intended for those students interested in careers in nuclear engineering, health physics or radiological engineering.

Three Executive MBA programs are also offered through the UT College of Business Administration.

Students may transfer up to six hours of credit from an accredited university to a UT master's degree program. In the Information Sciences program, some elective hours may be earned through directed independent study projects; such credits are generally transferable to other colleges and universities toward the completion of a degree.

Grad Certificate in Applied Statistical Strategies

UT's Graduate Certificate in Applied Statistical Strategies focuses on the practical application of advanced statistical tools useful in several professional career tracks.

Each student chooses three courses that best meet individualized needs, designing customized course tracks that focus on manufacturing & engineering data or service industry & business. Combining courses from both tracks is also possible.

Students learn at desktop computers using current Internet delivery technology or take an intensive short course on the University of Tennessee campus at Knoxville. In both cases, students participate in a class of working adults focused on practical answers to tough data analysis questions. More information about this certificate program is available on the Internet (http://www.outreach.utk. edu/cyberstats/).

Professional Certificates in Internet Technology

The Internet eLearning Institute (IEI) provides certificate programs, professional development courses and training for information technology professionals or individuals wanting expertise in Internet technology. Courses are offered over the World Wide Web in the areas of e-commerce, web databases, web mastering, network systems engineering, administrative technology, technical sales and instructional technology. For more information, students should consult the IEI web site (http://www.iei.utk.edu/).

Requirements for Admission

Application to the Graduate School is required for credit or audit of distance education courses. Admission requires a bachelor's degree with a minimum grade point average (GPA) of 2.7 overall (on a 4.0 scale) or 3.0 during the senior year of undergraduate study. Applicants must have a GPA of at least 3.0 or the equivalent in any previous graduate work. The various degree programs may have individual requirements.

Admission is not required to take undergraduate correspondence courses. Enrollees are encouraged to obtain an adviser's signature in support of taking courses via independent study enrollment. IEI web classes are designed for existing Information Technology (IT) professionals interested in updating their Internet skills and for students seeking quality web training to pursue new IT careers. Admission to the university is not required.

Tuition and Fees

In 2000–2001, in-state tuition at UT was US$118 per undergraduate and US$192 per graduate semester hour; out-of-state tuition was US$431 per undergraduate and US$584 per graduate semester hour. Undergraduate correspondence/independent study courses cost US$118 per undergraduate semester hour. IEI professional certificate course fees vary according to course.

University of Tennessee

•

Distance Education and Independent Study

Program Delivery and Student Support

University of Tennessee courses are delivered via videotapes, audiotapes, computer software and conferencing, the Internet and print. Students and teachers may meet in person or interact via audio conferencing, mail, telephone, fax, email and the World Wide Web. Students may require access to the following equipment: television, videocassette player, computer, modem, Internet access, email.

Students registered in UT distance education master's degree programs have access to university computer resources. A distance education librarian assists off-campus students with reference searches and obtaining materials through interlibrary loan. Academic advising is provided by telephone and e-mail, and through group sessions for students in interactive programs.

University and Location

The University of Tennessee is a state-supported university and is accredited by the Southern Association of Colleges and Schools. The university first offered distance learning courses in 1923 and currently delivers courses to homes, workplaces, military bases, hospitals, The University of Tennessee at Chattanooga (Chattanooga) and The University of Tennessee at Martin (Martin).

Contact Information

Distance Education and Independent Study
Outreach & Continuing Education, 1534 White Ave.
Knoxville Tennessee 37996-1525 USA
phone: 1-800-670-8657
fax: 1-865-974-6629
email: disteducation@utk.edu
internet: http://anywhere.tennessee.edu

Delivery Mode

• Videotape
• Audiotape
• Computer software
• Computer conferencing
• World Wide Web
• Print

Program Facts

	Program Entry	Program Length	Total Enrollment	# of Int'l Students	Total Program Costs	Application Fee	Prerequisites
Certificate in Applied Statistical Strategies	Aug, Jan, Jun	9 credit hours	–	–	US$192 (IS) US$584 (OS)	US$35	Undergraduate degree; minimum GPA of 2.7 overall or 3.0 in senior year
Executive MBA	Jan	1 year	–	–	US$192 (IS) US$584 (OS)	US$35	Requirements vary
MS Programs	–	–	–	–	US$192 (IS) US$584 (OS)	US$35	Undergraduate degree; minimum GPA of 2.7 overall or 3.0 in senior year
Professional Certificates in Internet Education	ongoing	varies	–	–	vary	US$50	working knowledge of computing

University of Wisconsin - Whitewater

●

College of Business & Economics

University Statistics

Year Founded:	1868
Total Enrollment:	9,915
Undergraduate Enrollment	8,726
Graduate Enrollment:	1,189
Distance Education Enrollment:	450

Program Overview

The College of Business and Economics at the University of Wisconsin - Whitewater (UW-Whitewater) offers a Certificate in Human Resources Management and an Online Master of Business Administration (MBA) through distance education. The Human Resources (HR) certificate program allows field professionals with bachelor's degrees in other areas to acquire HR management knowledge. Students enrolled in the Online MBA program at UW-Whitewater can select from one of four focus areas: Finance, International Business, Management or Marketing. Courses are delivered over the Internet and via CD-ROM, and students can undertake all requirements for the degree online.

Certificate in Human Resources Management

The HR certificate program requires the completion of five courses covering key areas of HR practice, including compensation & benefits, training & development, management & labor relations, strategic HR management and international management. Students enrolled in the HR Certificate program can enroll in the Online MBA program, provided they meet the necessary requirements for admission.

Online MBA Program

UW-Whitewater's Online MBA program provides students with the opportunity to undertake an MBA degree from virtually anywhere in the world. The program is designed for students who would like a flexible study schedule and who can effectively work on their own using a computer and communicating with classmates and instructors by email, phone and fax. The MBA program is accredited by the American Assembly of Collegiate Schools of Business.

The Online MBA program incorporates a case method approach and provides advanced understanding of how individual, team and organizational-level behavior affects organizational operations. Students develop skills in collecting, analyzing and interpreting data, as well as in addressing business problems through the conceptualization, evaluation and implementation of solutions. All course requirements can be completed online.

Program curriculum covers accounting, business education, economics, finance & business law, management and marketing. Students have the option of focussing their studies through advanced coursework in finance, international business, management or marketing. The degree comprises 36 credits, of which six credits can be designated for thesis work. At least 30 credits must be undertaken from breadth, elective and emphasis areas; for students without prior business preparation, a Common Body of Knowledge of 0–15 credits is required in addition to the standard degree requirements. A grade point average (GPA) of 3.0 is required for overall graduate coursework and must be maintained in core and emphasis courses.

Online MBA students can enter the program in August, January or May, and courses are offered in the fall, spring and summer semesters. Provided students meet the Common Body of Knowledge requirements, the degree can be completed in as little as one calendar year through full-time enrollment. The average period required to complete the program part-time is three to four years.

Application Requirements

Applicants to the Online MBA program should have a baccalaureate degree in arts, humanities, sciences, engineering, education or business from an accredited school. In addition to standard application materials, prospective students should submit Graduate Management Admission Test (GMAT) composite scores of 1000–1050. International students whose first language is not English must submit a paper-based TOEFL score of 550, or an equivalent score on another test. Due to increasing enrollment, these minimum requirements may not guarantee acceptance to the program. Exceptions to admission requirements may be made on a case-by-case basis.

HR certificate program applicants should have a bachelor's degree from a regionally-accredited school, and provide evidence of their ability to succeed in graduate level Human Resources coursework. This can be fulfilled by including outlined work experience, GMAT scores and evidence of professional certification (e.g. PHR, SPHR) with their admission application.

In addition to the materials listed above, applicants to the Online MBA and HR certificate programs should submit a completed graduate application form, official transcripts of all undergraduate and graduate coursework and the US$45 application fee. An online application is available at http://www.applyweb.com/aw?uww . Applications should reach the Graduate Admissions Office by the following deadlines: July 15 (fall), December 1 (spring), May 1 (summer).

University of Wisconsin - Whitewater

College of Business & Economics

Program Delivery and Student Support

The LearningSpace database system is the primary tool used by UW - Whitewater to deliver on-line courses. Through LearningSpace, students access print-based and multimedia course materials, take tests and exams, interact with fellow students and faculty both asynchronously and synchronously, and learn more about their cohorts through online profiles. UW-Whitewater instructors also supplement course materials on CD-ROM, providing an introductory course video and allowing students to view the course lectures/demonstrations as if they were in the classroom.

To access course materials, students should use a Pentium class PC with 32MB RAM (64MB preferred), a 28.8 kbps modem (56K preferred), a CD-ROM drive, Windows 3.1/95/98/NT, an Internet Service Provider (ISP) account and a properly-installed browser. Courses are accessed directly through the Internet, or via Lotus Notes Client software (provided free of charge).

University and Location

The University of Wisconsin - Whitewater was founded in 1868 as a normal school for teacher training. After progressing to State Teachers College, State College and State University status, the university became a member of the University of Wisconsin (UW) system along with nine other schools in 1972. The UW System now includes 13 universities and 13 two-year centers, and represents the fourth largest system of higher education in the US.

UW - Whitewater is situated in southeastern Wisconsin, approximately 45 miles southeast of Madison and 100 miles northwest of Chicago, Illinois. The university offers more than 60 majors in four undergraduate colleges—The Arts & Communication, Business & Education, Economics, and Letters & Sciences—and 16 disciplines of graduate study. UW - Whitewater's graduate school is the fourth largest in the UW system and has conferred over 9,000 master's degrees.

Contact Information

College of Business & Economics
800 W Main Street
Whitewater Wisconsin 53190 USA
phone: 1-262-472-1945
fax: 1-262-472-4863
email: zahnd@mail.uww.edu
internet: http://www.uww.edu

Graduate Studies Office
Roseman 2015
Whitewater Wisconsin 53190 USA
        1-262-472-1006; 1-800-628-4559 (toll free)
        1-262-472-5210
        gradschl@mail.uww.edu
        http://www.uww.edu/gradstudies

Delivery Mode

- Peer Interaction & Instructor Feedback
- Instructional CD
- Case Study
- Internet (Asynchronous)
- Group Projects

Program Facts

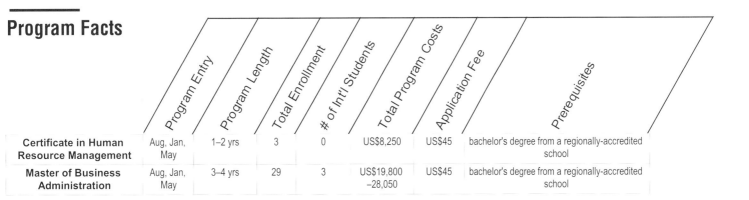

	Program Entry	Program Length	Total Enrollment	# of Int'l Students	Total Program Costs	Application Fee	Prerequisites
Certificate in Human Resource Management	Aug, Jan, May	1–2 yrs	3	0	US$8,250	US$45	bachelor's degree from a regionally-accredited school
Master of Business Administration	Aug, Jan, May	3–4 yrs	29	3	US$19,800 –28,050	US$45	bachelor's degree from a regionally-accredited school

University of Wyoming
•
The Outreach School

Highlights

- UW degrees earned through Outreach Credit Courses and UW/Casper College Center
- Admission to UW not required for flexible enrollment
- Innovative online degree and certificate programs
- Library Outreach Services provide research materials and database access

Programs Offered

Bachelor's Degrees:
- Business Administration
- Communication
- Criminal Justice
- Elementary Education
- Family and Consumer Sciences
- Humanities and Fine Arts
- Mathematics and Science
- Nursing
- Psychology
- Social Science
- Social Work

Certificate Programs:
- Early Childhood Program Director
- Land Surveying
- Real Estate

Master's Degrees:
- Adult and Postsecondary Education
- Business Administration (MBA)
- Counselor Education
- Curriculum and Instruction
- Instructional Technology
- Kinesiology and Health
- Nursing (Nurse Educator Option)
- Public Administration (MPA)
- Social Work (MSW)
- Special Education
- Speech-Language Pathology
- Teaching and Learning

University Statistics

Year Founded:	1886
Total Enrollment:	11,057
Undergraduate Enrollment:	7,686
Graduate Enrollment:	1,377
Distance Education Enrollment:	1,571

Program Overview

The Outreach School at the University of Wyoming (UW) offers distance education degree programs through two divisions and the UW/Casper College (UW/CC) Center. The Division of Outreach Credit Programs (DOCP) offers credit courses to students across Wyoming and the nation via compressed video, audio teleconferencing, flexible enrollment and Online UW, the university's virtual campus. DOCP also produces University of Wyoming Television. The Division of Community Service Education coordinates conferences, institutes and community enrichment programs and produces Wyoming Public Radio. Distance education at UW enrolls approximately 2,000 students.

Several special scholarships are available for distance education students including the Summer Session Extended Degree, Helen L. Hasbrouck and John Christopher Memorial scholarships. Students must have a minimum 3.0 cumulative GPA at the time of application for the Summer Session and Helen L. Hasbrouck scholarships, while the John Christopher Memorial Scholarship is distributed on the basis of financial need and academic performance.

Other educational institutions that prepare students for the UW degree programs via distance education include Central Wyoming, Eastern Wyoming, Western Wyoming, Northern Wyoming, Laramie County Community and Northwest colleges.

Outreach Credit Courses

UW offers the following degrees through The Outreach School: bachelor of arts in criminal justice, psychology, or social science; bachelor of science in business administration, social science, or family and consumer sciences (professional child development option); RN/BSN completion in nursing; master of arts in education with concentrations in teaching and learning, special education, or adult and post-secondary education; master of science in education with a concentration in instructional technology, speech and language pathology, kinesiology and health, or nursing (nurse educator option); master of business administration; master of public administration; or master of social work.

Nondegree credit programs include a certification in real estate, a land surveying certificate and an early childhood program director's certificate. The Western Integrated Resource Education (WIRE) program is also available. The program trains farm and ranch managers and is available through Online UW. It has been favorably reviewed not only in Wyoming, but elsewhere in the US (Idaho, Utah and Montana), Canada (Saskatchewan) and Australia (Queensland).

The DOCP incorporated over 50 courses into the division's 2000 Online UW curriculum. Online classes operate on a semester schedule and are primarily "asynchronous", which means students can participate in the class at their own convenience during a given week. Online degree programs include the bachelor's degree in business administration, RN/BSN completion, bachelor's degree in family and consumer sciences (professional child development option), nurse educator master's degree, master's degree in instructional technology, real estate certification or early childhood program director's certificate.

Beginning fall 2001, resident tuition plus an outreach delivery fee is charged to all students regardless of their location. Students seeking a degree through outreach credit courses must be admitted to UW before admission to The Outreach School is granted. The appropriate undergraduate or graduate application forms must be submitted to the UW Admissions office.

Flexible Enrollment Courses

UW addresses the needs of site-bound students by allowing six to nine months to complete flexible enrollment (FE) courses, formerly known as correspondence study. About 60 courses in agriculture, arts and sciences, business, education and health sciences comprise the FE curriculum.

FE courses have the same content and requirements as on-campus courses and are therefore designed for highly motivated students. Since registration in an FE course does not require admission, and the term of the course is not semester bound, students cannot obtain financial aid. Credit earned through FE cannot be applied to a graduate degree.

Students who have graduation or recertification deadlines or eligibility requirements must submit their final assignment at least two weeks before they need documentation of course completion.

UW/CC Center

The UW/CC Center is a residential campus located in Casper, Wyoming. It provides students from Casper and the surrounding areas the option of enrolling in UW courses leading to undergraduate or graduate degrees.

University of Wyoming

●

The Outreach School

Program Delivery and Student Support

UW delivers outreach credit courses through several electronic media and classroom settings. Electronic media include audio teleconferencing, compressed video and Online UW. Audio teleconferencing and compressed video courses usually require a minimum enrollment of 25 students from sites in Wyoming and nationwide. University of Wyoming Television is responsible for coordinating the DOCP's compressed video courses. Outreach credit courses are also delivered through on-site and intensive day and weekend classes in various regions around the state.

Students can obtain books, articles and audiovisual materials through the UW's Library Outreach Services. Reference or research assistance is also available. Electronic databases and the university's online library catalogs are accessible through a normal PC and modem.

University and Location

The University of Wyoming was founded as a public institution in 1886 and is located in Laramie, a community of approximately 27,000 in southeastern Wyoming. The university has a total enrollment of 11,057, 79 percent of whom come from Wyoming and three percent of whom come from countries other than the US. UW awards undergraduate and graduate degrees through seven colleges including agriculture, arts and sciences, business, education, engineering, health sciences and law. The university is accredited by the North Central Association of Colleges and Secondary Schools. UW is one of only 12 public universities to have been honored with two Rhodes scholars in the past seven years.

UW operates regional offices in Casper, Cheyenne, Torrington, Powell, Riverton, Rock Springs, Sheridan and Gillette. Seven libraries together containing 1.2 million books and bound journals, 12,960 active periodicals, 2.8 million microfilms and 165,900 maps serve UW students. The Centennial Complex houses the American Heritage Center and the UW Art Museum. The university operates six residence halls and 605 one-, two- and three-bedroom apartments. Support services include personal, career, academic and educational opportunity counseling, health care and resources for students with disabilities.

Contact Information

The Outreach School
Office of Outreach Credit Programs, PO Box 3274
Laramie Wyoming 82071-3274 USA
phone: 1-800-448-7801
fax: 1-307-766-3445
email: occ@uwyo.edu
internet: http://outreach.uwyo.edu

Delivery Mode

- Audio teleconferencing
- Compressed video
- Flexible enrollment
- Web-based instruction
- Regional on-site instruction

Program Facts

	Program Entry	Program Length	Total Enrollment	# of Int'l Students	Total Program Costs	Application Fee	Prerequisites
Bachelor of Arts or Bachelor of Science	any semester	120–130 credit hours	–	–	US$96.50/ credit hour	US$35	high school diploma with a 2.75–3.0 cumulative GPA
Early Childhood Program Director's Certificate	any semester	–	–	–	US$96.50/ credit hour	–	undergraduate degree with a 3.0 cumulative GPA or equivalent work experience
Land Surveying Certificate	any semester	24 credit hours	–	–	US$175/ credit hour	–	land surveying experience
Master of Arts, Science or Public Admin	any semester	30 credit hours minimum	–	–	US$160.85/ credit hour	–	undergraduate degree with a 3.0 cumulative GPA or equivalent work experience
Master of Business Administration	any semester	30 credit hours minimum	–	–	US$206.75/ credit hour	–	undergraduate degree with a 3.0 cumulative GPA or equivalent work experience
Master of Social Work	any semester	30 credit hours	–	–	$349.70/ credit hour	–	undergraduate degree with a 3.0 cumulative GPA or equivalent work experience
Real Estate Certification	any semester	18 credit hours	–	–	US$96.50/ credit hour	–	–
Western Integrated Resource Education	not applicable	varies	–	–	US$96.50/ to $160.85/cr hr	–	–

Upper Iowa University

•

Master of Arts in Business Leadership

- BS and MABL degree requirements are obtainable entirely online
- Students can begin the program during any one of six terms annually
- MABL Applicants with a GPA of 2.5 or higher need not take the GRE or GMAT
- Asynchronous classes eliminate isolation and allow students to log on at anytime, from anywhere with Internet access

Bachelor of Science:
  Accounting
  Management
  Marketing
  Technology & Information Management

Master of Arts in Business Leadership:
  (Now four areas of emphasis)
  Accounting Emphasis
  Human Resources Management Emphasis
  Organizational Development Emphasis
  Quality Management Emphasis

Year Founded:	1857
Total Enrollment:	4,860
Undergraduate Enrollment	4,660
Graduate Enrollment:	200
Distance Education Enrollment:	1,850

Program Overview

Upper Iowa University (UIU) offers a Bachelor of Science (BS) degree and a Master of Arts in Business Leadership (MABL) to distance learners.

BS degree students must complete a total of 120 semester credits, through transfer of not less than 36 semester credits and not more than 90 semester credits from regionally accredited colleges and universities, as well as completion of at least 30 semester credits through UIU online courses. The degree is offered in business, with majors available in Accounting, Management, Technology & Information Management, and Marketing.

The MABL degree consists of 36 semester credits of graduate work. Students without an undergraduate business degree may need to enhance their preparation with additional selected coursework. Students can opt for one of four emphases: Accounting, Human Resource Management, Quality Management or Organizational Development.

The learning experience for both programs is enhanced through the involvement of classmates with experience in business, government and nonprofit agencies.

Program Objectives

The BS program is designed to provide graduates with a sound background in the broad concepts of business and business management. Students are expected to develop a broad understanding of how businesses operate, the role of business in both the economy and society, how managers function to achieve business objectives, as well as specific technical strength in one of the major areas. Special emphasis is placed on the organizational, analytical and professional skills required for success in student's major area. Graduates are prepared to deal with individuals, groups and ideas.

The MABL program prepares graduates to successfully apply management theory to business and organizational problems. In addition to providing a strong theoretical foundation, the program focuses students on the analysis of issues, identification of solutions and implementation of appropriate actions. This blend of theory and practice is enhanced through interaction with an academically qualified faculty.

The Accounting emphasis is designed for students planning to sit for the CPA examination and includes a 150-hour education requirement. Students choosing this emphasis must have an undergraduate

accounting major or 30 semester credits of undergraduate accounting coursework. Course materials cover major aspects of the uniform CPA examination.

The Human Resource Management emphasis is designed to provide advanced managerial skills in professional HR functions such as employment laws, hiring practices, compensation & benefits programs, and tactical & strategic planning.

The Quality Management emphasis is designed to provide managers and executives with the knowledge and skills needed to integrate quality principles into all aspects of an organization. Organizations that can engage in quality-based competition are more likely to be successful and offer higher rates of return to their stakeholder groups.

The Organizational Development emphasis is designed to provide managers and executives with the ability to identify, plan and lead collaborative change within organizations, through the application of organizational development and intervention methods. This emphasis also addresses the skills needed to diagnose and correct problems related to organizational culture.

Prerequisites and Admission Procedures

Students entering the BS program must satisfy general education requirements outside the online program and have a 2.0 GPA in all prior undergraduate coursework. Learners must transfer at least 36 semester credits to the program, including satisfaction of all general education requirements, and not more than 90 semester credits.

MABL applicants with a bachelor's degree must have a minimum cumulative 2.5 grade point average (GPA) in undergraduate coursework, a minimum 2.7 GPA during the most recent 60 semester hours of coursework, or acceptable GMAT or GRE scores. Students who have not majored in business may need to take certain undergraduate prerequisites. Successful completion of CLEP testing will also satisfy prerequisites. Students with previous graduate-level academic experience must have attained a minimum cumulative GPA of 3.0. International applicants should submit TOEFL scores.

To apply, students submit an application form (which can be downloaded at www.uiu. edu/online/index.html), the US$50 nonrefundable application fee, and official transcripts of previous academic experience. The Online program accepts students on a continuous enrollment basis.

Upper Iowa University

Master of Arts in Business Leadership

Program Delivery and Student Support

Participants in the online MABL program use asynchronous communication. This mode of distance learning eliminates the isolation typical of independent study courses. Students can also contact instructors via telephone or email. Students can participate in class by logging on once each day, at any time, at least five days per week.

Program coordinators recommend that students have access to a Pentium processor, SVGA monitor, Windows 95, 32 MB RAM, free disk space and 28.8 or 56 baud modem. After enrollment, UIU provides each student with Convene, an online course access application.

The UIU bookstore accepts textbook orders by telephone or email. The university's library catalogs, electronic databases, career and counseling services, student writing labs and tutorial services are accessible online.

University and Location

Upper Iowa University was established in 1857 and has since become the second largest private university in the state. UIU is a four-year institution that confers degrees through four residential academic divisions, 11 off-campus centers throughout Iowa, Kansas, Wisconsin and Louisiana, three international sites in Hong Kong, Singapore and Malaysia; and an external degree program that offers independent study courses worldwide. Approximately 4,440 students are engaged in undergraduate programs and 150 students are enrolled in graduate programs. UIU is accredited by the Commission on Institutions of Higher Education of the North Central Association of Colleges and Schools (email: info@ncacihe.org; phone: (312) 263-0456).

One of the UIU libraries claims the distinction of being among the nearly 100 postsecondary libraries in the US endowed by Andrew Carnegie. Students wishing to improve or maintain their fitness can use tennis and volleyball courts, a softball field and an athletic complex and stadium on campus.

UIU is located in Fayette, a community of approximately 1,317 in northeast Iowa. Fayette is home to Volga River Lake State Park, which provides opportunities for canoeing, cross-country skiing, fishing, hiking and sailing.

Contact Information

Master of Arts in Business Leadership
PO Box 1857, 605 Washington Street
Fayette Iowa 52142-1857 USA
phone: 1-800-773-9298
fax: 1-319-425-5771
email: online@uiu.edu
internet: http://www.uiu.edu/online/index.html

Delivery Mode

- Asynchronous communication
- Commercial email
- Telephone

Program Facts

	Program Entry	Program Length	Total Enrollment	# of Int'l Students	Total Program Costs	Application Fee	Prerequisites
BS: Accounting	six times yearly	eight weeks per course	–	–	US$648 per course	US$50	UIU gen'l educ requirements (min 36 hrs); minimum 2.5 GPA in prior u/grad coursework
BS: Management	six times yearly	eight weeks per course	–	–	US$648 per course	US$50	UIU gen'l educ requirements (min 36 hrs); minimum 2.5 GPA in prior u/grad coursework
BS: Marketing	six times yearly	eight weeks per course	–	–	US$648 per course	US$50	UIU gen'l educ requirements (min 36 hrs); minimum 2.5 GPA in prior u/grad coursework
BS: Technology & Info Management	six times yearly	eight weeks per course	–	–	US$648 per course	US$50	UIU gen'l educ requirements (min 36 hrs); minimum 2.5 GPA in prior u/grad coursework
MABL: Accounting Emphasis	six times yearly	eight weeks per courses	–	–	US$870 per course	US$50	BA, BS or 30 u/grad sem cr in accounting; GRE, GMAT or a minimum 2.5 GPA
MABL: Human Resources Management Emphasis	six times yearly	eight weeks per course	–	–	US$870 per course	US$50	bachelor's degree; GRE, GMAT or a minimum 2.5 GPA
MABL: Organization Development Emphasis	six times yearly	eight weeks per course	–	–	US$870 per course	US$50	bachelor's degree; GRE, GMAT or a minimum 2.5 GPA
MABL: Quality Management Emphasis	six times yearly	eight weeks per course	–	–	US$870 per course	US$50	bachelor's degree; GRE, GMAT or a minimum 2.5 GPA

Vincennes University

•

Distance Education/Degree Completion Program

Programs Offered

Associate in Applied Science:
- Business Studies
- General Studies
- Law Enforcement Studies

Associate in Arts:
- Behavioral Science

Associate in Science:
- Behavioral Science
- Business Administration
- General Studies
- Health Information Management (HIM)
- Law Enforcement
- Recreation Management

Other Programs:
- Emergency Medical Services
- Fire Science & Safety Technology
- Surgical Technology
- Technology Apprenticeship

University Statistics

Year Founded:	1801
Total Enrollment:	6,134
Undergraduate Enrollment	6,134
Graduate Enrollment:	n/a
Distance Education Enrollment:	1,700

Program Overview

The Distance Education/Degree Completion Program (DE/DCP) at Vincennes University (VU) is delivered through traditional correspondence and electronic media courses. In conjunction with the Indiana Partnership for Statewide Education and Indiana Higher Education Telecommunications System, the university delivers distance learning programs to many sites across Indiana.

VU confers 14 associate degrees by way of the DE/DCP: an associate in applied science (AAS) in general studies, business studies and law enforcement; an associate in science (AS) in general studies, business administration, behavioral science, law enforcement, emergency medical services (EMS), fire science and safety technology, surgical technology, technology apprenticeship, health information management (HIM) or recreation management with an option in therapy; and an associate in arts (AA) in behavioral science.

Students can enroll in DE/DCP courses year round, but must complete their course within 12 months. The university will grant a six-month extension for a fee, and a second extension of the same duration for a fee, with a letter of explanation addressed to the program director. For a given course, students can submit lessons by mail, email or fax, but may not submit more than one quarter of the total number of lessons within a two-week period.

Entrance and graduation requirements are identical to those expected of main campus students. In order to graduate from the DE/DCP, students must acquire 62 to 69 credit hours, maintain a 2.0 cumulative GPA and fulfill the university's general education (GE) requirements. The GE curriculum consists of courses in writing, speech, mathematics, science, social science, humanities, and physical education–fitness/wellness. Prior to graduation, all students must take a test measuring basic skills and general knowledge.

Credit options include transfer, military and life experience credits, as well as a one-time postenrollment course examination, the College Level Examination Program (CLEP) and DANTES Subject Standardized Tests.

Tuition is equal to that charged for main campus courses: US$83.35 per credit hour. An additional US$25 nonrefundable handling fee is required for each correspondence, videotape or online course. To qualify for financial aid, students must complete coursework within one semester, rather than the one year otherwise permitted. Financial aid is released in two stages; the first with the student's successful completion of one quarter of the course work,

and again with the completion of three quarters of the course work.

Behavioral Sciences Program

The behavioral sciences combine the research of two fields, psychology and sociology. This program offers a crucial background for further study in public service, prelaw, teaching or any profession demanding significant interaction with the public. The behavioral sciences curriculum includes courses in micro- and macroeconomics, social problems, fitness and wellness, humanities, US history and world civilization, as well as psychology and sociology.

Business Administration

Business Administration is a two-year transfer program leading to an AS. This program should be the choice of students who intend to pursue a BS in business, accounting, management, finances, marketing, human resources management, management information systems, and those who might eventually enter career fields such as public relations, law or hospital administration.

Business Studies Option

The business studies option permits students to acquire an AS or an AAS by taking courses in the following subjects: business computing, word processing, desktop publishing, spreadsheets, databases, accounting, office management, applied management, human resource management, small business operations, organizational leadership and group dynamics.

Law Enforcement Option

The law enforcement curriculum offers a broad survey of criminal justice, including courses in criminology, substantive and procedural criminal law, criminal investigation, police operations and community relations, police administration and organization, forensic science, juvenile delinquency and traffic control. A law enforcement practicum is available to DE/DCP students.

Surgical Techology Option

The surgical technology option is designed for graduates of formal certificate programs who intend to acquire an AS in surgical technology. Certificates must have been issued by institutions recognized by the National Association of Surgical Technology.

Vincennes University

•

Distance Education/Degree Completion Program

Program Delivery and Student Support

VU delivers distance education through traditional means such as correspondence independent study and through electronic media such as videotape and online courses. Within Indiana, the university also utilizes satellite, cable television and video conferencing. DE/DCP students must have a computer capable of running the following software or more advanced versions: Microsoft (MS) Windows 95, Internet Explorer 4.0, MS Works 4.0 or MS Office 4.0 and MS Word 6.0.

The Learning Resources Center supports the technical elements of distance education and responds to student inquiries by email or telephone. Academic assistance consists of assessment services, a study skills department and use of library online services.

University and Location

Vincennes University is a two-year, public institution accredited by the North Central Association of Colleges & Schools. VU awards associate degrees in the following areas: business; health, physical education and recreation; health occupations; humanities; public service; science and mathematics; social science and technology. In addition to the main campus in Vincennes, Indiana, VU operates campuses in Jasper, Elkart and Indianapolis.

Founded in 1801, VU presently enrolls 6,134 students: 92 percent come from Indiana, 5 percent come from other states and 3 percent come from countries other than the US. Forty-six percent of students are registered in transfer programs, 30 percent are in occupational programs and 24 percent are in certificate programs. The university has a student to faculty ratio of 15 to 1.

Athletic facilities consist of an archery range, lighted tennis courts, baseball and soccer fields, an indoor swimming pool, bowling lanes and a fitness center. VU residence hall plans offer a student health plan, and furnished rooms with a kitchen, telephone jack, cable television, voice mail and Internet services. The university's six dormitories house 67 percent of the student body.

Annual student events at VU include a tube race, spring and winter formals, homecoming, variety shows, a fall musical, spring drama and dances, and year-round concerts and movies.

Contact Information

Distance Education/Degree Completion Program
CBA Room 202
Vincennes Indiana 47591 USA
phone: 1-812-888-5900 or 1-800-880-7961
fax: 1-812-888-2054
email: disted@indian.vinu.edu
internet: http://www.vinu.edu

Office of Admissions
1002 North First Street
Vincennes Indiana 47591 USA
          1-812-888-4313 or 1-800-742-9198
          1-812-888-5707
          askuce@indian.vinu.edu
          http:/www.vinu.edu

Delivery Mode

• Correspondence
• Online instruction
• Satellite and cable television
• Videotapes
• Video conferencing

Program Facts

	Program Entry	Program Length	Total Enrollment	# of Int'l Students	Total Program Costs	Application Fee	Prerequisites
Associate in Applied Science	year round	2 years	700	70	US$83.35/ credit hour	US$20	high school diploma, GED or good standing at other accredited institutions
Associate in Arts	year round	2 years	50	–	US$83.35/ credit hour	US$20	high school diploma, GED or good standing at other accredited institutions
Associate in Science	year round	2 years	950	50	US$83.35/ credit hour	US$20	high school diploma, GED or good standing at other accredited institutions

Virginia Polytechnic Institute & State University

●

Institute for Distance and Distributed Learning

Programs Offered

Certificate Programs
- Admin: Community Services for Older Adults
- Career & Technical Education License
- Computer Engineering
- Information Policy & Society Studies
- Networking
- Software Development

Master's Programs
- Business Administration
- Civil & Environmental Engineering
- Civil Infrastructure Engineering
- Computer Engineering
- Electrical & Computer Engineering
- Engineering Administration
- Health Promotion
- Information Technology
- Instructional Technology
- Ocean Engineering
- Physical Education
- Political Science
- Systems Engineering

University Statistics

Year Founded:	1872
Total Enrollment:	25,000
Undergraduate Enrollment	21,000
Graduate Enrollment:	4,000
Distance Education Enrollment:	7,300

Program Overview

The Institute for Distance & Distributed Learning (IDDL) was created in 1999 to provide leadership, coordination, management and support to the growing distance and distributed learning activities of Virginia Tech. The Institute provides a network to connect learners with distributed learning resources regardless of time and place, and supports teaching & learning, and research & outreach.

IDDL supports over 200 distance learning courses as well as thirteen degree and six certificate programs. Through distance learning, Virginia Tech extends its campus to communities everywhere, while providing an open-campus environment that allows students to learn anytime.

Study Options

Through Virginia Tech's distance learning programs, working professionals have the opportunity to obtain a master's degree in thirteen program areas that include a master of business administration, various master of science degrees, a master of arts in political science and a master of information technology. A certificate program is offered in the administration of community-based services for older adults, and a career and technical education license is also available.

Students taking coursework through interactive videoconferencing need to be present at a specific location and time each week. Courses proceed like regular college courses; however, students interact with the instructor or other students on camera rather than in the same room. This method of course delivery is outlined on the Virginia Tech website (http://www.vto.vt.edu/ivc.php).

In a web-based course, students access the course online anytime, from anywhere, via the Internet. Communication with the instructor and fellow students takes place through email, web-based chatrooms or other synchronous methods. Generally, students can work and complete assignments according to their own schedule, though some instructors require virtual meetings with their students. Most tests and quizzes are taken online, but some can be taken in a local center with a proctor. More information on web delivery is available online (http://www.vto.vt.edu/online.php).

Credit Transfers

At Virginia Tech, credits earned in distance learning classes are equivalent to those earned on site. Students are normally able to transfer earned credit to any other institution, though they are advised to check with the new school to determine which credits will be accepted. Following current university policies, students can transfer earned credits from other accredited postsecondary institutions to studies at Virginia Tech. Students who have completed the transfer module by the Virginia Community College System or Richard Bland College will receive a total of 35 transfer credits.

Admissions

To become undergraduate or graduate degree candidates at Virginia Tech, students must formally apply for admission; all student records are reviewed per current admission policies. Detailed information on admissions criteria is available online (http://www.admiss.vt.edu) or on the grad admissions website (http://www.rgs.vt.edu) for master's program admission.

As a member of the Commonwealth Campus of Virginia, Virginia Tech also allows qualified students at other Virginia institutions to enroll as non-degree-seeking students.

Tuition and Fees

Total undergraduate tuition and fees for in-state residents is US$350 per three-credit-hour course; non-VA residents pay US$1452 per course. Graduate tuition and fees for in-state residents total US$725 per three-credit-hour course; non-VA residents pay US$1220 per course. Additional information on tuition and fees is available online (http://www.bursar.vt.edu).

Financial aid is available to qualified Virginia Tech students, but is not offered to students from other universities, even if they are taking a distance learning course. For more information, students can visit the financial aid website (http://wwwfinaid.es.vt.edu/).

Virginia Polytechnic Institute & State University

●

Institute for Distance and Distributed Learning

Program Delivery and Student Support

Virginia Tech offers multiple methods of course delivery and student interaction such as CD-ROM, interactive videoconferencing, streaming video and threaded discussion. Net.Work.Virginia, a statewide high-speed broadband ATM network, supports different teaching and learning programs and allows faculty members to customize their courses depending on student needs.

The Virginia Tech Online Writing Lab (VT OWL) offers an electronic tutoring environment. As there are no fixed hours, students can schedule individual sessions with a tutor at their convenience. The OWL also includes a self-help area and grammar hotline. Virginia Tech provides extensive library services, such as an online library catalog and full-text electronic resources and databases. The library also has a distance learning librarian who supports off-campus students and faculty.

Contact Information

Institute for Distance and Distributed Learning
Cate Mowrey, 3044 Torgersen Hall (0445)
Blacksburg Virginia 24061 USA
phone: 1-540-231-9584
fax: 1-540-231-2079
email: catem@vt.edu
internet: http://www.vto/vt.edu

University and Location

Since its founding as a land-grant college in 1872, Virginia Polytechnic Institute and State University (Virginia Tech) has grown to become the state's largest university. With approximately 170 degree programs and $170 million in research projects allocated each year, Virginia Tech is the state's leading research institution.

Through its three missions of instruction, research and public service (outreach), Virginia Tech fulfills its motto: "Ut Prosim" — "That I May Serve." The university's satellite linking capabilities and teleconferencing facilities beam interactive classes across the state and allow participation in a variety of electronic forums.

Delivery Mode

• CD-ROM
• Interactive videoconferencing
• Online courses
• Streaming video
• Threaded discussion

Program Facts

	Program Entry	Program Length	Total Enrollment	# of Int'l Students	Total Program Costs	Application Fee	Prerequisites
Commonwealth Graduate Engineering	spring, fall	3 years	–	–	US$725–1220/ course	US$45	bachelor's degree in appropriate engineering subject, 3.0 GPA
Information Technology	summer, fall, spring	2 years	–	–	US$725–1220/ course	US$45	bachelor's degree, 3.0 GPA
Master's in Business Administration	fall	2 years	–	–	US$725–1220/ course	US$45	calculus & accounting, bachelor's degree, 3.0 GPA
Master's in Health Promotion	fall	2 years	–	–	US$725–1220/ course	US$45	bachelor's degree, 3.0 GPA
Master's in Instructional Technology	summer, fall, spring	2 years	–	–	US$725–1220/ course	US$45	bachelor's degree, 3.0 GPA, certified K-12 teacher
Master's in Ocean Engineering	fall	2 years	–	–	US$725–1220/ course	US$45	bachelor's degree in appropriate engineering subject, 3.0 GPA
Master's in Physical Education	summer	2 years	–	–	US$725–1220/ course	US$45	bachelor's degree, 3.0 GPA, certified K-12 teacher
Master's in Political Science	summer, fall, spring	2 years	–	–	US$725–1220/ course	US$45	bachelor's degree, 3.0 GPA

ei's guide to distance and online learning programs in the usa - 2001 edition

Waukesha County Technical College

•

Distance Learning

Programs Offered

Associate Degrees:
- Financial Planning
- Mortgage Lending
- Property Management
- Real Estate Brokerage

Certifications:
- Certified Novell Administrator
- Certified Novell Engineer
- Microsoft Certified Systems Engineer

Credit Courses:
- Business
- Communication
- E-commerce
- Economics
- Equine Genetics
- Home Care
- Human Anatomy
- Information Systems
- Investments
- Java Programming
- Management
- Marketing
- Medical Terminology
- Microcomputer Applications
- Non-traditional Career Explorations
- Psychology
- Sociology
- Statistics
- Unix
- US History

College Statistics

Year Founded:	1923
Total Enrollment:	33,128
Undergraduate Enrollment:	33,128
Graduate Enrollment:	n/a
Distance Education Enrollment:	675

Program Overview

Through distance learning at Waukesha County Technical College (WCTC), students have an opportunity to earn associate degrees through the School of Real Estate and the Academy of Financial Education. Individual courses, designed to enhance job skills, are available, as are specific computer certification programs.

Most academic courses and career-track degrees can be completed on the Internet. Some class lectures are available on videotape. Telecourses for credit, broadcast on public television (PBS), offer an alternative to on-campus courses. Technical training in computer skills, toward certification in Microsoft or Novell systems, is available via Computer-Based Training (CBT).

Courses and occupational training programs offered at WCTC can be delivered to specific sites in Wisconsin via interactive television. The Wisconsin Technical College Network (WTCN) brings together distance learning resources from colleges throughout the state.

WCTC believes all students have a "right to succeed." To ensure that students can do well in their chosen program of study, prospective students may be required to write a WCTC Admissions Assessment, which tests applicants' potential to meet WCTC standards. Internet students may have additional assessment instructions, and should contact the director of Admissions and Counseling. Some courses also require an Internet Written Communication Assessment Exam.

Application forms can be completed online, or requested by phone, and submitted with the US$30 application fee. Assessments are mailed to applicants, and should be returned as early as possible. For assessing advanced standing and transfer credits, applicants should also submit high school or other college transcripts.

Most Internet and CBT courses have set start dates, corresponding to a tri-semester system. A few have open entry dates. Some are open, with permission, to high school students who are 16 years of age or older.

Career-Path Degrees

Associate degree programs currently offered online provide students with specific knowledge and skills in the areas of real estate, property management, mortgage lending and financial planning. Upon completion of the real estate brokerage and financial planning degrees, students are prepared to write industry certification exams.

These degrees comprise approximately 67 credits designed to be completed in four semesters with five courses in each, or through a program of part-time study.

Many courses can be applied toward general education requirements of baccalaureate degrees, though students should investigate transfer agreements if they plan to use their distance learning credits as the basis for further study.

Computer-Based Training

Computer-Based Training offers programs online in technical computer skills, developed by CBT Systems, Ltd. Students can earn certification as a Microsoft Certified Systems Engineer (MCSE), Certified Novell Administrator (CNA) or Certified Novell Engineer (CNE). The MCSE program currently requires six courses, the CNA requires one, and the CNE requires seven.

Self-paced CBT courses provide training in Microsoft Office and Windows.

Credit Courses

Individual course offerings on the Internet vary between semesters. Topics covered usually relate to the associate degree programs mentioned above, as well as human anatomy, medical terminology, home care, respiratory assessment or equine genetic principles. A no-charge online course for one credit that explores non-traditional careers is offered through the Women's Development Center. It is open to both men and women.

Telecourses are offered in subjects of interest to a broad audience, such as business, economics, sociology, communication and psychology.

Waukesha County Technical College

·

Distance Learning

Program Delivery and Student Support

Students taking Internet courses need a modem to connect to the campus and a hard drive to save downloaded files. Internet access is required, as is a web browser, e-mail, and wordprocessing software. Some courses may require RealPlayer software, which can be downloaded from the Internet.

The WCTC website guides students through the application and registration process, and helps prospective students determine whether learning by Internet is the right format for them. Instructors' email addresses for student use are found on each departmental and course webpage, and admissions and counseling staff can also be reached by email or telephone.

The Student Services Center answers students' questions by phone, in person or by email. Textbooks can be ordered online by email, or by telephone; shipping and handling costs apply.

College and Location

Founded in 1923, WCTC delivers student learning-centered education in five university transfer programs, close to 70 associate degree areas, 13 advanced technical certifications, and an apprenticeship program. It assists individuals in securing entry-level employment or upgrading occupational skills. Its programs are organized around the teaching of four broad critical areas: communication, analytical, group effectiveness and personal management skills.

WCTC is a member of the Wisconsin Technical College System, and is accredited by the Commission on Institutions of Higher Education of the North Central Association of Colleges and Schools.

The college is a major employer in Waukesha County in the southeastern corner of Wisconsin.

Contact Information

Distance Learning
800 Main Street
Pewaukee Wisconsin 53072 USA
phone: 1-262-691-5566
fax: 1-262-691-5047
email: vbunker@waukesha.tec.wi.us
internet: http://www.waukesha.tec.wi.us/

Delivery Mode

- Online via Internet
- Videotape
- Interactive television
- Telecourses via PBS

Program Facts

	Program Entry	Program Length	Total Enrollment	# of Int'l Students	Total Program Costs	Application Fee	Prerequisites
Associate Degree programs	Fall, Spring, Summer	4 semesters	–	–	not avail	US$30	High school diploma or equivalent
CNE Computer-Based Training program	Fall, Spring, Summer	7 courses	–	–	not avail	US$30	High school diploma or equivalent
Internet computer 3-credit courses	Fall, Spring, Summer	1 semester	–	–	not avail	US$30	High school diploma or equivalent
Internet credit courses (1–3 credits)	Fall, Spring, Summer	1 semester	–	–	not avail	US$30	High school diploma or equivalent
MCSE Computer-Based Training program	Fall, Spring, Summer	6 courses	–	–	not avail	US$30	High school diploma or equivalent

Weber State University

•

Distance Learning

Program Overview

Through independent and online study, Weber State University (WSU) offers individual courses and certificate and degree programs in a wide range of academic disciplines. Special programs are available for health professionals and APICS (The Educational Society for Resource Management), and general programs are offered in areas such as criminal justice, driver's education and general studies.

WSU independent study courses can be completed in more than two dozen disciplines. Students receive course modules and materials by mail and follow step-by-step instructions for completing course requirements. Select courses include audiotapes, videotapes or computer software. Students complete their courses within six months of enrollment and have the choice, with approval, of enrolling on an accelerated schedule (http://www.weber.edu/dist-learn).

Through WSU Online, students can undertake semester-based courses through the Internet, allowing them to enroll, participate in course activities, purchase course texts, use library and other campus services and take part in extra-curricular activities online. New courses and activities are added each term; students are encouraged to contact WSU Online (http://wsuonline.weber.edu) for up-to-date course listings and tuition rates.

For admission to WSU degree programs, applicants should forward applications for admission and distance learning, US$30 admission and US$10 processing fees, and transcripts and course descriptions of previous education. Individual programs may require letters of reference and documentation, work history and/or the appropriate registry, status or credential in a given occupation. For some programs, deadlines apply. Admissions information can be accessed through the WSU online catalog (http://weber.edu/catalog/0102/catother.htm).

Health Professions Programs

WSU offers certificate, associate and bachelor's degree programs for students in the health professions. These programs allow students to complete courses and supervised work experiences while remaining on the job in their communities. Students admitted into a health sciences degree program have up to two years to complete the program.

Associate of Applied Science (AAS) degrees are offered in Entry-level Respiratory Therapist, Health Information Technology and Clinical Laboratory Technician (CLT).

Students can also earn the Associate of Science (AS) in Advanced Respiratory Therapist. Candidates for the AAS respiratory therapist degree complete a minimum of 63 credits including core and general education courses. The AS respiratory therapist degree comprises 60 credit hours, 25 of which are completed in upper-division respiratory therapy courses.

Bachelor of science degrees are offered in Clinical Laboratory Sciences, Health Administrative Services, Radiologic Sciences and Respiratory Therapy. BS students complete 120 credits, including a minimum of 40 credits of upper-division work. At least 30 credits must be taken through WSU. Majors in radiologic science have the option of seleting a minor in either advanced radiologic sciences or health administrative services.

APICS

WSU works in partnership with APICS – The Educational Society for Resource Management to provide certification (CPIM) exam preparation courses, which can be taken in series or individually. Designed for production and inventory management professionals, five two-credit courses are available and courses begin every month. Students can take up to three months to complete a course and must pass five CPIM certification exams offered through APICS (http://wsuonline.weber.edu/ce_center/apics/default.htm) for certification.

Other Programs

The AS in Criminal Justice prepares those working in law enforcement with coursework in areas such as criminal law, abnormal psychology and the technology of prevention and detection. Students complete 12 core credits (four courses) and nine elective credits in addition to general education requirements.

In cooperation with A-1 Driving Schools, Inc., WSU offers independent study driver education covering the fundamentals of safe and defensive driving. Students complete 30 hours plus required driving time (availability and regulations may vary by state).

The Associate of General Studies degree allows students to individualize the first two years of academic study. The degree requires 60 credit hours (minimum), of which 20 credits must be earned through WSU; general education requirements must be completed. Distance learning course areas include composition, American institutions, quantitative literacy, computer literacy (by examination), humanities, creative arts, social sciences, physical sciences and life sciences.

Weber State University

•

Distance Learning

Program Delivery and Student Support

Once registered, independent study students receive course modules by mail to complete on their own. Modules include the instructions and materials required to complete each course, which may take up to six months. Some courses include audiotapes, videotapes and software.

WSU Online courses generally follow the semester schedule and, with the exception of the course textbook, deliver course materials online. WSU Online students should have access to a Pentium 200 computer or higher with a 28.8 kbps (minimum) modem and Internet access through an Internet Service Provider (ISP).

The Stewart Library at WSU strives to provide academic library resources and services to independent study students that are equivalent to on-campus resources. The library website (http://library.weber.edu/) lists the library resources and services available.

University and Location

Founded in 1889, Weber State University (pronounced wee-ber) is accredited by the Northwestern Association of Schools and Colleges and is a member of both the American Council on Education and the American Association of State Colleges and Universities. WSU offers a variety of program streams: undergraduate liberal education in the arts, humanities and sciences; vocational and professional programs in education, business and technology; specialized education in the health professions; master's degrees in education and accounting; and lifelong learning opportunities both on and off campus.

Since early in its history, WSU has offered educational options for those who are employed, who have mobility problems or family commitments, who are military personnel, and those enrolled as students through Indian reservations and high schools. Computers have extended the possibilities of extending WSU distance learning programs to students with all interests and educational goals, wherever they are located.

Contact Information

Distance Learning
4005 University Circle
Ogden UT 84405-4005 USA
phone: 1-800-848-7770 ext. 6785
fax: 1-801-626-8035
email: dist-learn@weber.edu
internet: http://www.weber.edu/dist-learn

Delivery Mode

- Independent study (modules, textbooks, audiotapes, videotapes, computer software)
- Online (Internet delivery, textbooks)

Program Facts

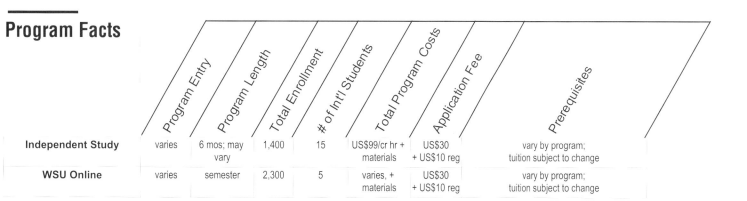

	Program Entry	Program Length	Total Enrollment	# of Int'l Students	Total Program Costs	Application Fee	Prerequisites
Independent Study	varies	6 mos; may vary	1,400	15	US$99/cr hr + materials	US$30 + US$10 reg	vary by program; tuition subject to change
WSU Online	varies	semester	2,300	5	varies, + materials	US$30 + US$10 reg	vary by program; tuition subject to change

Western Oklahoma State College

●

Distance Learning

- Small college setting allows quality interaction with instructors
- General education college credit courses for high school students
- Unique 2-way switching technology for interactive video networks

Programs Offered

Credit Courses:
- American History
- Drafting
- Federal Government
- High School-Level Education
- Introduction to the Child
- Literature
- Microcomputer Applications
- Nutrition
- Psychology
- Sociology

College Statistics

Year Founded:	1926
Total Enrollment:	2,463
Undergraduate Enrollment	2,252
Graduate Enrollment:	n/a
Distance Education Enrollment:	211

Program Overview

The Western Oklahoma State College (WOSC) offers distance learning courses for credit through the distance education component of the Information Systems department. Credit can be earned by adults and high school students toward existing vocational programs and in general education.

Distance learning courses are equivalent to on-campus courses in time spent, entry dates, evaluation and tuition, with the exception of a small distance learning fee. Students have the option of studying at times and places convenient to their schedule, via Internet connection, televised pretaped lectures or live interactive television from predesignated sites. WOSC follows a trisemester system, with an intersession period between spring and summer semesters.

Students may be able to apply previous education, such as training for the Military Airlift Command in Altus, to program credit requirements.

Technical programs at WOSC maintain current industry relevancy through technical advisory committees.

Application to the Office of Admissions and Records requires a high school diploma, GED and college transcripts, along with a US$15 application fee. Tuition for in-state residents is low, since the college is state funded; residents pay US$39.95 per credit hour, while non-residents pay US$102.85 per credit hour. Refunds of 100 percent are possible until the first day of classes except in the fall semester, when students have two weeks to drop classes before they are no longer eligible for refunds.

Internet Courses

Internet courses include drafting, nutrition and microcomputer applications. Drafting courses by distance education form part of the Associate of Applied Science – Drafting Option, while nutrition courses can be used toward study in the Associate of Science in University Studies. Other courses vary in availability; students should check with the distance learning coordinator.

Telecourses

WOSC offers telecourses in American history, federal government studies, introduction to literature, general psychology and sociology, and introduction to the child.

Telecourses are broadcast on cable channels by the Oklahoma Educational Television Authority and can be viewed at home, and by video either on campus or on the Altus Air Force Base. Prior to viewing the first course, students should obtain the study guide, which presents all relevant course information including lesson outlines, assignments, readings, pre- and post-tests, and reviews. Textbooks are also required; both the textbooks and study guide are available at the on-campus WOSC store.

Each telecourse has an on-campus component comprising a minimum of two exams, or other supervised work. A half-hour orientation session is conducted by the telecourse instructor on campus.

General Education Courses

WOSC general education courses are provided in 25–30 sections to interactive sites throughout Oklahoma. These courses are usually taken by high school students for college credit before they have completed their high school diploma.

The interactive distance learning studios provide two-way interactive audio and video between remote sites and studio classes on campus. Western's unique switching capacity allows the delivery of courses via multiple transmission technologies, which increases the ability to connect to multiple video networks serviced by WOSC.

Western Oklahoma State College

●

Distance Learning

Program Delivery and Student Support

Courses are delivered on the Web, via cable television or broadcast as interactive video courses. Students will require adequate computer technology with Internet access for the web-based courses. Telecourse students maintain regular contact with instructors by email, phone or fax, or in person. Textbooks and study guides support these courses, and should be purchased before the first broadcast. Interactive courses, which require links to interactive studios on the WOSC campus, are delivered to established sites throughout Oklahoma.

Students have on-campus access to the Learning Resource Center (LRC), which organizes resource material and equipment for WOSC students. It can instruct students on Internet use, catalog and database searching, and loans material from its 35,000-item collection. LRC users linked to the Electric Library can access books, magazines and other printed materials.

College and Location

Founded in 1926, Western Oklahoma State College is the oldest municipal college in the state of Oklahoma. It primarily serves the greater southwestern Oklahoma community, and is open to the rest of the state by virtue of its state funding. Accredited by the North Central Association, the college offers two-year programs in 34 areas, and currently enrolls approximately 2,500 students annually.

The college is located in Altus, the county seat, southwest of Oklahoma City and at the center of agricultural production in cotton, wheat and cattle. The Altus Air Force Base is a training center for the Military Airlift Command and is a major employer for the city of 26,000. The college operates an office on the base and offers courses for military personnel.

The Altus area, 30 miles north of the Red River that forms the Texas border, was a part of the historic Great Western trail, along which cattle were herded from the ranches of Texas to the stockyards of the north. The Quartz Mountain State Park north of Altus is a major source of outdoor recreation, including mountain climbing and sailing.

Contact Information

Distance Learning
Kent Brooks, Director, 2801 N. Main St.
Altus Oklahoma 73521 USA
phone: 1-580-477-7992
fax: 1-580-477-7861
email: kent@western.cc.ok.us
internet: http://www.western.cc.ok.us

Delivery Mode

- Broadcast on television/via videotape
- Online via Internet
- Interactive video networks

Program Facts

	Program Entry	Program Length	Total Enrollment	# of Int'l Students	Total Program Costs	Application Fee	Prerequisites
In-state courses	Jan, Jun, Aug	2–3 credit hours	211	–	US$39.85 per credit hour	US$15	High school diploma or equivalent
Out-of-state courses	Jan, Jun, Aug	2–3 credit hours	–	–	US$102.85 per credit hour	US$15	High school diploma or equivalent
Telecourse fee	n/a	n/a	n/a	n/a	US$17.50	US$15	n/a

Worcester Polytechnic Institute

•

Advanced Distance Learning Network

- Over 95 percent of MS and MBA program faculty have PhDs
- Continuing education students can audit ADLN courses at half tuition
- A maximum of nine credits from other schools can be applied to MS or MBA programs
- Financial aid may be available to students who take at least two courses per semester

Programs Offered

Advanced Certificate:
   Fire Protection Engineering
Graduate Certificates:
   Civil & Environmental Engineering
   Fire Protection Engineering
   Management
Master's Degrees:
   Business Administration
   Environmental Engineering
   Fire Protection Engineering

Institute Statistics

Year Founded:	1865
Total Enrollment:	3,805
Undergraduate Enrollment	2,754
Graduate Enrollment:	1,051
Distance Education Enrollment:	150

Program Overview

The Advanced Distance Learning Network (ADLN) at Worcester Polytechnic Institute (WPI) enables students to fulfill the requirements for a variety of certificates, as well as master's degrees in business administration, fire protection engineering or environmental engineering. Over 95 percent of the faculty teaching ADLN programs have PhDs.

Students applying for ADLN degree and certificate programs must seek admission to WPI. Applicants should submit a US$50 nonrefundable application fee, official transcripts from all academic institutions attended and three letters of recommendation. International students whose native tongue is other than English must submit TOEFL results. A paper-based score of 550 or a computer-based score of 213 is necessary.

Individual programs have additional admission requirements. Students applying for the business administration program must include Graduate Management Admissions Test (GMAT) results. Those applying for a fire protection engineering program who have no work experience in that field must include a statement of purpose. Students applying for the environmental engineering program are encouraged to submit Graduate Record Examination (GRE) results in order to secure financial aid.

The ADLN master's degree programs permit applicants to transfer a maximum of nine graduate-level credits from other institutions. At least two thirds of the required credit for degree programs and all the required credit for certificate programs must be obtained at WPI. All of the credits earned in a WPI certificate program can be applied to a master's degree.

Continuing education students can audit ADLN courses at half tuition. The tuition rate for the 2000–2001 academic year was US$703 per credit. Financial aid may be available to students who take at least two courses per semester.

Master of Business Administration

The master of business administration (MBA) is a 49-credit program in technology management. Twenty-eight courses are available via distance learning, including financial accounting, organizational behavior, quantitative methods, principles of marketing, domestic and global business environments, legal and ethical contexts of technological organizations, and telecommunications management and electronic commerce.

MBA applicants should hold a bachelor's degree. Under credit transfer options the Management Department may reduce the degree requirements to 31 credits. Students should have acquired these credits within six years of applying to WPI and have earned a minimum grade of B at the time.

MS in Fire Protection Engineering

The master of science (MS) in fire protection engineering is a 30-credit program that prepares students to apply current industry standards and research to real scenarios. A thesis is not required. Ten courses are available via distance learning, including: flammability tests, codes and standards; fire dynamics; fire protection systems; risk management; fire-safety engineering evaluation; building fire-safety; failure analysis and industrial fire protection. Applicants should have a bachelor's degree in the sciences, engineering or engineering technology.

MS in Environmental Engineering

The MS in environmental engineering is a 33-credit program that enhances the knowledge and skills of those currently employed in the field. A thesis is not necessary. Nine courses are available via distance learning, including integration of design and construction, geohydrology, biosystems in sanitary engineering, industrial waste treatment, hazardous waste, multiphase contaminant transportation and advanced project management. Applicants should hold a bachelor's degree.

Graduate and Advanced Certificates

WPI confers a graduate certificate (GC) in fire protection engineering, management, waste remediation systems or pollution prevention. Applicants considering the management program should hold a bachelor's degree, while those considering the fire protection engineering program should have a bachelor's degree in science or engineering technology. Applicants considering the waste remediation systems or pollution prevention program should have a bachelor's degree and be employed in one of these fields. To professionals who hold a master's degree, the institute confers an advanced certificate (AC) in fire protection engineering.

ei's guide to distance and online learning programs in the usa - 2001 edition

Worcester Polytechnic Institute

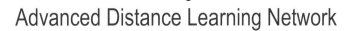

Advanced Distance Learning Network

Program Delivery and Student Support

The ADLN delivers campus-based courses to distance learners via the World Wide Web, interactive compressed video and videotapes. Traditional distance learning materials such as textbooks, handouts and supplemental readings are sent by fax, mail or email. ADLN students must have an email account and Internet service.

The library maintains an online catalog and databases, while the bookstore accepts orders via a toll-free line. Technical support is available from the institute's computer college center. Distance learners can obtain career guidance from career counseling and placement services.

Contact Information

Advanced Distance Learning Network
100 Institute Road
Worcester Massachusetts 01609-2280 USA
phone: 1-508-831-5220
fax: 1-508-831-5881
email: adln@wpi.edu
internet: http://www.wpi.edu/Academics/ADLN

Institute and Location

Founded in 1865, Worcester Polytechnic Institute (WPI) has contributed to the development of technological higher education. The university's distinctive outcomes-oriented approach to education is being viewed as a model for reform at the national level. WPI is fully accredited by the New England Association of Schools and Colleges.

Most of WPI's academic departments offer master's and doctoral programs and support current research in a broad range of fields. WPI strives to cultivate academic excellence, respond to the needs of the marketplace, and maintain renowned academicians and industry experts who are practitioners in their fields.

With a population of 170,000, Worcester is the second largest city in Massachusetts and New England. History buffs will appreciate Sturbridge Village and the exhibits of the American Antiquarian Society. Students interested in cultural attractions will appreciate the Worcester Art Museum and Foothills Theater. Skiers will enjoy the slopes of Wachusett Mountain.

Delivery Mode

• Compressed video
• Internet (online instruction, email, WWW)
• Textbooks
• Videotapes

Program Facts

	Program Entry	Program Length	Total Enrollment	# of Int'l Students	Total Program Costs	Application Fee	Prerequisites
AC in Fire Protection Engineering	Sep, Jan, May	varies	–	–	US$703 per credit	US$50	professionals with a master's degree in science, engineering or engineering technology
GC in Fire Protection Engineering	Sep, Jan, May	varies	–	–	US$703 per credit	US$50	professionals with a bachelor's degree in science, engineering or engineering technology
GC in Management	Sep, Jan, May	varies	–	–	US$703 per credit	US$50	professionals with a bachelor's degree
GC in Pollution Prevention	Sep, Jan, May	varies	–	–	US$703 per credit	US$50	professionals with a bachelor's degree
GC in Waste Remediation Systems	Sep, Jan, May	varies	–	–	US$703 per credit	US$50	professionals with a bachelor's degree
Master of Business Administration	Sep, Jan, May	varies	–	–	US$703 per credit	US$50	professionals with a bachelor's degree, GMAT
MS in Civil & Environmental Engineering	Sep, Jan, May	varies	–	–	US$703 per credit	US$50	professionals with a bachelor's degree, GRE recommended
MS in Fire Protection Engineering	Sep, Jan, May	varies	–	–	US$703 per credit	US$50	professionals with a bachelor's degree in science, engineering or engineering technology

More on the EI Group

The EI Group provides high-quality information on postsecondary study opportunities in the USA and Canada. A global leader in education services, The EI Group provides comprehensive, in-depth information on academic programs through print guides and the Internet.

EI's print and Internet guides for postsecondary study

www.SchoolsintheUSA.com
profiles undergraduate academic programs in the USA

www.GraduateBusiness.com
profiles graduate management programs

www.GradEducation.com
profiles graduate teacher education programs

www.GradSciEng.com
profiles graduate engineering and science programs

www.DistanceStudies.com
profiles distance learning degree and diploma programs

www.SchoolsinCanada.com
profiles undergraduate academic programs in Canada

www.GradFineArts.com
profiles graduate fine & performing arts programs

www.GraduateHealth.com
profiles graduate nursing and health programs

EI's magazine for careers and education

Campus Starter is **the** student magazine for career and education information. Published in full color, twice a year, with interesting features, useful tips, expert advice, and great contests and giveaways, *Campus Starter* is a fun and valuable tool for today's high school student interested in postsecondary education opportunities. Visit the magazine online at **www.campusstartermag.com**

Whether you are looking for an undergraduate or graduate program, we know that choosing the program suited to your unique needs is the key to your success. Our mission is to help make that process easier.

THE EI GROUP

Guiding Students to Success

3873 Airport Way, PO Box 9754, Bellingham WA 98227-9754 USA
phone: 1-250-658-6283 fax: 1-250-658-6285 email: service@theEIGroup.com

2001 Guide Series Order Form

	ISBN	Qty	Price	Total
Business & Management Programs				
Guide to Doctoral Programs in Business & Management in the USA	1-894122-80-1		US$29.95	US$
Guide to Graduate Management Programs in the USA	1-894122-82-8		US$29.95	US$
Guide to Graduate & Executive Management Programs in Canada	1-894122-84-4		US$24.95	US$
Guide to Undergraduate Business Programs in the USA	1-894122-86-0		US$14.95	US$
Guide to Undergraduate Business Programs in Canada	1-894122-88-7		US$11.95	US$
Engineering & Science Programs				
Guide to Graduate Engineering & Computer Science Programs in the USA	1-894122-90-9		US$29.95	US$
Guide to Graduate Engineering & Computer Science Programs in Canada	1-894122-79-8		US$24.95	US$
Guide to Undergraduate Engineering & Technology Programs in the USA	1-894122-83-6		US$14.95	US$
Guide to Undergraduate Engineering & Technology Programs in Canada	1-894122-85-2		US$11.95	US$
Guide to Undergraduate & Graduate Science Programs in Canada	1-894122-87-9		US$29.95	US$
Teaching and Education Programs				
Guide to Undergraduate & Graduate Teaching and Education Programs in Canada	1-894122-91-7		US$29.95	US$
Fine and Performing Arts Programs				
Guide to Undergraduate & Graduate Fine and Performing Arts Programs in Canada	1-894122-70-4		US$29.95	US$
Health Programs				
Guide to Undergraduate & Graduate Health Programs in the USA	1-894122-64-x		US$29.95	US$
Distance Learning Programs				
Guide to Distance Learning Programs in the USA	1-894122-94-1		US$29.95	US$
Guide to Distance Learning Programs in Canada	1-894122-96-8		US$24.95	US$
Canadian Schools				
Guide to Universities & Colleges in Canada	1-894122-93-3		US$24.95	US$
International Guide to Public & Private Secondary Schools in Canada	1-894122-92-5		US$16.95	US$

Shipping & Handling

*Add the appropriate charges to the total at right ***

	First Copy	Per Additional Copy
Within North America		
☐ Surface Mail	US$ 7.00	US$ 4.00
Outside North America		
☐ Surface Mail	US$10.00	US$ 5.00
☐ Air Mail	US$30.00	US$15.00

SUBTOTAL = US$ _____

* SHIPPING & HANDLING = US$ _____
(from charges shown at left)

TOTAL = US$ _____

Billing Address *(please print)*:

Name _____ Position _____

Organization _____

Address _____

Telephone (area code) _____ Email _____

Shipping Address *(if different from billing address)*:

Name _____ Position _____

Organization _____

Address _____

Telephone (area code) _____ Email _____

PAYMENT

All orders from outside of North America must be prepaid or accompanied by credit card information.

☐ Certified check or money order enclosed
(payable to: Education International)

☐ Please invoice:
Purchase Order # _____

☐ Please charge my: ☐ MasterCard   ☐ Visa

Credit Card # _____

Expiry Date _____   Card Holder Signature _____

We guarantee your satisfaction with our publications. If for any reason you are not satisfied with a book, you may return it, in resaleable condition, within 30 days, for a full refund. Substantial discounts are available on volume orders.

To order, mail or fax this form to: The EI Group
3873 Airport Way, PO Box 9754, Bellingham WA 98227-9754 USA
phone: 1-250-658-6283 fax: 1-250-658-6285 email: service@theEIGroup.com

INFORMATION

FOR

INTERNATIONAL

STUDENTS

English Language Tests: Steps to Success

International study is rapidly gaining in popularity as students worldwide recognize the cultural and educational advantages of overseas experiences. In 1998, more than 481,000 international students were pursuing studies at universities and colleges in the US.

Not surprisingly, international students who wish to pursue postsecondary studies in an English-speaking country sometimes view the language skills requirement as a barrier. Non-native speakers of English will almost always be required to prove their English language proficiency for admission into a postsecondary institution whose primary language of instruction is English. Conversational English abilities alone are not enough; when admitted to an institution in an English-speaking country, international students are competing at the same academic levels as native English speakers, and must have corresponding language skills. Required language skills are determined by each institution individually, and may vary from program to program within an institution.

Choosing a Proficiency Test

Although certain colleges and universities do administer their own institution-specific English language tests, there are several standardized international proficiency tests. For students who wish to improve their English language skills in an English-speaking environment, there are also several recognized institutes, such as the ELS Language Centers, designed to provide international students with the language skills necessary for university or college study. An individual university or college may request scores from one or several of the following tests.

TOEFL

The Test Of English as a Foreign Language (TOEFL) is the most widely accepted test of English proficiency in the world, and is offered 12 times per

> International students are competing at the same academic levels as native English speakers.

year at more than 1,200 test centers in 170 countries and regions. More than 2,400 universities in the US, Canada and other English-speaking countries require prospective international students to submit TOEFL scores. Many countries now offer the TOEFL in a computer-based format, allowing students to schedule their own exam appointments year-round in comfortable, computer-equipped cubicles. The computer-based TOEFL will gradually replace the paper-based exam over the next decade.

IELTS

The International English Language Testing System (IELTS) is accepted by most Commonwealth academic institutions and is becoming increasingly recognized for admission by colleges and universities in North America. The IELTS is available in over 250 centers across 100 countries. Testing dates are flexible and each IELTS center offers a testing date at least once per month.

MELAB

The Michigan English Language Assessment Battery (MELAB) is recognized by many educational institutions in the US and Canada as an alternative to the TOEFL. Though as of June 30, 1998, the MELAB has been available only at testing sites in Canada and the US, and at limited international locations where the TOEFL is not administered, international group MELABs may be arranged for institutions or organizations.

What to Expect

Most English language proficiency tests generally take between two and three hours to complete. Depending on the number of candidates present for a given testing date, students should normally expect to spend at least three and a half hours writing the test.

The majority of the English language tests are presented in multiple-choice formats and are divided into three general sections: listening comprehension, structure & written expression and reading comprehension. Students registered for certain TOEFL testing dates must also complete the Test of Written English (TWE), a short essay demonstrating their ability to write in English.

International students planning to pursue graduate studies in English-speaking countries are also often required to submit scores for the Test of Spoken English (TSE), a third optional element to the TOEFL. The MELAB, although similar in structure to the TOEFL, requires all students to complete a written examination. Similarly, all IELTS candidates complete a test module on spoken English.

English language test scores are normally valid for a maximum of two years after the testing date. There are generally no pass or fail marks: scores are given and evaluated according to each institution's English proficiency standards. The average paper-based TOEFL requirement for undergraduate students is a score of 550, while the average undergraduate IELTS requirement is a score of 6.5. The average undergraduate MELAB requirement is 85.

How to Prepare

Students with advanced English language abilities may only need to prepare for two to four months before writing a proficiency test. Students with elementary to intermediate abilities will need anywhere from six to 10 months of intensive language courses to achieve the skills they will need to succeed on a standardized English language proficiency test.

Students planning to write an English proficiency test should prepare to do so by writing the sample tests provided by most testing centers. Studying using a center's practice exams enables students to review their English language skills while becoming familiar with the format of the exam. By writing practice tests under the same circumstances they will experience on the actual testing day (completing a sample test within the set time limit, for example), students should gain useful insight into the nature of the exam, and be able to approach the actual testing day feeling confident, well prepared and relaxed.

Students should remember that they are not allowed to use dictionaries, watches with alarms, scratch paper, highlighters or notes during most English language tests, and should therefore avoid using these tools during their practice sessions.

What to Bring

Most testing centers will send admission tickets to all candidates. These tickets function both as receipt of payment and for examination entry.

> Students should be able to approach the actual testing day feeling confident, well prepared and relaxed.

Students who do not bring their admission ticket with them to the testing center may be unable to write their test. In addition to admission tickets, all test-takers should bring the following:

➤ Photo File Record—candidates will normally receive these in the mail along with their admission tickets and must attach current photos of themselves to each signed, completed form.
➤ Official Identification—as specified on their admission tickets, students are required to bring two pieces of official photo identification, such as a passport and driver's license, with them to the testing center.
➤ Pencils—most tests must be completed with soft-lead (#2 or HB) pencils. Students are advised to bring at least two pencils, a pencil sharpener and an eraser.
➤ Watch—although official time will be kept by the proctor, candidates may want to monitor their own progress. Students should remember to avoid bringing watches with alarms.
➤ Lunch—since cafeteria facilities are not available at all testing centers, students should bring snacks to eat after the test or during break periods.

Test Administration

Students registering for English language tests should remember to use the same form of their names on all testing and identification documents. Students using variant spellings or name orders may not be permitted to take the proficiency test.

Students are encouraged to register early for their chosen testing dates, as some centers fill up quickly.

English language test administrators inform students of their test scores within a varying amount of time. Students receive results from the paper-based TOEFL approximately one month after the testing date, and IELTS candidates receive their scores within a two-week period. The new computer-based TOEFL offers students the opportunity to view unofficial exam results immediately upon completing the exam.

Students should remember that in most cases they may rewrite the examination if necessary.

"Top 10" Reasons to Study in the USA

1	The US is one of the **foremost destinations** for international students and tourists.
2	The US is a country full of **world-famous attractions** and **spectacular geography**.
3	The US offers the **greatest number** of colleges and universities to choose from.
4	Many American universities are **very prestigious**, and degrees earned in the US are respected worldwide.
5	The US is **one of the world's leading nations** in industry and technology.
6	**Spaces are available** for large numbers of international students at many institutions.
7	The US is a nation of **diverse cultures**; more than 20 million people living in America were born elsewhere.
8	Many US schools have **strong links** with industry, business and commerce.
9	Admission standards vary greatly, thus **increasing your chances** of finding a school that will accept your qualifications.
10	You will have opportunities to take part in an **enormous range** of planned and informal student activities offered on American campuses.

ei's guide to distance and online learning programs in the usa - 2001 edition

The Real Secret to Succeeding in US Higher Education

I f you are considering applying to a US college or university to further your education, you are looking to join over 514,000 international students who are currently studying in the United States. Most of these students have chosen a US institution either because of its worldwide reputation for quality or because of a desire to broaden their life experiences. All of these students can benefit from a secret that is key to succeeding in reaching their goals once enrolled in a US institution: What will make your education come alive and enable you to truly understand the United States has nothing to do with the prestige of your professors or the diversity of students on campus. The secret to getting the most out of your college experience is to GET IN-VOLVED.

Success in American colleges requires an investment of time and effort. For students to succeed in college, they must take advantage of all that the college has to offer. This includes using the physical facilities such as science labs, the student union and the athletic and fine arts areas. Getting involved really means the investment of both time and effort in your studies. To take full advantage of the library, a student must visit the building and use its resources regularly throughout the school year. To have meaningful interaction with faculty, showing up— whether to classes or to meetings with professors—is half of the success. Academically, a student who rarely approaches a professor about issues or assignments that are difficult to grasp is simply not putting in the time necessary to make the most of the college experience. Unlike many educational systems, US faculties expect that students will actively participate in class. Classroom participation means speaking up, taking risks and entering into the give and take of discussion.

If showing up is half of the success, the other half is putting effort into the activity. It is a relatively small matter to show up for class regularly, still another to diligently take notes and participate, and yet another to do additional readings on class topics and to apply them in other classes or at work. The difference between the two is the difference in student effort. Responsible student behavior is defined by the time a student devotes to high-quality encounters both in and out of class with both faculty and peers.

Universities are communities in which all members play an important role in creating an ideal climate for healthy learning. There are four fundamental areas of involvement:

1. First, as a student you have the responsibility to attempt to understand yourself and your peers as learners. One of the most fundamental kinds of diversity is the difference in the way students engage with the class material. A well-educated individual should have an understanding of these differences.
2. Second, you have a responsibility to find connections with smaller groups of individuals. At all but the smallest campuses, it is quite possible for you to become isolated. Students should become actively involved with clubs, career organizations or academic fraternities to extend their learning beyond the classroom.
3. Third, as a student you have a responsibility to actively participate in the creation of a climate that fosters learning. As a member of the campus community, it is not enough simply to show up for class. The life of a campus depends on each member doing his or her part. Students who are mutually tolerant and supportive of honest efforts towards learning contribute to an atmosphere that encourages personal growth and real achievement.
4. Finally, you have a responsibility to become actively involved with peers and faculty in both academic and cocurricular activities. Students need to ask themselves: Am I actively participating in class, not just taking notes and staring blankly into space? Am I engaged with the material, posing questions and supporting fellow students in discussion? Do I seek out faculty members? Do I make friends with peers? Do I attempt to find connections between my academic work and other aspects of my life? Students who consider these questions and actively assist other students in realizing the value of involvement help to promote responsible student behavior.

The real secret to success in American higher education is actually quite simple. Learning in college requires your active participation. Learning requires that you involve yourself in class and take advantage of the opportunities provided by the college and the faculty. You must carry forward your studies into your own life and relationships. Ultimately, you are the secret to your own success.

Todd M. Davis is Director of the Higher Education Resource Group with the Institute of International Education.

Destination USA

Living in the US

The United States is an exciting country with a distinguished heritage. Those who visit the US appreciate its ethnic and cultural diversity and its expansive and spectacular scenery.

A country famous for its "firsts"—the first lightbulb was invented by Thomas Edison, the first airplane by the famous Wright brothers—the US is also the first choice of destinations for an increasing number of international students.

Country Facts

Though relatively young, the US is a nation rich in history and culture. International students studying and living in the US will have many opportunities to learn about its intriguing past— the colonial settlements, the American Revolution, the Civil War—and the history of its native people who arrived in North America 25,000 years ago, and who now represent less than 1 percent of the population.

The country's landscape is widely varied: expansive beaches, lush forests, fertile farmland, vast deserts, spectacular mountain ranges, tropical islands and subtropical wetlands. Hundreds of national and state parks offer unique geological and historic features.

Because the US is a relatively large country—half the size of South America and slightly smaller than China—its climate varies dramatically, from tropical in Hawaii to arctic in Alaska. Summer months (June to August) are warm to hot in most places, and winter (November to February) can be cooler with rain and snow in many areas. Generally speaking, it is colder in the East and the Midwest than in the South; the West includes dry regions and rainy forests. In summer, light clothing is sufficient, but warm clothes and raincoats are required in some places during winter months.

To provide a global description of all 50 US states would be impossible. The country can, however, be divided into four general regions: the East, Midwest, South and West. The West ranges from the hot, arid, mostly desert lands of Arizona and New Mexico

> The US is the first choice of destinations for an increasing number of international students.

(the "wild" part of the West that spawned the genre of American films known as "Westerns") to the lush, forested Pacific Northwest. Mountain ranges divide the Midwest from the West. The Midwest is characterized by flat plains and fertile farmlands, although the northeastern states, where the American auto industry is centered, are heavily industrialized. This region also features the Great Lakes. The East includes the New England states, where America's first immigrants, the Pilgrims, came

ashore. The South is a vast geographical region stretching from Virginia, with its snowy, picturesque winters, to Florida, parts of which are just 185 miles from the Tropic of Cancer. Sometimes called "the sun belt," this region is characterized by its warmer climate and slower rhythm of life, especially in the Deep South.

The country's diverse landscapes and dramatic variations in climate provide the perfect conditions for a wide variety of outdoor sports. Rock-climbing, downhill skiing, surfing and kayaking are all popular activities, but the possibilities are endless.

The multicultural US population comprises people of mainly European, African American, Mexican and Latin American descent. Nearly three-quarters of the country's 250 million inhabitants live in the cities. Over 20 million people living in the US were born elsewhere.

The United States of America is a federal republic with a strong democratic tradition. The nation's capital, Washington, DC, is nestled between Maryland and Virginia. The government is headed by the president and governed by Congress, which consists of the Senate and a House of Representatives.

The dollar or "buck" is the basic unit of currency in the US. All paper money is green and the most widely used denominations are the $1, $5, $10, $20, $50 and $100 bills. Coins come in a variety of sizes and denominations including the 1-, 5-, 10- and 25-cent coins. Banks throughout the US readily accept traveller's checks and most foreign currency. The most widely accepted credit cards include Visa, MasterCard and American Express.

People and Culture

The American people have always placed a high value on individual rights, freedoms and responsibilities. Americans are renowned for taking great pride in their accomplishments as a nation. Often referred to as a melting pot, the US has been greatly influenced by the customs and cultures of the many immigrants who now call it home. International students will feel welcome and comfortable in multicultural, perspective-rich, American cities.

Sports, a major component of US culture, are an integral part of university and college life. Many students regularly attend their school's football and basketball games, and participate in a wide range of athletic endeavors themselves. Fraternities and sororities are also important to student life on US campuses. These student organizations, known as the "Greek" system, provide member students with social activities, support, and, in some cases, even housing.

Because the US is a multicultural society, many of its customs are unique to the various ethnic and cultural groups. However, in general, Americans tend to treat each other informally in their business or social dealings, even given a difference in their ages or social standings. This informality often extends into the classroom, though polite forms of address such as "Mr/Ms" or titles such as "Dr/Professor" are usually used. Americans are often outgoing, friendly and quite direct. A handshake and a smile are the normal response when meeting someone for the first time.

> ## Most institutions have an international student office that provides an extensive range of services.

Americans have never adopted the metric system; new arrivals will have to adapt to reading measurements in miles, feet, pounds, cups, and temperatures in Fahrenheit. Tipping about 15 percent at hotels and restaurants is customary and usually expected.

Hamburgers and French fries are known worldwide to be staple items of the American diet; in fact, a wide variety of foods are readily available in the US. International cuisine is popular in most cities, and regional dishes, like New England clam chowder, spicy Cajun and New Mexican dishes, and Pacific smoked salmon, are served in restaurants all over the US. Americans generally eat three meals a day: breakfast, lunch and dinner. Dinner, or supper as it is sometimes called, is the main meal. On weekends, many Americans eat brunch, a combination of late breakfast and early lunch. Eggs Benedict—poached eggs served with hollandaise sauce—first served at New York City's Waldorf Hotel in the 1890s, is a favourite brunch dish.

Day-to-Day Living

American clothing is generally more casual than clothing in Europe. It is not unusual for women to wear their skirts above knee length and, in warm weather, to wear sleeveless shirts.

Many domestic, as well as international, students travel long distances to attend college or university in the US, and many schools have on-campus residence halls or dormitories to accommodate these students. Some schools offer separate residence halls or on-campus apartments for graduate students and families. Students may also choose to live in an apartment or shared house off campus, or, through special arrangement, with an American family in a room and board or homestay situation. Most universities operate a housing office which can offer assistance and advice regarding accommodation options.

Most international airlines service the larger cities in the US, and many domestic airlines link major cities. When traveling in the US, overseas students should keep in mind the size of the country. Air travel is now quite common, and since the airlines were deregulated, air travel has become more reasonably priced. Travel by train is not as popular as it once was, though it can still be a comfortable way to travel, offering students a unique opportunity to see the American landscape. One of the most extensive and cheapest means of travel is by coach (long-distance bus); Greyhound-Trailways is the major international bus company.

Although not as widespread as the European network, the Hostelling International-USA system offers opportunities to make touring the country more economical. For travel within a city, buses and cars are the most common forms of transportation.

Studying in the US

Internationalization of Education

People from all over the world choose to study in the US. Many universities, recognizing the unique and important contributions international students make to education in the US, have begun offering courses with a global or multicultural focus.

In 1998, there were more than 481,000 international students studying in the US at over 3,000 colleges, universities, English language schools and postsecondary institutions.

To assist students who come to study in the US, most institutions have an international student office that provides an extensive range of social, academic and personal services. Often, institutions will also offer an orientation program to familiarize new arrivals with the campus and US academics.

Overview of Education System

There is no national education system in the United States, as there is in some countries. Instead, each state has its own education department which sets state guidelines for schools.

Universities are the largest and most complex of the country's higher education institutions. They comprise colleges, schools, departments and faculties, which deliver undergraduate, graduate and professional programs. Universities place a heavy emphasis on research; most are publicly supported and funded by the state. Private institutions have more selective admission policies and often significantly higher fees. Some are affiliated with religious groups, but

International students are advised to apply as early as possible.

normally welcome all students regardless of whether or not they are church members. Colleges tend to be smaller than universities and offer a more specific range of degree programs.

Master's programs normally take two years to complete; some schools offer accelerated, one-year programs and many offer part-time options. PhD degrees can take anywhere from three to seven years to complete. Professional programs can range from intensive weekend seminars to part-time, one- to four-year degree programs.

English as a Second Language, or ESL, courses are offered by all types of institutions. Some schools allow students with insufficient English language test scores to enroll conditionally in a program while upgrading their language skills through an ESL program.

US colleges and universities use one of three systems to divide the academic year: the semester, the trimester or the quarter system. Whatever the system, the academic year is approximately nine months long, from late August or September to May or June. Many schools operate year-long, offering some courses over the summer (May to August). International students are often advised to enter in the fall

term, when many year-long classes start. By starting in the fall, new arrivals can participate in all of the university's orientation programs. ESL programs offer many entry dates throughout the year.

General Admission Requirements

Each school in the US evaluates students by its own admission standards, which vary according to the program. Undergraduate applicants must normally have the equivalent of a US high school education. Master's program applicants usually require an undergraduate degree earned in a related discipline. Doctoral program applicants usually require a master's degree in their field of study; many universities and colleges require either an honors graduate degree or significant related employment experience. At a number of US universities, exceptional students may be permitted to enter a doctoral program with only an undergraduate degree. US schools recognize a wide range of secondary school certificates and degrees (International Baccalaureate, for example) as equivalent to the US high school diploma. Generally, international applicants are required to submit official academic records and certified translations, where necessary, along with their application forms.

International applicants to both undergraduate and graduate fine arts programs are often required to submit additional admissions materials or participate in additional admissions procedures. These can range from portfolios (for example, for applicants to visual arts, electronic media and some music programs); audio- or videotapes of live performances (for applicants to music, dance or theater performance programs); participation in telephone interviews; and live auditions or in-person interviews once students arrive at the school.

International students are also required to meet the institution's and program's minimum English language requirements. The most widely accepted test of proficiency in the US is the Test of English as a Foreign Language (TOEFL), though some institutions also accept the Michigan English Language Assessment Battery (MELAB) results or ELS Language Centers English proficiency recommendation. Generally, for admission to undergraduate programs, applicants are required to have a minimum TOEFL score between 500 and 550 on the paper-based test; applicants to graduate programs normally must have a minimum TOEFL score of 550 to 650 on the paper-based test.

Fees and Cost of Living

Annual tuition fees for international students vary widely, ranging from just over US$4,000 to nearly $30,000. Many schools charge a higher rate to international students, and some require payment of a tuition deposit or of the entire year's fees in advance.

Depending on their lifestyle, students will require between US$9,000 and $13,000 yearly for living expenses; this will cover room and board, books and supplies, transportation and other personal expenses. Living costs in large cities may be higher. Some schools also require students to have guaranteed, unlimited access to a personal computer for the duration of their studies.

Need-based financial assistance for international students is limited; some international students may be eligible for merit-based scholarships,

International students may be eligible for merit-based scholarships, fellowships or assistantships.

fellowships or assistantships.

Health Insurance

Health care in the US is advanced, progressive and potentially expensive for anyone who encounters an accident or illness requiring medical treatment. In the US, a visit to the doctor may cost US$100, and an overnight stay in the hospital is typically US$1,000 per night.

Because of the expensive nature of US medical care, international students should obtain some form of health insurance coverage, effective for the length of their stay in the US. Medical insurance is currently required for all J-1 visa holders and their spouses and dependents, and is expected to become mandatory for F-1 visa holders and their spouses and dependents as well.

Most colleges and universities in the US offer a health insurance plan for both domestic and international students. The cost for such insurance is approximately US$600 per year for the student alone; coverage for spouses and dependents is available for an additional fee. Alternatively, students may choose to purchase or continue coverage from an insurance company in their home country; however, the terms of these agreements must match or exceed the specifications set by the

university that the student will attend. Most schools require students to provide proof of adequate medical coverage before enrolling.

While the exact terms of insurance plans can vary greatly from school to school, students should be aware that coverage does not always extend to dental and eye care, or to pre-existing conditions, such as pregnancy, which the student may have had prior to obtaining insurance. In addition, insurance usually covers approximately 80 percent of the cost of medical expenses; the remaining 20 percent must be paid by the student.

Visa Requirements

In order to study in the US, international students will require one of the three types of student visas. Most international students obtain an F-1 visa for full-time academic or language studies. A J-1 visa is required for students participating in an exchange program. An M-1 visa is necessary for individuals pursuing vocational studies.

In order to obtain a student visa, international students must submit an I-20 form (for an F-1 visa) or an IAP-66 (for a J-1 visa) to the US embassy or consulate in their home country. These forms are sent to students by US universities and colleges only after applicants have been accepted to a school and have demonstrated financial resources sufficient to cover the cost of studying in the US.

With few exceptions, US law generally prohibits students from outside the US from working. Students may be allowed to work part-time on campus after one year of study; outside employment generally requires government approval.

Before You Go

O nce you have received an acceptance letter from your school, there are several things you can do to prepare yourself for a rewarding international experience. The following is a short list of some of these considerations:

> ➤ ***Learn more about where you are going.*** It is important to invest time into researching and reading about the USA. Learn about its culture, geography, economy, and political and legal systems. The more you learn about where you will be living, the more you will appreciate the experience and the more quickly you will adjust to your surroundings. Everyone experiences a different degree of culture shock, but certainly the more you learn about the culture, the better prepared you will be for your new way of life. Talking to other people who have visited, lived and studied in the USA is one of the greatest sources of information—but remember, everyone has different experiences.

> ➤ ***Make sure your passport is in order.*** You will need your passport to enter the USA, as well as for other things like banking. It can take quite some time to obtain a passport, so be sure to apply early. If you already have a passport, you may want to make sure that it will not expire while you are overseas. Have a plan to keep your passport in a safe place. It would be wise to make several photocopies and you may want to consider keeping your passport in a safety deposit box at a bank.

> ➤ ***Obtain a student authorization.*** You will need a visa to live and study in the USA for more than three months. Visit an education center or embassy to obtain an application and to learn exactly what is needed to apply. This process can be very lengthy, so apply as early as you can.

> ➤ ***Book your flight.*** It is worthwhile to invest time in booking a flight. Often as a student, you can find low-cost flights, but they sell out quickly. If you begin your search early enough, you may learn of a special seat sale that could save you hundreds of dollars.

> ➤ ***Buy additional health insurance.*** Students may be required to purchase health insurance. You can organize this from your home or you may be able to purchase a health plan when you arrive. Keep a copy of your insurance plan in a safe place.

> ➤ ***Make money arrangements.*** Once you are in the USA, you will want to open a bank account. Before you go, however, you should arrange to obtain US currency and traveler's checks to use during the first few days after your arrival.

> ➤ ***Prepare an arrival plan.*** Before you leave, you will want to know that all arrangements for your first few days or weeks in your new home have been made. Some schools offer airport pickup or provide very detailed directions on how to get from the airport to your destination. If you do not yet have permanent accommodation organized, you may want to reserve a few nights at a local hotel or International Youth Hostel.

While You Are There

O nce you arrive at your university, there are a number of steps that you can take to ensure a safe and rewarding international experience. The following list includes some of the most important things to consider:

➤ **Register at your country's mission or embassy, if there is one.** You will find people there who may be able to help you in an emergency, as well as provide information on local customs, laws, health insurance, etc.

➤ **Check in with a contact person at the institution you will be attending.** Contacts can help orient you to the city and your new lifestyle, and provide details about the school year.

➤ **Take extra precautions—foreigners are sometimes at greater risk of theft than locals.** Do not carry or show large amounts of money. Never carry all your information (passport, ID, cash, credit cards, etc.) together.

➤ **While you are in a foreign country, you are subject to its laws.** Make sure you know them and abide by them. If you find yourself in an illegal situation, contact the nearest embassy of your home country.

➤ **Familiarize yourself with the country's culture, laws, regulations and structure.** Always ask before you take a picture of someone and be respectful of religious sites.

➤ **Don't forget to reconfirm any onward flights you are on.** Usually, you should do this 72 hours before the flight's departure.

➤ **You may want to arrange to have your mail forwarded to a post office box.**

Dealing With Culture Shock

Almost everyone who studies, lives or works abroad experiences some degree of culture shock. This period of cultural adjustment involves everything from getting used to the food and language to learning how to use the telephone. No matter how patient and flexible you are, adjusting to a new culture can, at times, be difficult and frustrating. It is easy to get lost, or feel depressed. You may even want to return home!

These are normal reactions and you are not alone. You are about to enjoy a wonderful opportunity to grow and learn—even though it does not always seem that way. Although you cannot avoid culture shock entirely, the following tips may help:

> ➤ *Start a journal* of your new experiences and challenges. Writing things down will help keep them in perspective, and journal entries are rewarding and entertaining to look back on!

> ➤ *Be patient with your ability to speak a new language*. It is easy to get frustrated, but there is no reason to. It takes everyone time to adjust and become comfortable with a new language.

> ➤ *Be physically active!* Walk, swim, run, play tennis or take part in some other physical activity you enjoy. You will feel better, meet new people and keep in shape.

> ➤ *Keep your sense of humour.* Try, no matter how hard it is, to see something of value in every new experience and challenge you come across. Laugh now, not just later!

> ➤ *Take advantage of services that your university and community offer.* Contact a counsellor at the International Students Office, a resident advisor if you live in residence halls, someone at your church, etc. If you have a problem with something, tell someone! That person will want to help, and you will feel a lot better having people to support you. Don't be afraid to speak up.

Adjusting to a new culture can be difficult and frustrating, but it can also be a wonderful, intellectually challenging time of your life. Living in a foreign country will open new doors, introduce you to new ways of thinking and give you the opportunity to make life-long friends.

REMEMBER: All international students share what you are going through; you are not alone. More importantly, it is only a matter of time before you feel adjusted and comfortable in your new home.

ei's guide to distance and online learning programs in the usa - 2001 edition

ADDITIONAL
RESOURCES

USDLA Member Institutions

This list (as of April 2001) appears courtesy of the United States Distance Learning Association (USDLA).

Alberta Correspondence School
Distance Ed Resource Centre
Box 4000
Barrhead, ALB T0G 2P0 Canada

American Open University
5400 Payne Street
Suite 200
Falls Church, VA 22041 USA
http://www.open-university.edu

American University in London
97-101 Seven Sisters Road
London, N77QP, England
http://www.aul.edu

Arkansas State University
Department of Nursing
PO Box 69
State University, AR 72467 USA
http://www.astate.edu

Ball State University
Science Department
BC213
Muncie, IN 47306 USA
http://www.cics.bsu.edu

Barrington University
808 Executive Park Dr.
Mobile, AL 36606 USA
http://www.barrington.edu

Bellevue University
1000 Galvin Road South
Bellevue, NE 68005 USA
http://www.bellevue.edu

Bethany Bible College & Seminary
Bethany Theological Seminary
2573 Hodgesville Road
Dothan, AL 36301 USA
http://www.bethanybc.edu/

Bienville University
778 Chevelle Drive
Baton Rouge, LA 70806 USA
http://www.bienville.edu

Binghamton University
Telecommunications Dept.
Vestal Parkway East
Binghamton, NY 13902-6000 USA
http://www.binghamton.edu

Bob Jones University
1700 Wade Hampton Blvd.
Greenville, SC 29614 USA
http://www.bju.edu

Bryant College
1150 Douglas Pike
Smithfield, RI 02917 USA
http://www.bryant.edu

California State University
Monterey Bay
100 Campus Center
Seaside, CA 93955-8001 USA
http://www.calstate.edu

Central Michigan University
Academic Tech. Svcs.
Park Library 102
Mt. Pleasant, MI 48859 USA
http://www.cmich.edu

Central Missouri State University
Extended Campus
Humphreys 403
Warrensburg, MO 64093 USA
http://www.cmsu.edu

Central Pacific University
1188 Bishop St., Suite 3001
Honolulu, HI 96813 USA
http://www.central-pacific.edu

Chadwick University
2112 11th Ave, S, Suite 504
Birmingham, AL 35205 USA
http://www.chadwick.edu

Chapman University
333 N. Glassell Street
Mem Hall Room 221
Orange, CA 92666 USA
http://www.chapman.edu

Cheyney University of PA
Cheyney & Creek Road
Cheyney, PA 19319 USA
http://www.cheney.edu

City University
Distance Learning Center
1107 SW Grady Way, Ste.206
Renton, WA 98055 USA
http://www.cityu.edu

Colorado State University
Instructional Services
A-71 Clark Building
Fort Collins, CO 80523-1023 USA
http://www.colostate.edu

Columbia Southern University
PO Box 3110
Orange Beach, AL 36561 USA
http://www.colsouth.edu

Community College of Southern Nevada
Distance Education
6375 W Charleston Blvd. W3D
Las Vegas, NV 89146 USA
http://www.ccsn.nevada.edu

Cornell University
3- 27 MVR HAll
Ithaca, NY 14853-4401 USA
http://www.cornell.edu

USDLA Member Institutions

This list (as of April 2001) appears courtesy of the United States Distance Learning Association (USDLA).

Defense Acquisition University
Directorate of Academic Affairs
2001 N. Beauregard Street
Alexandria, VA 22311 USA
http://www.dau.mil

Dekalb College
3251 Panthersville Road
Decatur, GA 30034 USA
http://www.dc.peachnet.edu/

Drake University
Education Extension
School of Education
3206 University Ave.
Des Moines, IA 50311 USA
http://www.drake-extension-ed.org

Elizabeth City State University
1704 Weeksville Road
Elizabeth City, NC 27909 USA
http://www.ecsu.edu

Faulkner State College
Hammond Circle
Bay Minette, AL 36507 USA
http://www.faulkner.cc.al.us

Florida Gulf Coast University
10501 FGCU Blvd.
Ft. Myers, FL 33965-6565 USA
http://www.fgcu.edu

Golden Gate University
School of Technology & Indust.
536 Mission Street
San Francisco, CA 94105 USA
http://www.ggu.edu

Hamline University
1536 Hewitt Ave.
St. Paul, MN 55104 USA
http://www.hamline.edu

Harold Washington College
Vice President Office
30 E. Lake Street
Chicago, IL 60601 USA
http://www.ccc.edu/hwashington

Heartland Community College
1226 Towanda Ave.
Bloomington, IL 61701 USA
http://www.hcc.cc.il.us

Indiana Academy
Outreach Programs
Ball State University
Muncie, IN 47306 USA
http://www.academy.bsu.edu

Indiana University
Owen Hall 205
Bloomington, IN 47405 USA
http://www.indiana.edu

Kansas University
School of Nursing
3901 Rainbow Blvd.
Kansas City, KS 66160-7502 USA
http://www.kumc.edu

Keio University
Graduate School of Business Administration
2-1-1 Hiyoshihoncho, Kohoku-Ku
Yokohama-shi, Kanagawa-Ken, 223-8523 Japan
http://www.keio.ac.jp

Lambuth University
705 Lambuth Blvd
University Advancement
Jackson, TN 38301 USA
http://www.lambuth.edu

Louisiana State University
347 Pleasant Hall
Baton Rouge, LA 70803 USA
http://www.lsu.edu

Mercy College
555 Broadway
Dobbs Ferry, NY 10522 USA
http://www.mercycollege.edu

Mississippi State University
P.O. Box 5247
Division of Continuing Ed
Mississippi State, MS 39762-5247 USA
http://www.mc.edu

Missouri Western State College
4525 Downs Drive
St Joseph, MO 64507 USA
http://www.mwsc.edu

Mohawk Valley Community College
1101 Sherman Drive
Utica, NY 13501-5394 USA
http://www.mvcc.edu

Murray State University
4th Floor Sparks Hall
Murray, KY 42071 USA
http://www.mursuky.edu

National Technological University
700 Centre Avenue
Fort Collins, CO 80526 USA
http://www.ntu.edu

New Mexico State University
Box 30001 / MSC 3 CED
Las Cruces, NM 88003-001 USA
http://www.nmsu.edu

Northern Virginia Community College
8333 Little River Turnpike
Annandale, VA 22003 USA
http://www.nv.cc.va.edu

USDLA Member Institutions

This list (as of April 2001) appears courtesy of the United States Distance Learning Association (USDLA).

Ohio University
133 McCracken Hall
Athens, OH 45701 USA
http://www.ohio.edu

Oklahoma State University
Educational Television Services
100 Telecommunications Center
Stillwater, OK 74078-0585 USA
http://www.okstate.edu

Owens Community College
PO Box 10000
Toledo, OH 43699-1947 USA
http://www.owens.cc.oh.edu

Portland Community College
Distance Learning
12000 SW 49th Avenue
Portland, OR 97219 USA
http://www.distance.pcc.edu

Rend Lake College
Learning Resource Center
Route 1
Ina, IL 62846 USA
http://www.rlc.cc.il.edu

Rensselaer Polytechnic Institute
110 8th Street, CII Suite 4011
Troy, NY 12180 USA
http://www.pde.rpi.edu

Rogers State College
Dept. KXON TV 35
Will Rogers and College Hill
Claremore, OK 74017-2099 USA
http://www.rsu.edu

San Diego City College
1313 - 12th Ave.
A1A
San Diego, CA 92101-4787 USA
http://www.city.sdccd.cc.ca.us

San Jose State University
One Washington Square
San Jose, CA 95192-0169 USA
http://www.sjsu.edu

SE Louisiana University
Dept. of Special Education
SLU Box 879
Hammond, LA 70402 USA
http://www.selu.edu

Shawnee State University
940 Second Street
Portsmouth, OH 45662 USA
http://www.shawnee.edu

Southwest Tennessee Community
5983 Macon Cove
Memphis, TN 38134 USA
http://www.stcc.cc.tn.us

Stanford University
School of Engineering
Durand Building
Stanford, CA 94305-4036 USA
http://www.stanford.edu

State University of New York
SUNY Plaza, T-301
Albany, NY 12210 USA
http://www.alis.suny.edu

Texas A&M University
106 Fermier Hall
College Station, TX 77843-3367 USA
http://www.tamu.edu

Texas State Technical College
300 College Drive
Sweetwater, TX 79556 USA
http://www.tstc.edu

Trinity College
300 Summit Street
Hartford, CT 06106-3100 USA
http://www.trincoll.edu

Troy State University
In Service McCartha Hall
Troy, AL 36082 USA
http://www.troyst.edu

UNISINO
College of Economics
Avenida Unisinos, 950
Sao Leopoldo, RS 93022-000 Brazil

Universidad de Belgrano
Zabala 1837
Buenos Aires, 1426 Argentina
http://www.ub.edu.ar

University of Arizona
1955 E. Sixth Street
Tucson, AZ 85719 USA
http://www.arizona.edu

University of Arkansas, Monticello
Information Technology
P.O. Box 3490
Monticello, AR 71656 USA
http://www.vamont.edu

University of Asia
International Business
PO Box 148
Campbelltown, SA 5074 Australia

University of British Columbia
2053 Main Mall
Vancouver, VAN V6T 1Z2 Canada
http://www.ubc.ca

University of Central Florida
Ctr. for Distributed Learning
12424 Research Pkwy, Suite 264
Orlando, FL 32826-3269 USA
http://www.ucf.edu

USDLA Member Institutions

This list (as of April 2001) appears courtesy of the United States Distance Learning Association (USDLA).

University of Delaware
CE-Distance Learning
211 Clayton Hall
Newark, DE 19716 USA
http://www.udel.edu

University of Florida
Division of Cont. Education
2209 NW 13th Street Ste. A
Gainesville, FL 32609 USA
http://www.ufl.edu

University Of Kentucky
4 Frazee Hall
Lexington, KY 40506-0031 USA
http://www.uky.edu

University of Louisville
Special Education
158 Education Building
Louisville, KY 40292 USA
http://www.louisville.edu/edu/edsp/
distance

University of Massachusetts, Amherst
Video Instruct. Program Dept.
113 Marcus Hall, Box 35115
Amherst, MA 01003-5115 USA
http://www.umasss.edu

University of Miami
PO Box 248005
Coral Gables, FL 33124-1610 USA
http://www.miami.edu

University of Minnesota
P.O. Box 141717
Minneapolis, MN 55414 USA
http://www.umn.edu

University of North Carolina, Chapel Hill
Campus Box 7400
University N. Carolina Chapel Hill
Chapel Hill, NC 27599-7400 USA
http://www.unc.edu

University of North Carolina, Charlotte
Continuing Education & Exten.
202 King Bldg.
Charlotte, NC 28223 USA
http://www.uncc.edu

University of Notre Dame
Executive Education
126 Mendoza College of Business
Notre Dame, IN 46556 USA
http://www.nd.edu

University of Pittsburgh
A114 LIS Bldg.
135 N. Bellefield Street
Pittsburgh, PA 15260 USA
http://www.pitt.edu

University of Southern California
Center for Telecom Mgmt
3415 So. Figueroa Street
DCC-217
Los Angeles, CA 90089-0871 USA
http://www.usc.edu/ctm

University of Tennessee, Knoxville
440 Comm & Univ Ext Bldg
Knoxville, TN 37996 USA
http://www.utk.edu

University of Texas
TeleCampus
201 W. 7th Street
ASH 426
Austin, TX 78701 USA
http://www.telecampus.utsystem.edu

University of Wisconsin, Milwaukee
PO Box 413
Milwaukee, WI 53201 USA
http://www.uwm.edu

Walden University
24311 Walden Center Drive
Suite 300
Bonita Springs, FL 34134 USA
http://www.waldenu.edu

Glossary

Definitions

Academic Advisor – an appointed university representative who provides guidance to students in designing an academic program and selecting courses to meet program requirements

Accredit – to render credible; programs are often accredited by regional and/or general bodies, ensuring that specific curricular standards are met

Advanced Standing (Advanced Placement, Accelerated Study) – direct entry into more advanced levels in the program (bypassing initial components) based on performance on advanced placement tests or academic credit previously earned

Affidavit – a written statement confirmed by oath

Associate Degree – degree granted after completion of a two-year postsecondary program (sometimes used as a transfer degree)

Asynchronous Communication – two-way, "non-synchronous" communication that involves a time delay between the transmission and receipt of a message (e.g., email and voice messaging)

Audioconferencing – voice communications, either through standard telephone lines or through Internet-based software

Audiographics – type of audio-based technology that uses phone lines to transmit visual information, such as drawings and charts

Baccalaureate – a bachelor's degree level of study

Baud – a unit of digital transmission used to describe the rate at which information flows between two electronic devices such as modems.

Case Study – the application of management principles to simulated or real-life situations in order to give students

practice in applying their analytical and presentation skills as well as theoretical knowledge

College – institution offering associate and bachelor's degrees focusing on education rather than research; also refers to divisions within a university system (e.g., College of Business)

Compressed Video – Video images processed to remove extraneous information, facilitating the transmission of information over telephone lines or other narrow bandwidth carriers.

Concentration – a focus undertaken within a major; for example, a student pursuing a degree with a major in business might undertake a concentration in human resources management

Concurrent – simultaneous; occurring at the same time or together

Conditional Acceptance (Admission) – offer of a place in a university/institution degree program to an academically qualified student subject to meeting a specified condition, often completion of English language studies or achievement of a minimum English proficiency test score

Consortium – an association of several bodies

Cooperative or Co-op (Program) – education program that combines theoretical learning with practical experience, generally via alternating periods of classroom study and paid work placements

Core Course – course addressing the main components of a program, generally as a requisite for graduation

Courseload – the number of courses taken or credits earned within a period of study (semester, term, quarter, etc.)

Credit – a measure granted for each course completed; most academic programs require students to complete a certain number of credits for graduation

Credit Hours – a system of measuring credit by the number of hours spent in class a week

Curriculum – subjects included in a course of study; plural: curricula

Deferred Admission – postponing enrollment into an academic program after acceptance for a specified period of time (usually one year)

Digital Technology – allows compression of communication signals for faster, easier transmission of information

Distance Education (Learning) – education program whereby students may complete all or part of an educational program in a geographical location apart from the institution hosting the program; the final award given is equivalent in standard and content to an award program completed on campus

Double Major – the pursuit of two majors during the course of one degree program

Early Admission – acceptance into a postsecondary institution before completion of secondary school; admission standards are usually higher than for regular admission

Early Decision – a system in which applicants apply earlier than the posted deadline, and, if accepted, withdraw all other applications and agree to enroll at the university

Elective Courses – optional courses that complement the core components of a degree program; credit earned is applied to the final degree

Entrepreneurship – the undertaking of a business or enterprise with chance of

Glossary

profit or loss; a common specialization in business programs; program participants study the traits of successful entrepreneurs as well as what is needed to establish a new business

Exchange (Program) – agreement between institutions that permits students to move from one institution to another for short- or long-term periods of study or employment; may offer credit towards a degree earned at the original institution

Faculty – the professors and researchers employed by a university; also refers to divisions within a university system (e.g., Faculty of Engineering)

Foundation (Studies/Year) – preliminary general or specific course of study that forms the basis of subsequent education; frequently offered as a qualifying year for candidates who require skills/knowledge upgrading for entry into a desired degree program

GPA – grade point average; the average grade achieved by a student during the course of an educational program, calculated on various scales determined by individual institutions

Graduate Study – postbaccalaureate program, usually leading to master's or doctoral degrees

Honors Program – programs of particularly challenging coursework (and often including a major project or thesis) offered to high-achieving students; achievement is recognized on the degree

Interdisciplinary (Curriculum) – study of all aspects of a particular field (e.g., business, engineering) rather than complete specialization in a single area (e.g., marketing, electrical engineering); gives students a broad, well-rounded education

Internet – electronic communications network that connects computer networks and organizational computer facilities around the world

Internship – concentrated period of degree-related, industrial or business placement, for which participant may or may not be remunerated

Joint Degree – pursuit of two degrees (e.g., business and law) at the same time; students achieving joint degrees frequently benefit from special programs enabling a shortened period of study

Liberal Arts – nontechnical work conducted in the humanities and social and natural sciences

Major – the primary academic focus pursued within a degree program; often combined with general education requirements

Matriculation – qualifying by examination or otherwise for admission to a university

Mechatronic – the use of computer hardware and software to control mechanical systems

Minor – a secondary academic focus pursued as a supplement or accent to a major program

Modem – a device used to convert digital information for transmission over a telecommunications channel

Open Admissions – admissions policy under which there are no academic prerequisites with the exception of secondary school completion

Orientation – an organized introduction for new students to the campus, resources and surrounding area; usually occurs just prior to the onset of classes

Parallel-time Co-op – cooperative education system in which students complete classroom instruction and acquire degree-related work experience during the same time period

Placement Test – a test used to determine a student's level in a particular skill area; commonly used for placement in English

language programs for non-native speakers; conducted after a student's arrival on campus

Pool (Selection) – determination, with academic advisory assistance, of a schedule of required and elective courses and the appropriate order of completion to fulfil degree requirements

Postgraduate Study – see graduate study

Practicum – concentrated period of degree-related, practical work experience; plural: **practica**

Prerequisite – course required as preparation for entry into a more advanced academic course or program

Private Institution – an institution that relies primarily on non-governmental sources of financial support

Prorated – proportionally; for prorated refunds, the amount of money refunded is proportional to the amount of time passed from a specified date

Public Institution – an institution that receives the majority of funding through the government

Reference (Recommendation) – a commendation from a former teacher or counselor in the form of a letter attesting to the student's academic and/or personal merits

Registrar – the person responsible for records of enrollment and academic achievement at an institution

Residence Hall (Dormitory) – accommodation located on campus; students usually live in shared or private rooms; cooking facilities are not generally supplied, though many institutions offer cafeteria meal plans

Rolling Admissions – a policy with no set deadline for application submission

Self-catering – accommodation type in which housing may or may not be furnished and students are responsible for

Glossary

upkeep as well as food purchase and preparation

Specialization – a focus undertaken within a major; for example, a student pursuing a degree with a major in engineering might specialize in computer science

Standardized Tests – tests administered by an outside body that are used in the admissions process in conjunction with academic transcripts; these include the SAT and ACT

Study Abroad (Program) – agreement between institutions in different geographical locations enabling students to move from one to the other for short- or long-term study periods within a single degree program

Syllabus – program or outline of a course of study

Teleconferencing – the use of sophisticated telecommunications to link remote sites; examples are audioconferencing and videoconferencing

Terminal Degree – the highest degree that may be obtained in a field (usually, but not always, a doctoral degree)

Tertiary – postsecondary education; education pursued after secondary school (usually in reference to college or university education)

Transcript – official academic records detailing place and time of study, courses completed and grades achieved

Tutor – a qualified person who provides academic assistance to students, and may also grade assignments; a tutor generally provides one-to-one assistance to individual students, or, less often, teaches in a more formal classroom setting.

Twinning (Program) – arrangement between institutions in different geo-

graphical locations in which students complete up to two years of study in a college in their home countries, followed by guaranteed admission to the partner university for completion of a degree program; the degree is granted by the latter institution

Videocassette – cartridge containing taped video and audio information often used as a distance learning delivery mode owing to its adaptability to the distance learner's study methods

Videoconference – a conference conducted in "real time" through the use of video technology, allowing individuals to participate from separate locations; frequently used by distance education programs

WWW – a system of hypertext links used to facilitate navigation of the Internet

Abbreviations

acc	accounting	econ	economics	org	organizations
adm	admission	educ	education	ops	operations
admin	administration	elect	electrical	phil	philosophy
adv	advanced	elem	elementary	poli	political
ag	agriculture(al)	eng	engineering	priv	private
app	application	env	environmental	prod	production
arch	architecture	fin	finance	prog	program(s)
asst	assistant	ha	hectare(s)	psych	psychology
assoc	associate/association	Hons	Honors	res	resources
avg	average	HR	human resources	qtr	quarter
begin	beginner	info	information	rehab	rehabilitation
bio	biology(ical)	int	intermediate	res	residence
bldg	building	ind	industrial	sci	science(s)
bus	business	IS	information systems	sem	semester
chem	chemistry(ical)	int'l	international	soc	sociology
comm	communication(s)	km	kilometer(s)	stats	statistics
comp	computer(ing)	lang	language(s)	tech'n	technician
des	design	mech	mechanical	tech	technology
dev't	development	med	medical	uni	university
dom	domestic	mgmt	management	yr	year
dorms	dormitories	mktg	marketing		

Glossary

Accreditation Bodies, Associations, Councils & Societies

AACSB   The International Association for Management Education

ACSDE   American Center for the Study of Distance Education

ADEC   American Distance Education Consortium

AECT   Association for Educational Communications and Technology

AAIEP   American Association of Intensive English Programs

ABET   Accreditation Board for Engineering & Technology

ACPE   American Council on Pharmaceutical Education

DETC   Distance Education and Training Council

ECE   Education Credentials Evaluators

FIYTO   Federation of International Youth Travel Organizations

GATE   Global Alliance for Transnational Education

ITCA   International Teleconferencing Association

ITC   Instructional Telecommunications Consortium

NAFSA   Association of International Educators

NSF   National Science Foundation

TESOL   Teachers of English to Speakers of Other Languages

UCIEP   University & College Intensive English Programs

USDLA   United States Distance Learning Association

Acronyms

ACT   American College Test

CALL   Computer-Assisted Language Learning

CD-ROM   Compact Disk-Read Only Memory

EMAIL   Electronic Mail

ESL   English as a Second Language

GCSE   General Certificate of Secondary Education

GEC   General Education Curriculum

GED   General Educational Development (test)

GMAT   Graduate Management Admissions Test

GPA   Grade Point Average

GRE   Graduate Record Examination

HND   Higher National Diploma

IB   International Baccalaureate

IEE   Institution of Electrical Engineers

LAN   Local Area Network

MIS   Management Information Systems

NAFTA   North American Free Trade Agreement

NASA   National Aeronautical & Space Administration

NCUR   National Conference for Undergraduate Research

PC   Personal Computer

RAM   Random Access Memory

SAT   Scholastic Assessment Test

TOEFL   Test of English as a Foreign Language

UFC   University Funding Council

UHIP   University Health Insurance Plan

UMAP   University Mobility in Asia Pacific Scheme

VLSI   Very Large Scale Integration

WWW   World Wide Web

Additional Resources

EDUCATION-RELATED ORGANIZATIONS

American Association for Higher Education (AAHE)

One Dupont Circle, Suite 360
Washington, DC 20036-1110
phone: 1-202-293-6440
fax: 1-202-293-0073
email: info@aahe.org
internet: http://www.aahe.org/

The American Association for Higher Education includes students, policymakers, and leaders from government, accrediting agencies, business and the media. AAHE promotes the changes needed in education to ensure that it remains effective in a complex and interconnected world.

American Association of Community Colleges (AACC)

One Dupont Circle, NW, Suite 410
Washington, DC 20036
phone: 1-202-728-0200
fax: 1-202-833-2467
internet: http://www.aacc.nche.edu/

The American Association of Community Colleges, founded in 1920, is a national voice for two-year associate degree granting institutions. AACC works with associations of higher education, national associations representing the public and private sectors, the federal government, and Congress to promote the goals of community colleges and higher education.

American Council on Education (ACE)

One Dupont Circle NW
Washington, DC 20036
phone: 1-202-939-9300
fax: 1-202-833-4760
email: web@ace.nche.edu/
internet: http://www.acenet.edu

The American Council on Education seeks to advance the goals and interests of higher and adult education by providing leadership and advocacy on important issues. Its membership includes approximately1,800 accredited degree-granting colleges and universities and other education and education-related organizations.

DISTANCE LEARNING RESOURCES

Distance Education and Training Council (DETC)

1601- 18th Street NW
Washington, DC 20009-2529
phone: 1-202-234-5100
fax: 1-202-332-1386
email: detc@detc.org
internet: http://www.detc.org/

The Distance Education and Training Council, formerly the National Home Study Council, serves as an information source for the field of distance study and correspondence education. DETC sponsors the Accrediting Commission of the Distance Education and Training Council.

Instructional Telecommunications Council (ITC)

Contact: Christine Dalziel
phone: 1-202-293-3110
fax: 1-202-833-2467
email: cdalziel@acc.nche.edu
internet: http://www.itcnetwork.org/

Nearly 600 American and Canadian institutions are represented by ITC in its work to raise awareness about the benefits and future of distance learning and instructional telecommunications. ITC conducts professional development meetings, tracks legislation, supports research and provides a forum for shared expertise and materials in the field of distance learning.

United States Distance Learning Association (USDLA)

PO Box 376
Waterton, Maryland 02471-0376
phone: 1-800-275-5162
fax: 1-781-453-2533
internet: http://www.usdla.org/

The United States Distance Learning Association promotes the development and application of distance learning for education and training. National recommendations, developed and published by USDLA, have become the basis of legislative and administrative education and telecommunication policy.

Fields of Study Index

A

Fields of Study Index

ei's guide to distance and online learning programs in the usa - 2001 edition

Fields of Study Index

Southern New Hampshire University 108
University of California Extension 124

Computer Networks
Colorado Electronic Community College 44
Community Colleges of Colorado 48
New Jersey Institute of Technology 84
Rensselaer Polytechnic Institute 96
Virginia Polytechnic Institute & State University 154

Computer Science
Bellevue Community College 32
Colorado State University 46
Harvard University 60
National Technological University 82
New Jersey Institute of Technology 84
Rensselaer Polytechnic Institute 96
Rogers State University 98
University of California Extension 124
University of Illinois at Urbana-Champaign 134

Conflict Resolution
Adams State College 30
Duquesne University 54

Construction Technology
Colorado Electronic Community College 44
Community Colleges of Colorado 48

Contemporary Topics in Biology
Adams State College 30

Convergent Technology
Community Colleges of Colorado 48

Correctional Administration
Salve Regina University 104

Counseling & Human Development Services
University of Georgia 132

Counselor Education
University of Wyoming 148

Criminal Justice
Caldwell College 36
Central Missouri State University 38
Southwest Texas State University 112
Southwestern Adventist University 114
Teikyo Post University 118
University of Wyoming 148
Weber State University 158

Criminal Justice Administration
Bellevue University 34

Criminology
Southern Oregon University 110

Critical Thinking
Clayton College & State University 42

Crop Sciences
University of Georgia 132
University of Illinois at Urbana-Champaign 134

Current Issues in Education
Adams State College 30

Current Perspectives in Nursing
University of Delaware 130

Curriculum & Education Reform
University of Illinois at Urbana-Champaign 134

Curriculum & Instruction
Central Missouri State University 38
University of Illinois at Urbana-Champaign 134
University of Wyoming 148

Cyber Law Concentration
Bellevue University 34

D

Dance
Southwest Texas State University 112

Data Telecommunications
University of Massachusetts Lowell 138

Database Systems Design
Rensselaer Polytechnic Institute 96

Dealing with Change
Adams State College 30

Decision Making & Problem Solving
Duquesne University 54

Diagnostic Medical Sonography
Weber State University 158

Dietetics & Food Systems Management
Kansas State University 68
The Pennsylvania State University 92

Digital Media Communication
Saint Mary-of-the-Woods College 102

Drafting
Western Oklahoma State College

Driver's Education
Weber State University 158

Drug Abuse
Rogers State University 98

E

Early Childhood Education
Saint Mary-of-the-Woods College 102

E-Business
Bellevue University 34

E-Commerce
Champlain College 40
Jones International University®, Ltd. 66
National American University 80
New Jersey Institute of Technology 84
University of California Extension 124
Waukesha County Technical College 156

E-Commerce Analyst
University of Tennessee 144

Early Childhood Education
Teikyo Post University 118

Early Childhood Program Director
University of Wyoming 148

Earth Literacy
Saint Mary-of-the-Woods College 102

Economics
Adams State College 30
Colorado Electronic Community College 44
Northwest Missouri State University 86
Rogers State University 98
Southern New Hampshire University 108
Waukesha County Technical College 156

Education
Central Missouri State University 38
Indiana Wesleyan University 64
Jones International University®, Ltd. 66
Saint Mary-of-the-Woods College 102
Southern Oregon University 110
Southwestern Adventist University 114
University of California Extension 124
University of Colorado at Denver 128
University of Georgia 132
University of Maine 136

Education Administration
Central Missouri State University 38

Education Database Systems
University of Maine 136

Educational Psychology & Measurement
University of Georgia 132

Educational Psychology & Organization
University of Illinois at Urbana-Champaign 134

Fields of Study Index

Educational Trends
Adams State College 30

E-Learning
Jones International University®, Ltd. 66

Electric Power Engineering/Systems
Rensselaer Polytechnic Institute 96
University of Maine 136

Electrical & Computer Engineering
Georgia Institute of Technology 58
University of Illinois at Urbana-Champaign 134
Virginia Polytechnic Institute & State University
   154

Electrical Engineering
Colorado State University 46
Kansas State University 68
National Technological University 82
Purdue University 94
Rensselaer Polytechnic Institute 96
University of Maine 136

Electronics Engineering Technology
Central Missouri State University 38

Emergency Management & Planning
Colorado Electronic Community College 44
Community Colleges of Colorado 48

Emergency Medical Services
Vincennes University 152

Emerging Technologies
Rogers State University 98

Engineering
Kettering University (formerly GMI) 72

Engineering (Interdisciplinary)
Purdue University 94
University of Colorado at Denver 128

Engineering Administration
Virginia Polytechnic Institute & State University
   154

Engineering Management
Colorado State University 46
Kansas State University 68
National Technological University 82
New Jersey Institute of Technology 84
Syracuse University 116

Engineering Science
Rensselaer Polytechnic Institute 96

English
Adams State College 30
Caldwell College 36
Colorado Electronic Community College 44
Saint Mary-of-the-Woods College 102
Southwest Texas State University 112
Southwestern Adventist University 114
University of Georgia 132
University of Maine 136

Entrepreneurship
Jones International University®, Ltd. 66
Northwest Missouri State University 86

Environmental Engineering
Colorado State University 46
Georgia Institute of Technology 58
Worcester Polytechnic Institute 162

Environmental Science
Adams State College 30

Environmental Systems Management
National Technological University 82

Equine Genetics
Waukesha County Technical College 156

Ethical & Spiritual Dimensions
Duquesne University 54

F

Family & Consumer Sciences
University of Wyoming 148

Family Financial Planning
Kansas State University 68

Federal Government
Rogers State University 98
Western Oklahoma State College 160

Film
University of California Extension 124

Finance/Financial Planning
Bellevue University 34
University of Wisconsin – Whitewater 146
Waukesha County Technical College 156

Fire Protection Engineering
Worcester Polytechnic Institute 162

Fire Science & Safety Technology
Vincennes University 152

Fire Services Administration
Eastern Oregon University 56

Firefighters Certificate
Kentucky Virtual University 70

Food & Agribusiness
Purdue University 94

Food Science & Human Nutrition
Kansas State University 68
University of Georgia 132
University of Illinois at Urbana-Champaign 134

G

Gerontology
Colorado State University 46
Saint Mary-of-the-Woods College 102

French/German/Latin/Spanish
University of Georgia 132

Fundamentals of Supervision
Rogers State University 98

General Arts
Colorado Electronic Community College 44

General Business (University Transfer)
Bellevue Community College 32
Kansas State University 68
Saint Mary-of-the-Woods College 102

General Engineering
University of Illinois at Urbana-Champaign 134

General Environmental Biology
Rogers State University 98

General Studies
Indiana University 62
Madonna University 76
Mott Community College 78
University of Nevada, Reno 140
Vincennes University 152
Weber State University 158

Geographic Information Systems
University of Colorado at Denver 128

Geography/Geology
Southwest Texas State University 112
University of Georgia 132

Gifted & Talented Endorsement
University of North Texas 142

Global Business Management
Bellevue University 34

Fields of Study Index

Fields of Study Index

ei's guide to distance and online learning programs in the usa - 2001 edition

Fields of Study Index

Library Technician
Community Colleges of Colorado 48

LionHawk
The Pennsylvania State University 92

Literature
Colorado Electronic Community College 44
Western Oklahoma State College 160

M

Maine Studies
University of Maine 136

Management
Bellevue University 34
Caldwell College 36
Champlain College 40
Indiana Wesleyan University 64
Jones International University®, Ltd. 66
Northwest Missouri State University 86
Purdue University 94
Rensselaer Polytechnic Institute 96
Rogers State University 98
Salve Regina University 104
Southern New Hampshire University 108
Teikyo Post University 118
Thomas Edison State College 120
University of Colorado at Denver 128
University of Wisconsin – Whitewater 146
Upper Iowa University 150
Waukesha County Technical College 156
Worcester Polytechnic Institute 162

Management Advisory Services
Southern New Hampshire University 108

Management Conflict
Jones International University®, Ltd. 66

Management of Digital Information
Drexel University 52

Management Information Systems
Bellevue University 34
Northwest Missouri State University 86
Teikyo Post University 118

Management/Marketing
University of Georgia 132

Managerial Accounting
Northwest Missouri State University 86

Managing Information Technology
Jones International University®, Ltd. 66

Kentucky Virtual University 70
National Technological University 82

Manufacturing Management
Kettering University (formerly GMI) 72

Manufacturing Systems Engineering
Lehigh University 74
National Technological University 82
Rensselaer Polytechnic Institute 96

Marketing & Retailing
Caldwell College 36
Northwest Missouri State University 86
Rogers State University 98
Saint Mary-of-the-Woods College 102
Southern New Hampshire University 108
University of California Extension 124
University of Wisconsin – Whitewater 146
Upper Iowa University 150
Waukesha County Technical College 156

Mass Communication
Rogers State University 98

Master Reading Teacher Program
Southwest Texas State University 112

Materials Science & Engineering
National Technological University 82

Mathematics
Adams State College 30
Central Missouri State University 38
Clayton College & State University 42
Saint Mary-of-the-Woods College 102
Southwest Texas State University 112
Southwestern Adventist University 114
University of California Extension 124
University of Georgia 132
University of Wyoming 148

Mechanical Engineering
Colorado State University 46
Georgia Institute of Technology 58
National Technological University 82
Purdue University 94
Rensselaer Polytechnic Institute 96
University of Illinois at Urbana-Champaign 134

Media Communication & Technology
Bellevue Community College 32

Medicaid Fraud Prevention
Southwest Texas State University 112

Medical Terminology
Waukesha County Technical College 156

Merchandising
University of North Texas 142

Microcomputer Applications
Rogers State University 98
Waukesha County Technical College 156
Western Oklahoma State College 160

Microelectronics & Semiconductor Engineering
National Technological University 82

Microelectronics Manufacturing Engineering
Rensselaer Polytechnic Institute 96

Microelectronics Technology & Design
Rensselaer Polytechnic Institute 96

Microsoft Certified System Engineer
Community Colleges of Colorado 48
Waukesha County Technical College 156

Microsoft Network Management
National American University 80

Modern Languages
University of Maine 136

Molecular Biology
Lehigh University 74

Mortgage Lending
Waukesha County Technical College 156

Multidisciplinary Studies
Caldwell College 36

Multimedia Applications
University of Massachusetts Lowell 138

Multimedia Development
Rogers State University 98

Museum Studies
Harvard University 60

Music
Colorado Electronic Community College 44
Southwest Texas State University 112

Music Appreciation
Rogers State University 98

Music Technology
Indiana University 62

Music Therapy
Saint Mary-of-the-Woods College 102

ei's guide to distance and online learning programs in the usa - 2001 edition

Fields of Study Index

N

Natural Resources
University of Illinois at Urbana-Champaign 134

Natural Science (Science)
Bellevue Community College 32
Clayton College & State University 42
Harvard University 60
Mott Community College 78
Southwestern Adventist University 114
Thomas Edison State College 120

Negotiations
Jones International University®, Ltd. 66
Northwest Missouri State University 86
Purdue University 94

Network & Information System Technology
Kentucky Virtual University 70

Network Systems Engineer
University of Tennessee 144

New Communications Technologies
Jones International University®, Ltd. 66

Non-Traditional Career Explorations
Waukesha County Technical College 156

Non-Profit Studies
Saint Mary-of-the-Woods College 102

Nuclear Engineering
University of Tennessee 144

Nuclear Medicine
Weber State University 158

Nursing
Central Missouri State University 38
The State University of New Jersey – Rutgers 100
Syracuse University 116
Thomas Edison State College 120
University of Maine 136
University of Wyoming 148

Nursing Informatics
University of Delaware 130

Nursing Research Applications
University of Delaware 130

Nutrition
Central Missouri State University 38
University of Maine 136
Western Oklahoma State College 160

O

Object-Oriented Design, Programming & Principles
New Jersey Institute of Technology 84
Rogers State University 98

Occupational Safety & Health Technology
Colorado Electronic Community College 44
Community Colleges of Colorado 48

Occupational Safety Management
Central Missouri State University 38

Occupational Therapy
Creighton University 50

Ocean Engineering
Virginia Polytechnic Institute & State University 154

Office Systems Administration
Southwestern Adventist University 114

Office Systems Technology
Kentucky Virtual University 70

Office Technology
Southwestern Adventist University 114

Operations Management
Kettering University (formerly GMI) 72

Optical Sciences
National Technological University 82

Organizational Communication
Duquesne University 54

Organizational Development Emphasis
Upper Iowa University 150

Organizational Theory, Policy & Decision Making
Northwest Missouri State University 86

P

Paralegal & Legal Assistant Training
Kentucky Virtual University 70
Saint Mary-of-the-Woods College 102

Parenting
Adams State College 30

Pathophysiology
University of Delaware 130

Peace Studies
University of Maine 136

Personal Development
University of California Extension 124

Pharmaceutical Chemistry
Lehigh University 74

Pharmacy
Creighton University 50
Purdue University 94

Philosophy
Harvard University 60
Southwest Texas State University 112
University of Georgia 132

Philosophy, Politics & Economics
Eastern Oregon University 56

Photography
Colorado Electronic Community College 44

Physical Education
Central Missouri State University 38
Eastern Oregon University 56
Virginia Polytechnic Institute & State University 154

Plastics Technology
University of Massachusetts Lowell 138

Political Science
Caldwell College 36
Colorado Electronic Community College 44
Saint Mary-of-the-Woods College 102
Southwest Texas State University 112
University of Georgia 132
University of Maine 136
Virginia Polytechnic Institute & State University 154

Positive Classroom Discipline
Adams State College 30

Postsecondary Teaching
Colorado State University 46

Pre-Law Track
Saint Mary-of-the-Woods College 102

Preparing for Today's Students
Adams State College 30

Production Operations Management
Northwest Missouri State University 86

Fields of Study Index

ei's guide to distance and online learning programs in the usa - 2001 edition

Fields of Study Index

SchoolsintheUSA.com

the website of US undergraduate programs

SchoolsintheUSA.com is designed exclusively for students who are searching for undergraduate university and 4-year college programs in the USA.

Check out the website to

 Search for business, engineering and technology, fine arts, health, teaching and education programs

 Find in-depth information for each program on admission requirements, program options, student services, tuition and more

 Link directly to school websites and other useful websites

 Request application packages online from each school via an automated email system

SchoolsintheUSA.com has the most up-to-date and accurate information available on US undergraduate programs. All information is verified by the schools.

Guiding Students to Success

General Index